Dog Driver

A GUIDE FOR THE SERIOUS MUSHER

Dog Driver

A GUIDE FOR THE SERIOUS MUSHER

MIKI AND JULIE COLLINS

Alpine Publications

Dog Driver: A Guide for the Serious Musher

Library of Congress Cataloging-in-Publication Data

Collins, Miki, 1959-
  Dog Driver: a guide for the serious musher / by Miki and Julie Collins.
     p.   cm.
  Includes bibliographical references and index.
  ISBN: 0-931866-48-0
  1. Sled dogs.   2. Dogsledding.   I. Collins, Julie, 1959-
  II. Title.
  SF428.7.C65   1990
  636.7'3—dc20   90-523
                                                                       CIP

Design and Layout:
  Dianne J. Borneman, Shadow Canyon Graphics, Evergreen, Colorado
Typography:
  Ruth Koning, Shadow Canyon Graphics, Evergreen, Colorado
Cover Photo:
  Julie and Miki Collins
Other Photo Credits:
  All photographs by the authors unless otherwise credited

Printed in the United States of America
First Edition
          5   6   7   8   9

"How far is it," the Arctic explorer asked the Eskimo,
"to that next mountain range?"
Responded the Eskimo,
"No good dogs, long way . . . good dogs, close to."

Reprinted from THE WORLD OF SLED DOGS, *From Siberia to Sport Racing,*
by Lorna Coppinger, with The International Sled Dog Racing Association.
Copyright 1977 by Howell Book House, Inc., with special permission of the
publisher.

CONTENTS

FOR LOKI
The best, and the worst

PREFACE

My sister Miki and I learned to run dogs on our own. This often meant improvising, learning the hard way, and improving by trial and error. There weren't many mushers around where we grew up, and few mushing books were available. Even today, with a burst of mushing books coming out, there are few, if any, comprehensive references for the serious musher.

We wrote this book for mushers who are tired of gleaning information from newsletters, advertisements, and pet-owner handbooks. We have attempted to compile information that, until now, has been widely scattered and not readily available. Veterinarians, top mushers, canine-nutrition experts, and supply-store owners have generously helped us. Hopefully this will get information to mushers while saving them the trouble of doing all the research.

We wrote this book for mushers who already know how to hook up their dogs and stand on a sled. We assume that the reader has a basic working knowledge of terms, gear, and techniques. This information is available in other books. The beginning musher will find our book useful but should couple it with a book covering the more elementary details. (A glossary at the back of this book will help beginners, and additional books are listed in the references.)

Dog Driver is not just for competitive mushers; it is for mushing adventurers and mushers who run dogs for transportation or as a source of income, and for recreational mushers who want to understand their dogs and the sport better.

How can a musher make his dogs do what *he* wants them to do — all sixteen of them at once? How does training for mid-distance races differ from training for sprint or long-distance races? What kind of plastic should go on the sled runners? We try to answer these questions and many others asked by mushers who have gone beyond the stage of hooking up a couple of dogs on a Saturday afternoon. We show how to understand the dogs as individuals and as a team, how to care for them and get more out of them, and how to correct problems as they come up so that there isn't as much brainwork to do along with the footwork.

Some mushers are more interested in running dogs than in reading, but a comprehensive knowledge of the dog is needed to reach the top of the profession. For the most part, we have limited this book to matters related directly to dog mushing. We recommend that you study other sources of information concerning cold weather survival and trail food and nutrition for humans, as well as other aspects of dog ownership and handling, such as nutrition, psychology, genetics, breeding, medical problems, anatomy and physiology, conformation and gaits, and training methods.

Since we are lifelong Alaskans who rarely venture outside our state, this book is necessarily written from a northern point of view. Thanks to input from mushers across the continent, we have also included information that is more pertinent to stateside, southern Canadian, and European mushers than to northerners. In most respects, mushing in the states is similar to mushing in Alaska, but southern dog drivers must cope with a warmer climate, a denser population, and land use limitations.

While we have attempted to present all viewpoints, you need not accept everything in this book. Dog mushing is a dynamic, constantly evolving sport. Also, what works for one musher may not work for another. Each team is unique, and you must do what works best for yourself and your team.

Although this is a joint effort between my sister, Miki, and me, for clarity it is written from my point of view. In the past sixteen years, we have put more than 25,000 miles on our team, including numerous cross-country trips in Alaska and Canada. The knowledge that we gradually accumulated through our experiences (with many a bumped shin and bruised ego), and the knowledge that we gained from other dog drivers and literature, has moved us to share with other mushers — novices and professionals alike. This book is the result. Let's hook up and get going.

Miki and Julie Collins
June 1990

ACKNOWLEDGEMENTS

Although we have been running sled dogs since 1974, we could not hope to know everything that there is to know about mushing. In writing this book, we went to a number of experts for help. Each person reviewed one or more chapters covering their field of expertise, answered our numerous questions, or forwarded material from their own research.

We were greatly flattered by the compliments and encouragement given to us by our advisors. However, we do not expect them to agree with every point in this book, and you should not assume that any one musher endorses any specific suggestion in this book.

We are especially grateful to the following people: Rick Atkinson, Jack Beckstrom, Susan Butcher, Charlie Champaine and Roxy Wright-Champaine, Jane and Bruce Cosgrove, Patty Doval, Harris Dunlap, the Fairbanks North Star Borough Public Library, Paul Farmer, Noël Flanders, Dr. Fred Husby, Carol Kaynor, Dave Ketscher, Jeff King, Marvin Kokrine, Bob Lugo, Joe May, Lynn Orbison, the Oregon Dune Mushers, Dr. Terry E. Quesnel, B.Sc., DVM, Sue Renkert, Clyde Risdon, Joe Runyan, Dr. Karin Schmidt, DVM, Mary Shields, Mary Beth Smetzer of the *Fairbanks Daily News-Miner*, Rick Swenson, Dr. Val Stuve, DVM, Dick Underwood of the Alaska Feed Company, Jack Utton of Superior Hardwoods, Dr. R. W. Van Pelt, DVM, Ph.D., Janet Ward, and Tim White.

We are also indebted to Betty Jo McKinney of Alpine Publications for her invaluable editorial assistance.

CHAPTER 1

THE ESSENTIAL SLED DOG

My sister Miki and I use our dogs for transportation along an eighty-mile trapline in the Alaskan bush. From November until March, our dogs move regularly on the ten-day round trip out the line and back. In addition, they freight tons of supplies and feed from the tiny bush village six miles away. They have pulled us on sled trips ranging from 300 miles to nearly 2,000 miles and have occasionally competed in long-distance races.

Our dogs have pulled sleds over glare ice, gravel bars, bare tundra, silt, ice bridges, sea ice, sandy seashores, flooding creeks, piled driftwood, log bridges, and thirty-foot snowbanks. One of our teams jumped from an expanse of lake ice into the frigid water to swim ashore, pulling the sunken sled behind them (without our approval). Another team chased a grizzly down a creek glazed with ice (also without our approval). Some loose dogs ran a black bear out of our cranberry patch, our little Siberian leader chased another bear away from a picnic, and two big wheel dogs valiantly drove a marauding grizzly away from our home. A big old Malamute saved my life (not quite on purpose) when I fell through weak ice into a lake. He buckled down and pulled me to safety when I grabbed his tail.

Our dogs have ridden in trucks, canoes, riverboats, and small airplanes. They have hauled freight ranging from alfalfa, wood stoves, and an eighteen-foot canoe to a dog with one leg in a cast, a hundred pounds of unruly puppies, day-old chickens, and a small cat. They have cheerily pulled through snow, sleet, and rain and splashed through hip-deep flowing water. We have traveled over mountains and tundra, rivers, forests, and sea ice at temperatures ranging from fifty above to fifty below zero.

Some mushers may never go beyond their local trails. Others have done more than we ever could do. They have taken their dogs across the Bering Straits from Siberia to Alaska. They have mushed to the top of the continent's tallest mountain, the 20,320-foot Mount Denali (McKinley). They have trekked to the North and South poles. They have crossed continents. They have raced their dogs on the rivers and over the hills, through cities and suburbs, from the Alaska Range to the Alps.

Sled dogs can do all this and more. Not only that — they and their drivers enjoy sledding with a boundless enthusiasm.

Basic Uses of a Dog Team

Dog teams today have three uses — recreation, racing, and working. The recreational teams are a motley group — often mismatched, but joyful and dearly loved. A team may be no more than a child with his spaniel or shepherd. Some recreational teams are perfectly trained, while others fly off half-cocked. Some go to the mailbox, others go into the wilderness. Some recreational mushers are part-time trappers in Alaska, while others are white-collar workers in New Jersey. All have one thing in common — they're in it for the sheer fun of it.

Race dogs are small, high-strung athletes and often represent years of hard work and high investments. Competitive mushers must constantly stay on top of the sport as new races, new feeds, and new materials evolve. Care and training must be considered to the minutest detail. The intoxicating challenge of racing has turned many casual mushers into serious dog drivers, experts in their field.

Working sled dogs are generally larger, more controlled, and powerful. Mushers use them for freighting, packing, pulling clients, checking traplines, and running rescue missions. The dogs must be willing to work long hours, frequently on poor trails. The runs may be repetitive and boring. For some teams, camping out is second nature. Endurance, patience, and loyalty are necessary qualities in these dogs.

Any musher can benefit by learning more about his dogs. While this book is aimed at the serious musher who runs his dogs regularly and is seeking to improve his team, even the weekend novice will find mushing more fulfilling if he learns more about the sport.

Notes for the Novice

Don't let us scare you if you haven't had dogs very long. You don't need to know the subtle differences between dog foods or sled plastics

Our team cheerfully trots over ice and through water on our many adventures.

if you aren't going to demand much from your team. You can use this book to deepen your understanding and clarify your methods, but don't worry about the technical details. A clean environment, reasonable feed, serviceable equipment, and a healthy attitude are simple requirements.

Some Common Misconceptions About Mushing

The term "Mush!" was only occasionally used in decades past. "Hike!" is easier to say when you're galloping up a hill behind a tired team. "Mush" is only used jokingly, as in "Mush, you mally-mutts!" Once, a young dog was named Mellow so that his master could say, "Mush-Mellow!" but that was quite the exception.

A common misconception among nonmushers is that only huge dogs pull sleds. Dogs weighing eighty to one hundred pounds were popular as freighters in the old days, but some race dogs today weigh less than thirty pounds. Another myth is that female dogs are too delicate to be worked. This is untrue; some mushers prefer females over males.

You do not have to be a keen young athlete to enjoy the sport. Although physical conditioning is important when you handle dogs, mushing is enjoyed by six-year-old school children and sixty-year-old schoolteachers. Norman Vaughan, one of the oldest mushers in the field, has competed regularly in the rigorous 1,100-mile Iditarod Sled Dog Race, and he is in his eighties.

Nor do you need a northern breed to run dogs. If you own Dalmatians, Pointers, Coonhounds, Standard Poodles, Collies, Labrador or Golden Retrievers, German or Belgian Shepherds, Airedales, Weimaraners, Greyhounds, Targhees, Salukis, Borzois, Russian or Irish Wolfhounds, Cocker Spaniels, Norwegian Elkhounds, Irish Setters, Saint Bernards, Spitz, Akitas, Newfoundlands, mongrels, or any of a number of medium-size to large breeds, then you own dogs whose peers have proven themselves in harness.

Breeds

Ideally, you will stick with one breed to ensure uniformity within your team. Even subtle differences between two strains of one breed can disrupt the balance of a finely tuned race team. For most mushers, performance is the ultimate goal, and if this means crossing a regis-

Our first team consisted of three Siberians (lead and swing); two Alaskan huskies (team); and two Alaskan Malamutes (wheel). We didn't pay a penny for any of these dogs, but all were good workers and four became good leaders.

tered Siberian Husky with a mongrel and adding a dash of hound, so be it. While conformation has some bearing on performance, a bow-legged mutt that runs twenty miles per hour is better than an eighteen-mile-per-hour purebred with impeccable conformation.

Unless a specific breed is mentioned, when we use the word "husky" we are referring to any of the miscellaneous strains of Alaskan husky or mixed-breed northern dogs.

Alaskan huskies come in many varieties, depending upon where they are bred, the amount of interbreeding with outside dogs, and the purpose for which they are bred. These are Alaskan huskies at Unalakleet, Alaska.

Bingo comes from an old line of Indian dogs in the Dawson City, Canada, area.

Natalie Norris, pioneer dog musher and early breeder of Alaskan Malamutes, Siberian Huskies, and Eskimo Dogs, remains active in working, showing, and judging dogs after more than fifty years of involvement in the sport. Natalie is shown with her choice for "Best Puppy in Match" at the Alaskan Malamute Club of Fairbanks' 50th Anniversary Match in 1985. The dog, Trillium's Yukon Pride Kalluk, owned by Rudy and Sue Renkert of Fairbanks, went on to become American/Canadian Champion. *Courtesy Sue Renkert.*

Probably the best all-around sled dog is the Alaskan husky, whose combination of speed, endurance, and natural drive makes it the most successful and popular dog for racing and other work. These dogs originated from strains of native northern dogs mixed with an assortment of other breeds introduced by white settlers. It is not a recognized breed because the strains are so varied and versatile — the dogs are bred for performance, not for conformational standards, color, or ear set. Because of their diverse background, a wide variation is seen within the breed and sometimes even within a litter. They come in all sizes, from the heavy descendants of old-time trapline and freighting teams to little sprint dogs weighing thirty-five pounds. Decades of breeding and selection specifically for harness work have all but eliminated undesirable traits, such as poor feet, poor stamina, and lack of speed.

Hans Oettli's team at the start of the 1987 Yukon Quest, including (from left to right): Polar and Nanook (Alaskan Malamutes); Jack and Odin (Eskimo Dogs); Dasher (Siberian Husky); and Tok (Alaskan Malamute). *Courtesy Sue Renkert.*

Other northern breeds also make good sled dogs but often lack the sheer speed of the Alaskan husky. Most of the purebreds make better pets than do high-strung race dogs, and registered breeds can go in the show ring as well as on the trail. Alaskan Malamutes excel at freighting, packing, and weight pulling, although they tend to be slow and some are fighters. Siberian Huskies, smaller and lighter, boast more speed, but only a few lines are fast enough to be competitive against Alaskan race huskies. Samoyeds are also small but have a stouter build than Siberians, making them unable to maintain the high speeds required in most races yet too light for serious freighting. Their fluffy, snowball appearances and friendly, loyal personalities make them popular among some recreational mushers.

These pure breeds, recognized by the American Kennel Club, have become popular as show dogs and pets as well as sled dogs. Unfor-

Dawn Maddex and her half-grown wolf hybrid, Athena. Wolves typically have very narrow chests, long legs, long, narrow heads, light amber eyes, and a peculiar gaze. Athena is 93% wolf.

tunately, many breeders have no knowledge of the demands made of sled dogs. Their stock is never trail-tested or raced. Emphasis is frequently on appearance. This results in dogs that have poor angulation, weak pasterns, and short bodies and that lack the required attitude for good sled dogs.

The Eskimo Dog, also called the Greenland Husky in some areas, is another arctic breed similar to the Malamute, with extra-long fur and a wiry, powerful build. These dogs are less common, but their toughness, ability in harness, and resistance to cold made them desirable among early polar explorers, especially in northern and eastern Canada. Farther inland, the MacKenzie River Husky resulted from mixing native sled dogs with large breeds such as Saint Bernards, Newfoundlands, Eskimo dogs, and, some say, a bit of wolf. This produced a tremendously powerful dog often weighing more than 100 pounds.

A number of sled dogs have some wolf breeding from distant relatives. However, wolf hybrids with more than one-quarter to one-half wolf usually do not measure up in harness. Although the feet of these hybrids are reputedly nearly indestructible, the wolf nature often leads to fighting and aggressiveness and to restlessness when confined. They may be quick to attack when another animal (or even a small human) is injured or incapacitated. In their relationships with humans, they can be distrustful, unpredictable, challenging, and stubborn. Wolf hybrids — and especially pure wolves — are not dogs and cannot be handled the same way as dogs. A sound understanding of wild canine psychology and behavior is required to maintain an agreeable, productive relationship.

While many non-northern breeds are used in harness, they usually have more problems. For instance, they may have trouble coping with cold weather. Soft-furred dogs tend to develop icy snowballs on their feet and legs. Many lack stamina or the innate desire to pull. In spite of this, many mushers run the breed of their choice, from Borzois to Weimaraners.

In 1988, John Suter of Chugiak, Alaska, ran some Standard Poodles on his Iditarod team, and three of them went the 1,100 miles to Nome for a thirty-eighth-place finish out of fifty-two starters. Although the fifty-below weather did not bother them, the poodles did have trouble with snowballing in their hair, and several were dropped due to foot problems. In training, Suter discovered that while poodles do not have the inherent desire to run and pull that huskies have, their intelligence and willingness overcame the drawback.

I once saw a team of German Shepherds and have heard that they make good workers with tough feet. However, they are slow and have poor endurance. In the 1940s, my father ran his pet Cocker Spaniel in the lead of his team on the Kobuk River. (The gentle bird dog was horrified when her husky teammates ripped up a ptarmigan that my father had shot.) Norwegian Elkhounds, with their arctic appearance, make good recreational sled dogs despite their lack of speed.

Irish Setters have been popular among racers, either as purebreds or mixed with husky strain. The long, soft coats and leg fringes of setters tend to collect snowballs, but these dogs have a strong desire to run, a certain amount of speed, and a friendliness lacking in huskies. Gareth Wright, a Fairbanks sprint racer, developed a strain that he called Aurora huskies, which is one-fourth Irish Setter, one-fourth wolf, and one-half husky. The dogs proved to be fast with tough feet.

Hounds are a controversial bunch. Some breeds have lots of stamina; others, notably the sprinting Greyhounds and other coursing dogs, lack stamina. They exhaust all of their energy in a burst of incredible speed in the first few minutes of a run. Some hounds give out when asked to pull a load. Many have different strides and gaits that may not fit in smoothly with a team of huskies.

Targhee hounds, a cross between Staghounds and Irish Setters, originated in Idaho and are fast as sprinters but reputedly have poor feet and cripple more easily. The Quebec hound, or Canadian hound, is a hound crossed with huskies, producing a long-legged, racy dog. Of the pure hounds, perhaps Dom Blodgett's Walker Coonhounds were the most famous. They were once clocked at thirty-two miles per hour while pulling a sled and driver.

Finding the Right Dog

When you want to start a team or add to an existing one, you need a clear idea of what you are looking for. The dog must be suitable for the work intended, and he must match your other dogs. The more competitive you intend to be, the more critical this matching is.

Sled dogs are easy to obtain in northern areas, but if they are selling for a dime a dozen, that's about what they are worth to the serious competitor. However, they still may be great for a recreational team. Top-notch race dogs, especially proven breeding stock, are more difficult to purchase.

Ads for dogs appear in mushers' magazines and newsletters, in the classified section of newspapers, and on bulletin boards at

Comet and Streak, from the first litter that we raised, grew into dedicated companions, pack dogs, bear dogs, watch dogs, and, in the team, outstanding wheel dogs. They are Malamute-husky crosses.

mushers' meeting places and feed stores. A recreational musher willing to go with less competitive dogs can often pick from "free" ads or even from the dog pound. On rare occasions, a good dog can be found on "death row." We once got a handsome, sharp leader from the pound, but he turned out to have bad feet. You always run a risk when getting a dog with a questionable or unknown background. Problems in temperament or health are common. Be wary of "freebies." Some may have been pampered pets incapable of comprehending the work that you expect of them.

Unless someone is selling out his whole team, he is not going to part with his best dog. A dog is sold for a reason, and you will have to deal with that reason — whether it is a problem with speed, attitude, or health. A top dog might cost thousands of dollars. One hundred to five hundred dollars are reasonable prices to pay for good, trained dogs.

Leasing is another option. You can lease a good dog or even a team of dogs for a race or for a period of time. Except for any winnings that the dog gains you, you will be out the investment when the dog is returned, but you also will not have that hungry mouth to feed over the summer. You may be liable for the dog's full value if something happens to him while in your care. If a leased dog does not actually improve the performance of your team, you may be better off without him.

Untrained dogs come cheaper than trained dogs, not only because they have not had the time and work invested in them, but also because they are unproven. You may get an outstanding dog or a complete dud. This risk can be greatly decreased by buying from a reliable musher selling a proven strain of dogs. You also run the risk of ruining a green dog through improper training or unreal expectations and demands. An inexperienced musher would be wise to purchase experienced dogs that already have good habits and that can in effect teach the musher.

Buying puppies is even riskier because of the training factor and because it is difficult to predict size, build, and temperament in pups. Of course, you might raise a litter of your own pups, but this is an expensive way to obtain dogs, and some might not fit into a cohesive team. However, most serious mushers do breed many of their own dogs, and this is discussed in Chapter 8.

Before the Purchase

Keep in mind the dog's purpose. He must fit into your team physically and psychologically. He must fit the position that you are trying to fill. Some dogs will not run in wheel or in swing. A dog who leads for one musher will not necessarily lead for another.

Ask many questions before buying a dog, especially "why are you selling him?" (See the Buyer's List of Questions and Checklist on the following pages.) Be sure to check the dog's medical background, because serious lameness, kidney disease, and other health problems can recur. Abnormal heat cycles or infertility can indicate low thyroid, infections, or other problem conditions. If possible, look at the dog's relatives to get an idea of breeding potential.

The best way to tell if a dog will work for you is to try him out, but give him the advantage of a familiar position, pace, and distance to run. Some mushers offer guarantees, but they need to be specific. A dog may be guaranteed sound, but that doesn't mean that he will work for you. A trial time period is very beneficial for both you and

A half-wolf husky in harness. Note the chewed harness and the chain collar used to prevent collar-chewing.

the dog, yet some mushers are reluctant to lend a dog on trial because they do not know how he will be treated.

A thorough physical examination by a veterinarian before the purchase is good insurance, but the layman can catch many weaknesses. Most mushers prefer to forego a costly professional job. In an older dog with a high price tag, a veterinarian now may save you grief later if blood chemistries reveal early stages of liver or kidney problems, or if X-rays show early stages of arthritis.

Go over the dog, feeling and examining every part of the body. Start with the feet; if they are bad, you might not even want to bother looking at the rest (see Chapter 7). *Feel* the dog. The musculature on the limbs should be uniform on both sides; if one side seems underdeveloped, the dog may be lame. Arthritis can cause swollen wrists. An enlarged joint has probably been traumatized. Flex and extend each leg, watching for pain or stiffness. The mouth, teeth, and gums should be clean and free of redness, swelling, discharge, or bad smells. Check the dog's eyes and ears for signs of infection and make sure that they work.

Feel over the dog's body for abnormal lumps, looking also for raw skin or sores. An unhealthy skin and hair coat often indicate health problems such as digestive enzyme deficiency or malnutrition. External parasites occur more frequently on dogs in poor condition. You should be able to feel the dog's ribs and pelvic bones, but he should not appear starved. A thin dog may have malnutrition, internal parasites, or a chronic disease, or he may be naturally thin, just as some people are.

Sometimes, well-known mushers raise the price of any dog because they are selling a "name brand." These mushers have their reputations at stake, and they did not reach the top with bad dogs — but even that is no guarantee that the dog will work for *you*. Beware of unscrupulous mushers who mask physical problems with steroids, analgesics, or other tricks. A guarantee offers some protection.

Attitude makes or breaks a sled dog, but unfortunately, attitude is difficult to judge when the dog is confined. Neither a wildly excited dog nor a quiet, subdued one will necessarily pull and run his best. If all of your dogs are quiet, you may find that an excitable one gets on your nerves. Getting the dog out and testing him on the trail is the best way to judge attitude. Make sure that the dog has the drive to keep going, even if he is tired or bored. Attitude is even more important in race dogs. This is discussed in more detail in later chapters.

Buyer's List of Questions

You may not want to ask all of these questions, and you may wish to add questions of your own.

- Why are you selling the dog?
- Can I try him in my team before buying him? Will you offer a guarantee?
- What position does he run? What size team and what speed is he used to? How much training/conditioning has he had recently? How many miles has he run this year? How many miles has he run in his life?
- Has he been run in the lead? Trail or command leader? Single or double lead? In front of how many dogs? Under what trail and weather conditions (high wind, no trail, icy trail)?
- Has he been raced, and what is his track record?
- Does he prefer the right or left side of the towline?
- Has he been run with a wheeled rig?
- Has he been on difficult trails that are icy, rough, or covered with deep or drifted snow or overflow? Will he go through water?
- Was he primarily run by a man or a woman? Does it make any difference to him? How does he handle children?
- Has he ever camped out?
- Has he ever had sore feet? Under what conditions?
- What is his medical record? Are his vaccinations current? When was he last wormed? With what wormer? Has he had any severe or chronic injuries or health problems? Is he currently on any medications (heartworm, thyroid, antibiotics, etc.)? What veterinarian has his medical records?

Buyer's List of Questions
(continued)

● How old is he?

● Is he neutered—spayed? If a female, are her heat cycles normal? Has the dog been bred, and how did the pups turn out? If a female, did she care for her pups properly?

● What is his breeding lineage? Does he have any outstanding dogs in his ancestry?

● What feed is he used to? Does he eat well when stressed? Does he maintain his weight easily?

● Does he have any personal idiosyncrasies? Does he fight or chew harnesses? Does he chase other dogs? Has he ever bitten anyone and if so, under what circumstances?

● If he's loose, will he run away or come when called?

● Has he had any previous owners — names, phone numbers?

Buyer's Checklist

When examining a dog that you hope to buy, watch for these good point and bad points.

Good Points
- Matches your team.
- High withers with back sloping gently to croup.
- Good angulation, front balanced with rear.
- Legs balanced with length of back.
- Body balanced with bone size.
- Deep chest.
- Elbows close against chest.
- Sloping croup (especially in sprint dogs).
- Strong, supple pasterns.
- Good feet — tight, tough, supple, nails not too long (see Chapter 7).
- Healthy coat and skin.
- Healthy mouth and teeth.
- Proven track record (for racers).
- Glowing performances by relatives.
- Good attitude — happy, eager, responsive.
- Smooth gaits, supple movement.
- Record of regular vaccinations and medical history.
- Good overall health.
- Normal, firm stools.
- Reasonable price (one that you can afford, as well as one that the dog is worth) and acceptable guarantee.

Buyer's Checklist
(continued)

Bad Points

• Level back with low withers, or back abnormally arched.

• Flat croup (although trotting dogs do not need the steeper slope of sprinters).

• Chest shallow or too wide (allow for a wider chest in freighters).

• Elbows splayed outward, loose or wobbly.

• Hock too long.

• Straight shoulders.

• Back pain.

• Musculature on one side unequal to that on the other.

• Abnormally excessive or shrunken musculature.

• Swollen or malformed joints.

• Lame.

• History of chronic disease, lameness, or other medical problems.

• Evidence of disease — diarrhea, abnormal discharges, poor coat, fever, lethargy, unusual lumps, sores, or excessive thirst.

• Choppy, short, awkward, stiff, or uneven gaits.

• Rough, coarse, sparse, itchy, or patchy coat and skin.

• Scars on face or missing teeth, indicative of fighting.

• Evidence of destructive behavior — torn-up dog house, battered feed pans.

• Poor attitude — scared, sullen, aggressive, hyperactive, withdrawn.

• Evidence of abuse — starving, shyness, a filthy dog yard, no available water.

Conformation

Experienced mushers can frequently look at a dog and know whether it is well built, but it helps to understand how bone structure and build affect a dog's performance.

A dog with poor conformation may be slower, less muscular, badly gaited, or prone to injury. He may work hard, but if he has to expend more energy than his teammates, he may turn sour. In some cases, bad conformation impedes the dog's actions, speed, and stamina. Because it is primarily hereditary, conformation is a major consideration in breeding.

The angles formed by the junction of the shoulder with the upper arm, and the pelvis with the rear leg, influence the stride of a dog.

Look for a trim body, hard muscles, and a firm, tucked-up belly in working dogs. Oly has the flatter back and larger size of a distance dog, but he has straight shoulders and is "out at the elbows," which are faults. Oly is an Alaskan husky.

Proper, balanced angulation allows a smooth, extended stride with correct timing and placement of the feet.

Angulation can be judged roughly by viewing a dog from the side; however, even a slight change in foot placement or balance can change the appearance of the angles. Study a dog carefully, preferably several times, before making a judgment. You can also assess the angle by feeling from the top of the shoulder blade (scapula) to the point of the shoulder (lower forward end) and then to the elbow while the dog is standing square (see Figure 1-1). Practice on several dogs so that you can easily find the landmarks and estimate angles on different dogs.

Shoulder blades that are sloped instead of vertical will connect to the upper arm at a more acute angle. This allows muscles to pull across the angle instead of paralleling the bones, giving the muscles

Left: Pasterns should not be too straight or they will not absorb shock; nor should they be too sloping or they will be weak and prone to overextension. These are acceptable. *Right:* "Out at the elbows," a serious fault. The elbows should lie closely against the chest wall.

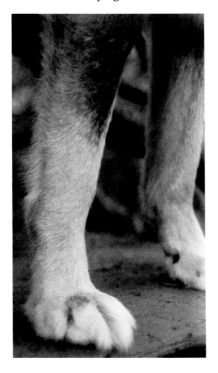

Figure 1-1
Shoulder Conformation

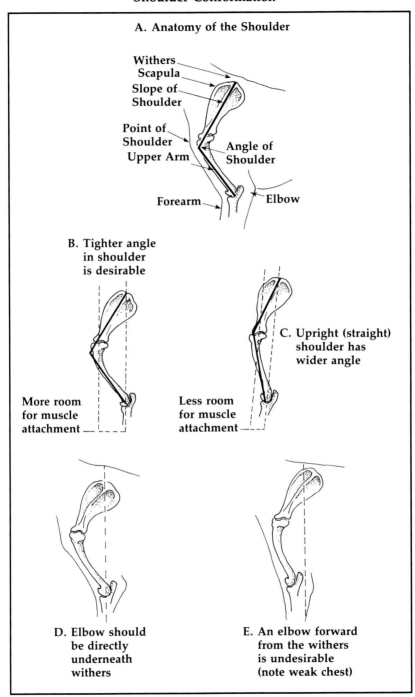

A. Anatomy of the Shoulder

Withers
Scapula
Slope of Shoulder
Point of Shoulder
Upper Arm
Angle of Shoulder
Forearm
Elbow

B. Tighter angle in shoulder is desirable

C. Upright (straight) shoulder has wider angle

More room for muscle attachment

Less room for muscle attachment

D. Elbow should be directly underneath withers

E. An elbow forward from the withers is undesirable (note weak chest) more leverage on the bones. This also provides more room for muscle attachment, facilitating muscle development. The angled bones have more spring to absorb shock. A dog with straight shoulders is more likely to pound (land hard on the front feet) and is thus more prone to front-end injury.

A dog with good angulation has distinct withers, with the point of the shoulder well forward and the elbow directly below the top of the withers. If the angle is too acute, however, the dog will not be able to open the joint fully, and his stride will be shortened.

In the rear, a sloping croup is desirable, especially in sprint (running) dogs. When the croup slopes, tail placement is lower, while a flat croup (caused by a level pelvis) results in a high tail.

Balance between front and rear angulation is very important (see Figure 1-2). When the shoulders have poor angulation and the hindquarters have good angulation, the front legs have a relatively shorter stride. This causes pounding, and the dog may crab (run sideways) to prevent the overreaching hind feet from striking the front feet. Movement is bouncy, mincing, and inefficient. (Pups tend to develop faster in the rear than in the front, but they usually outgrow this; therefore, do not be too quick to judge them.)

The overall bone size and structure should match the size and structure of the dog. The length of the back must conform to the length of the legs, with both preferably fairly long and limber. The withers should be higher than the croup, and the back should slope gently from front to rear. A short rib cage and longer loin weaken the back, and provide less bone for muscle attachment.

A deep chest allows for heart and lung development. If it is too wide, it will interfere with the free movement of the front legs. A dog that runs wide in the front lames more easily. (A freighting dog often develops a wider, more heavily muscled chest, making his legs look farther apart.) The front legs should be set well under the dog — close together but not "coming out of the same hole." The tops of the shoulder blades should also be close together.

Elbows must move closely against the rib cage, without splaying outward as the dog moves. Strong, well-formed pasterns (wrists) are important to absorb shock. Faulty pasterns may look as though the wrist collapsed ("down at the pastern") or as if the leg is "over at the knees," causing the pastern to slope back from the knee. In the rear, a long femur and shorter lower leg are preferred.

Sprint dogs, who lope most or all of the time, have slightly different builds than distance-racing dogs who primarily trot, and these are discussed in the chapters on racing.

Figure 1-2
Good Versus Poor Angulation

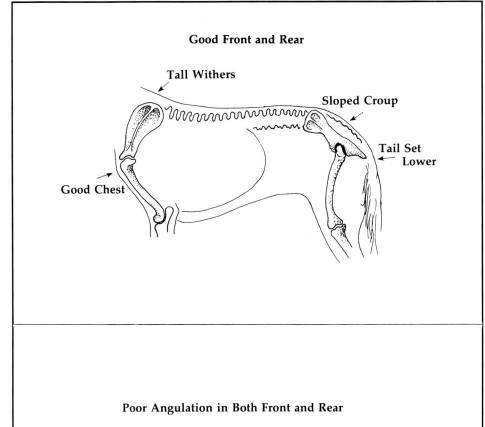

Good Front and Rear

Tall Withers

Sloped Croup

Tail Set Lower

Good Chest

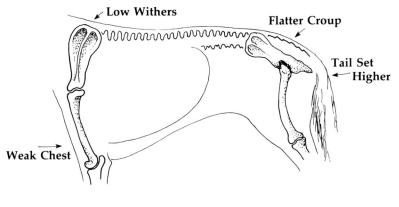

Poor Angulation in Both Front and Rear

Low Withers

Flatter Croup

Tail Set Higher

Weak Chest

Gaits

Walking, trotting, and cantering (loping) are the three primary gaits. The trot is critical in a long-distance or working dog, while the lope is critical in a sprint dog. Conformation, physical condition, age, and other factors affect a dog's gait. A sled dog traveling with his head up probably is not pulling. A high head also shortens the stride. (Some leg muscles attach to the neck, and when the neck is up, the legs go more up and down. When the head and neck are held low and forward, the legs are pulled forward instead of upward.) A jerky gait may be caused by poor conformation or by pain or fatigue.

A walking dog should have a smooth, easy stride with no jerking, loose, or waddling motions. He lifts only one foot at a time so that he is supported by three feet at any given moment.

At the trot, the dog balances on two feet at a time, relying on forward momentum to maintain his balance. Faults show up more readily at a trot because it is a more dynamic gait than the walk. Movement should be lithe and effortless without pounding. Good extension of the limbs is essential. Front and rear legs should fly straight and true, without flicking sideways or twisting, and each stride should cover a lot of ground.

The diagonal legs (front left and right hind, for instance) move together at the trot. Some dogs prefer to pace instead of trot; their legs swing as a pair on the same side (left front and left rear moving in unison — see Figure 1-3). In a dog team, this gait is less efficient. Energy is lost in the side-to-side motion, and a pacing dog is more likely to slip or lose his balance. We have a natural pacer who is always the first to fall flat on glassy ice.

Dogs may pace naturally to avoid interference between the front and rear feet. This interference can be caused by a number of conformational problems: a back too short for the legs, withers lower than the croup, or rear legs better angulated than the shoulders. Pacing keeps the feet on each side separated so that they will not hit each other.

Fatigue or pain can make a dog switch from a trot to a pace. Pacing uses alternate muscles and allows the fatigued muscles to rest. Pacing also reduces back pain (perhaps caused by a kidney infection or a bone spur), because the back is stiffened at the pace. It rolls from side to side instead of twisting, as it does in a trot. When a dog that normally trots suddenly begins to pace, suspect a physical problem. Because a dog can usually pace faster than he can trot, he may pace

Figure 1-3
The Dog at a Trot, Pace, and Slow Lope

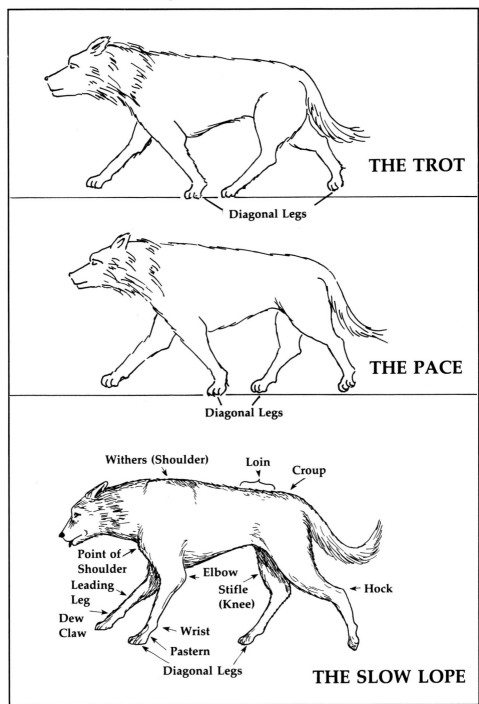

THE TROT

Diagonal Legs

THE PACE

Diagonal Legs

Withers (Shoulder)   Loin   Croup

Point of
Shoulder
Leading   Elbow
Leg   Stifle   ← Hock
               (Knee)
Dew
Claw   ← Wrist
               Pastern
               Diagonal Legs
                                THE SLOW LOPE

The two lead dogs are both on a left lead. The entire weight of the body is breaking over that left wrist. Dogs in a left turn should lead with the left leg. John Urquhart at the North American skijoring event, 1988. *Courtesy* Fairbanks Daily News-Miner.

instead of breaking into a lope when stiffness or pain interferes with his lope.

Like other gaits, the lope should be smooth and effortless, without wasted motion. This requires good shoulders and legs, a good back, a sloped croup, and a well-formed chest. A well-built dog can really stretch out, covering a lot of ground with every stride. A dog with a short, bobbing gait tends to be slower and cannot maintain high speeds. If the withers bob up and down, the dog is wasting energy and is not stretching out; this can indicate fatigue. Bobbing can also be caused by unequal angulation between front and rear limbs: the thrust (rear) and lift (front) are not equalized.

The leading leg (the front leg that stretches the farthest forward and hits the ground just *after* its partner) can be injured, because the full weight of the dog breaks over it at every stride. The opposite leg is susceptible to sprains, because it absorbs the forward momentum of every bound as the dog lands. On a corner, dogs lead with the inside leg. Dogs on a sharp sprint team taking a corner will change leads in rhythmic synchrony. Often on a straightway, dogs in a pair lead with opposite legs.

Ideally, each dog matches his gait to that of his partner. Dogs can move in synchrony at any gait, with walking or trotting dogs matching each forward step and loping dogs matching each forward leap. This not only contributes to the efficiency of the team but to the grace and beauty of the team as well. It can only be accomplished if the dogs are well-matched — by breed, by size, by conformation and build, by gait, and even by attitude and willingness to cooperate with and depend upon their partners and teammates. This synchrony cannot be taught, but it does come naturally when the dogs are matched closely enough — and that is your goal when choosing new dogs.

CHAPTER 2

SLED-DOG PSYCHOLOGY

Our dogs slumped late one year after an unusually difficult season. Miki was mushing home one day, and every dog was messing up. The dogs had been working hard, and with warm weather, a soft trail, and fresh memories of unpleasant experiences, they looked ready to quit. They hated Miki, they hated each other, and they hated their job — the job that sled dogs are born to love. A crisis was at hand.

In desperation, Miki aimed for a shady spot, and the disunited dogs managed to reach it. That was enough. She stopped, walked up, and hugged her wheel dogs. "Comet, Streak!" she cried with fake enthusiasm. They were surprised. Miki went on up the line. Every dog heard his name and felt a special touch. Did they deserve it? No. But when Miki hiked them up again, they cut for home with spirited dedication.

It pays to know how to get performance from your dogs. A dog will perform differently for each driver, and the person who knows a dog best will get the most from him. A dog's behavior is based more on instincts and conditioning rather than on reasoning. Their *actions* are usually *reactions* to stimuli ranging from a distant howl to the scent of game. By controlling the stimulus in training, or by breaking the chain of events, you can often stop a dog from slacking, ducking off the trail, or chewing the towline.

Dogs sometimes behave like small children, but they differ from humans in many ways. Their eyes are on a lower level, so they have a close-up horizon and rely on nearby landmarks. (This is why some leaders cannot cross trackless lakes and fields — they do not focus on the far side.) Dogs have tremendous senses of smell and hearing and can react to something that you cannot sense. Their goals are short-term. As hunters, most dogs are opportunistic and easily distracted by new scents and sounds.

Squat when you want to have a heart-to-heart talk, especially if the dog is shy or anxious.

A dog's instincts are very powerful, and he must develop considerable willpower to overcome them. He jumps after a rabbit instinctively, not to mess up the team. Firmness, understanding, and consistency are required if you are going to train a dog to ignore his instincts. Even marking a well-used scent post is a powerful instinct in the male dog.

You can use some instinctive behaviors to your advantage. Originally roving hunters, dogs take naturally to traveling. A fast trot is their natural gait. They naturally follow trails. They naturally work as a pack. Your job is to mold these characteristics to fit your own plan and to limit undesirable instincts like dominance fighting and stopping to investigate objects or scents of interest. Although these instincts are strong, dogs are highly adaptable and can comply with many demands if properly trained.

One musher would call "Moose!" when his dogs winded game so that he could use the command near a race finish. We take advantage of natural instincts by saying, "Look! Look!" instead. Spoken in a sharp, deep voice, it sounds like the alarm bark, "Woof!" Even untrained pups respond with full power.

A Dog's Psychological Needs

All dogs have certain needs that, if not met, can result in problems ranging from major psychoses to disciplinary trouble to a simple lack of fulfillment. In large kennels, these needs might be overlooked from sheer lack of time or attention if the kennel operator is unaware of them.

Most dogs need a relationship with humans. Unlike wolves, they are domestic animals that by definition rely on humans for their upkeep and security. This relationship is special to the musher because the dogs give so much in return.

Dogs also require hierarchy. They need to know that you are the boss. Some give and take is desirable, but *you* must be the ultimate authority. Some dogs respect only one person and have trouble shifting their respect to a new owner. Others respect men but not women, who have softer, higher voices. Long ago, an untrained Malamute named Yukon accepted us without any respect or affection. He often growled when we disciplined him. But when our brother whipped him for fighting, the effect was astonishing to us. Yukon turned to Ray with *adoration*. Later, when Miki and I learned to discipline him sternly, he came to admire us as well. He only needed to know who was boss.

Dogs also need a sense of security. They need to know that you will care for them when they are hungry, tired, or getting dragged by a tangled towline. They need their companions to bark at intruders with them. They need houses to hide in. Knowing that you are in control gives them security. If they think that you have lost control, they are put in the uncomfortable position of trying to take over. Sometimes you may have to fake it so that the dogs will not lose their confidence in you.

Some (not all) dogs that are abused or have changed owners often, or that are driven too hard, lose their security. All dogs lose some security on trips away from home, and your calm presence and encouragement will reduce their anxiety. Security reduces stress and gives dogs a strong, adaptable psyche.

Similarly, dogs need to play. Playing releases stress and energy, and dogs that have no toys or playmates might turn to more destructive entertainment like chewing on dog houses, digging holes, or

These pups gain security as well as warmth from each other. They are happier this way than if they were separated.

barking. Destructive behavior can be reduced by running the dogs regularly and by giving the dogs toys, a long cable run, or playmates.

Praise and Punishment

We are firm believers in swift, honest, and meaningful praise. We are also firm believers in swift, honest, and meaningful punishment. Together, discipline and praise build character, self-control, and a strong — very strong — desire to please. Both must follow a dog's action within seconds so that the dog makes the connection. Both must be given for a reason, with sincerity and consistency, if they are to have the desired impact. If you want consistent behavior from your dogs, you must show consistent behavior yourself.

A very basic rule in dog handling is that *you must know what a dog is thinking to discipline him effectively*. It seems reasonable to punish a dog for doing the wrong thing, but if he misbehaved because he was afraid or confused, punishing him will frighten or confuse him even more and might even exaggerate his behavior. You must interpret a dog's behavior, determine the cause of his action, then decide how to handle the problem.

For instance, a dog that looks backward might be uncertain. Punishment makes him scared and even more uncertain. He looks backward to see if it will happen again. Instead of punishing the dog, move him back where he will feel more secure. As another example, if a dog chews his harness in frustration because he cannot go yet, try hooking him up last so that he will not have time to get frustrated. Also, a dog that runs away will not understand if you punish him after he returns. You must instead teach him to "Come" and avoid turning that dog loose without supervision.

In many cases, you can avoid using ineffective punishment by changing the situation or the events leading to the problem. We will point out some of these situations in other chapters.

It takes time to really understand your dogs, but until you do, you will not get the most from them. For example, some dogs respond very well to praise but are overly sensitive to stern punishment. Others, like Yukon, have no respect unless you prove yourself dominant by swift, meaningful correction. The majority of dogs, however, respond best to a healthy balance of praise and discipline.

Our old dog Legs did not respond to praise, and he did not like to be touched. As a leader, he obeyed commands only to avoid punishment, not to please us. When he did disobey a command, he ignored shouting, yet a single hard swat on the rump would miraculously put everything right. No praising, coaxing, or pleading ever had any effect.

On the other hand, Tonto, our first leader, was overly sensitive. He was afraid of making a mistake and eventually refused commands for fear of making the wrong choice. With him, *asking* for a turn produced better results than *demanding* one. Spanking him made him freeze up, while wheedling and coaxing made him shine.

Praise is usually given on the run and limited to a pleased word or two. Keep it short: "What a *good* dog!" The tone of voice is very important; also, remember that babbling makes the praise ineffective. (Many mushers think that you should only speak to your dogs to give commands, because the dogs stop listening if you babble. We feel that on a long run, a one-way conversation is more relieving than staring blankly down the trail. The dogs understand from the tone of voice whether we are giving a command or easing boredom on a day-long run.)

Occasionally, you may want to stop the team to praise a leader, especially a young one. Or you may want to pat everyone while giving them a breather. When you step among your dogs, they realize that they have more than a couple of seconds to rest, and you can see the tension roll off as they dive into the snow, lift a leg, or bite snow to cool off. It keeps them happy, especially if you let them know that you are proud of them.

When you discipline a dog, make the punishment suitable to the situation. A small mistake can be corrected by a sharp word. Repeat mistakes can be corrected by stopping the team, anchoring it, then giving the offender a whack on the rump. This will be a light swat or a hard spank, depending upon the crime. Aim for the rump, because striking a dog's head can make him hand-shy. A panicky dog should be restrained, given one swift smack, then quickly released; he will feel foolish for making such a fuss.

Severe punishment is rarely necessary. It is better to take a problem dog out as an individual or in a small team and repeatedly give him a gentler form of discipline. Before you really whip a dog, be sure that you are justified and that you haven't merely lost your temper. Maybe a dog is lagging because his feet are sore; maybe a dog chewed the line because he was caught in a painful tangle that you never saw. Dog fighting usually requires harsh punishment, and this is discussed later in the chapter.

A whip is an effective tool and can be used as a warning, as punishment, or as encouragement. When using it as punishment, you must double it up in your hand; do not crack and snap it on the dog, and do not club him with it. Although a whip can excite and encourage the dogs (if they are not afraid of it), a jingler, made from bottle caps or bells strung together, is also effective.

Kicking is a bad idea. A swift shove on the rump is acceptable to some mushers, but kicking can injure a dog fatally by rupturing internal organs.

Never fly into a rage and mindlessly punish your dogs. They will stop trusting you, become cowed and hand-shy, and may even turn vicious in their own defense. Certainly they will lose their drive and their desire to please you. Punishing the wrong dog or a dog that does not understand why he was punished can have these effects, too. If your whole team falls to the ground when you rush up to discipline one dog, this is a sign that you could be overdoing it.

It is easy to get frustrated when every dog is going in a different direction. You must learn self-control so that you can reason out the problem and the solution instead of grabbing a stick and swinging it. Some people are naturally more excitable, timid, or quick-tempered than others, just as dogs are. Know yourself and your weaknesses, and be prepared to stop and think before administering punishment.

Panicking will also upset your dogs and impede your progress. Dogs are very sensitive to your emotions. Stop. Practice self-discipline and objectivity. You will feel better, your dogs will appreciate it, and other mushers will admire you. Seeing the humor in any situation will help get you through it.

The key to effective praise and punishment is consistency and knowing when and how much to use for any given dog. Most dogs grudgingly appreciate being set straight; they feel more secure knowing that someone reliable is in charge, and other members of your team will appreciate your effort to right a bad situation.

Compromise

Certainly you must be in command, but often you will get better results if you compromise with your dogs. In certain situations, you must be willing to forgive infractions. Minor problems should be ignored if you are disciplining a major problem, because the dogs only can handle so much. Minor problems can also be ignored when the dogs are being stressed, such as in hard physical training or in races.

If a dog is making the same mistake repeatedly but is showing some understanding and improvement, let the mistake slide once in awhile. He may have forgotten himself for a moment (witness the guilty look afterward), or he may be gently testing his independence. Like a child, he wants to feel that he *can* do it, but he no longer feels good about it. For instance, let's say that you shout at him three times for barking, then spank him. A moment later you hear a small "Woof." Let it slide. He might decide that he does not want to bark after all. This is compromising.

Again, if you are on the trail and the situation is improving, let it go for awhile. Dogs tend to "space out" and forget what they were doing. If you constantly wake them up by shouting, they will continue looking backward or goofing up.

When your dogs are tired or are feeling rebellious from being over-trained, they may try to quit on you. Generally, you must discourage this, but if the problem is severe, let your dogs stop. Just do not rest very long. Then after a short distance tell them to stop again. The dogs are not winning, and you are not losing. In a distance race, dogs might try to stop at people's houses where they should not, because they think that the houses are checkpoints and honestly expect a rest. If you try to drive them, they will get sullen. So tell them to stop, but not for very long — just enough to pat them and say, "What good boys." The art of compromise can generate dogs that take advantage of you if you are not careful, but it also will reduce friction and improve the attitude of your team.

Communicating

You can communicate with dogs in two ways — your way and their way. Dogs can learn a number of words, even the names of their close companions. They also respond strongly to tone and inflection. They pick out key words and let the rest of your sentences slide, as in, "You want to go *out*?" or, "Stay *out*!" (This is why you should not say, "You can't go *out*" — the dogs will not understand.) The natural human tendency to repeat short phrases helps dogs to pick up words. We say, "Good boy, yes, what a good boy."

In the following series of photographs, the dogs are all communicating. These two are saying hello.

These two are indicating
recognition and
friendliness with their
tongues.

Trapper is enjoying
himself and releasing
stress as well as calling
to nearby dogs.

Loki might just be sleepy, but dogs also yawn when you look at them — when they are just a little excited because *you looked* at them.

Dogs stretch when they have been a bit excited and are relaxing again.

If you also understand how *dogs* communicate, you have an extra edge in training them. Body language and physical contact play a greater role here than voice. Drooling, panting, and shivering are natural processes, but they can also indicate fear or anxiety. Stretching, licking his nose, or shaking off also occur naturally, but they can happen when a dog recognizes a friend that he admires (you). A dog will also shake off after a bad experience. If you have just freed a dog from a choking tangle and he does not shake off, suspect a possible problem, such as shock or depression. (Know the dog — not all will reliably shake off even when they feel great again.)

Tail-wagging can indicate either friendliness *or* aggression, depending upon whether the tail is waved loosely like a flag or tautly like a wire. Eye contact, or avoidance of it, shows full attention, dominance, subordinance, or confusion. No driver likes a dog who constantly looks backward, but unless it has become a habit, the dog is trying to make eye contact for some reason.

Howling brings dogs together and appears to relieve stress. We like to make our dogs howl (by imitating a howl) during long trips; it unites the team and keeps the dogs happy and secure.

Physical communication on your part includes petting for a reward or throwing a dog to the ground as punishment or to establish your authority. Pinning down a rebellious dog proves your authority by sheer physical control. A dog understands this — you are talking his language. Some experienced mushers bite a dog's ear to punish him and feel that it is a natural form of communication. While it is effective, I personally would hesitate to inflict sudden pain with my face so close to a dog's jaws.

When you resort to your own language, you can only expect the dogs to obey commands that they know. Teaching them a few extra words helps you communicate with them better. For example, on a long trip, our dogs learn the words, "We're going to *camp* now." They willingly leave the trail to struggle through deep snow to the campsite if they know the reason for it.

Our leaders learn that "Trail!" means a broken path to follow. If they lose the trail and we spot it, we say "Gee, trail!" and the dogs watch for it on the right. With just a trace of the trail on drifted snow or ice, the dogs may wander away, but a sharp "Trail!" wakes them up and gets them back on line. When breaking trail across an untraveled field, our dogs cross animal tracks without a glance, but if the track is going our way, the command "Trail!" makes the dogs stay on it.

We also say "Mm, yummy!" at feeding time. Even if we say it at

Although these dogs are resting in a strange place, their howling indicates a sense of security and togetherness. They act more relaxed and playful after a concert.

an odd time, the dogs are up and yowling. We use this to lure in runaway dogs. We also use it to gauge how tired they are. If we stop to snack and they do not respond to the words, we know that we have pushed them too hard.

By communicating with your dogs, you will build a stronger rapport with them. They will better understand what you want. Dogs, especially young ones, sometimes disobey simply because they do not understand what you want.

Attitude

Many mushers believe that attitude is critical to a strong team. Others think that, compared to physical potential and training, attitude is much less significant; that is, a dog cannot run on heart alone. Since every team takes on a unique character, often complementing the driver's character, the importance of attitude probably varies among teams.

At the same time, most mushers today run dogs primarily because they *like* dogs. They want their dogs to be happy. For the recreational musher, attitude is rarely a problem unless severe disciplinary or training problems arise. Hard-working dogs, however, can get so tired of the daily grind that they slip into a depression exacerbated by fatigue. The problem may affect a single dog (see "Burnout") or the whole team (see "The Slump").

Mushers look for a good attitude; dogs should *want* to work. The moment Amber is harnessed and turned loose, she heads for the sled.

Burnout

Learn to recognize depression *before* a major burnout, and rest the dog *before* he goes sour. Symptoms include a reluctance to be harnessed, irritability, anxiety, apathy, lack of appetite, decreased performance, rebellion, a refusal to take commands, or a change in character. A sober dog might act goofy — looking backward, leaning on his partner, or plunging off the trail. The hyper dog may turn sober, apathetic, and sluggish.

If the dog is just trying to avoid responsibility, he needs discipline, but if he is truly burned out, discipline will only depress him more. You cannot cure fatigue by whipping, kissing, or giving drugs. Only rest will cure it. After a tough trip or race, a dog needs time to recover. It may take three weeks for him to fully regain his vitality. If you demand too much, or try to bring him back too soon, he may never completely recover psychologically.

Sometimes a dog tries too hard in a team that is a little too fast for him. Perhaps new dogs outclass him this year and he is burning his heart out trying to keep up. Or maybe he is older and is slowing down. It is not fair to drive this dog; put him in a slower team before he burns out.

A dog that is simply bored is helped by time off. You can also run this dog in a different position, behind other dog teams, on different trails, or even on the same loop in reverse. Remind the dog that you really do care. Spend extra time with him — bring him inside and make him feel good.

I will take a burned-out dog on a private walk. After he entertains himself for awhile, I squat and call him with open arms, hug him, and let him go. Soon this dog is flinging himself into my arms, wriggling with joy. When I leap up and cry, "Let's go!" that fatigued, depressed dog is running in circles of insane joy.

Just playing with a dog on the chain helps — it stimulates him. When men are caught in survival situations, experts recommend play periods to relieve stress. Dogs are the same way. Play relieves their tension and helps to reestablish your rapport with them.

The Slump

"Has your team slumped yet?" is a common question in January. After heavy training in November and December, the whole team can go into a slump. In a way, the slump is good, because the dogs learn that they must work whether they enjoy it or not. The trick is to pull them out of it before the Big Event!

First, recognize the problem. The dogs are eager on the chain but lack spirit on the trail. You climb a hill and there is no power. They have no rhythm or unity. Tugs go slack, and enthusiasm wanes. They bicker, goof off, and look for excuses to mess up.

Next, you must determine the cause of the problem. Are the dogs fatigued, dehydrated, on a poor diet, or suffering from infections or bad feet? Or are they simply bored? Only in the last case is your problem psychological, and this usually goes together with general fatigue.

Rest your dogs for a few days, then run them on new trails even if you have to truck them somewhere. Surprise them — head out the

Stopping occasionally to let the dogs breathe, and maybe walking among them for a pep talk, will keep them moving readily. Dogs that travel for hours without a stop begin to get discouraged. *Photo by Pat Brawand; courtesy Oregon Dune Mushers.*

These dogs are very tired after a tough run, but with time in the house, depression will lift and they will be ready to go in the morning.

twenty-mile trail but turn back after three miles. Time off is your best bet. The dogs will bounce back eager and responsive, without backsliding much physically. This is called peaking your team and is discussed more fully in Chapter 11.

Pep talks along the trail can work wonders. Walk among your dogs, telling them how fantastic they are (lie if you must). This works well after a bad session. Maybe you pushed them too hard on a hot day, or maybe the dogs had a fight and are now shooting dirty looks at each other. After the discipline has sunk in and the dogs are going reasonably well, stop and walk among them. They will not feel so bad. On a long, tough pull, frequent stops keep the dogs motivated. They will not worry that you will *never* stop, so they slack off less. (Do not stop too often or you will break their rhythm and annoy them.)

If your dogs rebel during a slump, do not demand too much. But do not let them take advantage of you, either — just cut the run short.

Keep the trip home upbeat, because the dogs go to sleep remembering the last lesson of the day, not the first. If you must run them the next day, go on a different trail or you will certainly have a repeat disaster.

Before I ran the Yukon Quest race, I asked a veteran musher for advice, and he said, "Make the dogs think you're holding them back, even when they're tired." That's fine, I thought, but how? The answer is by using reverse psychology. When your dogs are tired, they are glad to stop, but after a few minutes, they are usually ready to go again. This time lapse is called the recovery time. If you ask the dogs to go *before* they recover, they have no enthusiasm. If you ask them to go *afterward*, they need no second bidding; this is reverse psychology. Like children, they are trying to get the better of you. If they think that you want to go, they want to stay, and vice-versa. The turning point in their mood comes after they have recovered, when they feel like going again. Standing up, shaking off, harness-banging, barking, and looking back are signs that they have recovered.

By stopping when the dogs are not ready to stop, and by resting longer than they feel is necessary, you are using reverse psychology to make them want to go. It keeps them willing on a tough trail. If you know your dogs well, you will know when they have recovered, even if they do not stand up together. Shaking the handlebow or clucking brings them to their feet readily. The recovery period varies considerably, but half a minute to five minutes is usually all it takes.

Leaders require special attention, because their attitude can hold together a ragged team. Depressed leaders often turn a deaf ear to commands. They must be replaced to avoid a worsening problem. Just moving them back in the team can work a miracle. Or, ask the dogs to go slower so that they are not pushing the front end so hard.

Problem Dogs

It is far easier to prevent a bad habit from developing than it is to erase a set behavior pattern. Starting with pups, teach your dogs discipline. When problems do arise, deal with them promptly to prevent bad habits from forming. As mentioned before, you can often change the situation to eliminate incorrect behavior instead of using punishment.

Aggression
Dog fighting was once a common problem but is rarely seen in today's teams. Fighters have been culled, because serious mushers

will not tolerate them. Some recreational teams have fighters because it is difficult for the recreational musher to get rid of dogs that are so much like pets. However, once the decision is made to cull them, it usually is followed by profound relief.

Whether you tolerate a fighter is your own choice. If you keep one, you must be willing to endure the frightful tasks of breaking up fights, patching injuries, paying veterinarian bills (maybe even doctor bills), and perhaps facing the death of a dog. Owning a dog that grabs animals in passing teams will make you some enemies, too.

Perhaps huskies fight more than other dogs because they are more closely related to the dominance-oriented wolves. Wolves often avoid fights by avoiding conflicts, but dogs are forced into close company, without the space to avoid each other. In the dog yard, in the team, and even in your own home, they cannot get away from each other.

Squabbling dogs come apart with a sharp command, but a true fight often requires brute force to break up the dogs. If the dogs hear your shouts, they may take them as encouragement. If they bite you, it will be an automatic reaction, not a deliberate one. Pulling one dog by the tail and kicking off the other might break them up if you are alone. In a bad fight, you must jerk the dogs out one at a time and tie them off. Some dogs fight until they are literally knocked unconscious.

Whipping dogs with a hose or dousing them with water will work sometimes, but not always. Pulling by a hind leg can dislocate the hip, while grabbing the collar can get your hand bitten. A musher once stopped a fight by firing a pistol, but the second time he tried it, the dogs ignored him. I have thrown dogs into deep water with immediate results, but once, old Loki bobbed up, seized Trapper, and drove him back underwater for five seconds!

Young dogs testing their strength by fighting will benefit from severe discipline. However, if two dogs are just starting to dislike each other, a major whipping will imprint the incident in each dog's mind, and he will blame his opponent instead of learning from the punishment. An immediate return to work distracts the dogs so that they forget the grudge.

Neutering is often successful in preventing dogs from fighting (see Chapter 6). It works best in males, especially young ones. However, once the fighting instinct becomes ingrained, the only real solution is to get rid of the dog. (If you sell him, inform the new owner of the problem.)

A dog aggressive toward humans must be dealt with before he becomes a menace. Prove your authority physically by shaking him

Julie and Legs demonstrate two ways to approach a scared dog: the wrong way — hand over the head, with good intentions, but overwhelming the dog —

and the right way — hand under the chin, inviting a positive response. Once the dog's fear is allayed, he can be petted on the head.

hard or throwing him to the ground. When he growls, slap his muzzle hard and shout, "No!" If you are actually afraid of a dog, get rid of him.

Shy Dogs

Dogs can be shy or spooky due to an inherited tendency, environmental factors, or both. A shy dog has not necessarily been abused. Some dogs are afraid of everything, while others are afraid only of humans, or only of men. Some mushers will not keep a spooky dog, but those who are willing to work with them often have good success. Prevention is easier than cure, and this means handling pups frequently (see Chapter 8).

When approaching a scared dog, squat so that you look less imposing. Offer a hand, stroking him underneath the jaw instead of over his head. Some people march up to any dog, even a strange one, and thump his side without so much as an introduction. This just is not smart. Most dogs tolerate or enjoy it, but a few cannot handle it and may panic or even snap at the offending hand.

Shy dogs need lots of handling and encouragement. Tie them where you can pet them frequently. Work with them one-on-one. Bring them inside and offer treats from your hand. Do not discipline them physically if a sharp word gets the desired response.

We have had many shy dogs. Legs made friends with us when we discovered that he liked gloves. We would give him a glove; he would bury it and return for another. That simple game laid the foundation of his trust. Sky was afraid of men. Two days after we got him, he decided that he was *not* afraid of girls. Loki acted as though he had been abused; it took him months to overcome his fear. These three dogs all matured into good leaders.

Hyperactive Dogs

Some mushers like "crazy" dogs and allow jumping, chewing, squabbling, and screaming. This excitement enhances the dogs' spirit, but too much of it tires the dogs and lessens their sense of responsibility.

Handling and exercise will tone down hyperactive dogs. Picket them along the main trail in your yard and make a point of handling them. Make them stand to be petted; do not encourage roughhousing. A big bone, a hunk of rawhide, or even wood will deflect their destructive energy from your equipment. Hooking up screamers last will reduce tangles and chewed lines.

Sprint dogs need to be hyper because their spirit plays a big part in winning a race. How much harness-banging a musher tolerates is up to the individual. In a freighting team, this business would soon quiet down. *Courtesy* Fairbanks Daily News-Miner.

When my dogs are not happy, I am not happy. The keys to keeping your dogs happy and productive lie in understanding your dogs in particular and dog behavior in general. Be consistent, patient, and observant when handling your dogs. Be cautious when handling dogs during hard training. If you pay attention to them, they will pay attention to you — and you will all be happy.

To be a dedicated musher, you must really like dogs and get along with dogs. You must also have a sense of responsibility and a sense of humor.

CHAPTER 3

SLEDS, RIGGING, AND GEAR

You do not need much equipment to run a dog team. What you do need is gear of good quality, in good condition, and suitable to your needs. To see what works best, go to races, feed shops, swap meets, and club meetings. Ask questions, but do not take anything for granted. If you are not sure about some gadget, try to borrow it before buying one. Much of the paraphernalia is very useful but not necessary.

Sleds

Most mushers use the modern toboggan or the traditional basket sled. Select a sled with which you feel comfortable and that suits your purpose. Racers want light, maneuverable sleds. A recreational musher must consider strength and versatility, while a freighter needs a heavy, durable sled.

Sled Types
Different sleds are adapted to various conditions. Toboggans and long, narrow sleds with wide runners handle soft snow better. In open, drifted areas, mushers tend to use long, inflexible sleds. Toboggan sleds and sleds with long runners travel well over hummocks and rough country, but the old-style, runnerless toboggans skid into ruts too easily.

Basket Sleds. The basket or stanchion sleds are used by sprint racers, by some recreational mushers, and by traditional mushers who prefer wood over the modern shiny, angular contraptions of metal and plastic. Basket sleds may or may not be faster and easier to handle, depend-

Although sprint
sleds come in many
styles, they all are
lightweight, supple,
and maneuverable.
Courtesy Fairbanks
Daily News-Miner.

ing upon the load, the trail conditions, and the musher with whom
you are talking. They do perform well on glare ice, hard-pack, and
sidehills and in high wind conditions. The sleds are lightweight, and
the high basket keeps your gear above any overflow water. But they
carry less and are more top-heavy than toboggans.

In the summer, basket sleds should be protected from rain and
dampness and from sunlight, which dries the wood and ages the
finish. Varnishing the sleds before storing them helps to preserve
them; wood becomes brittle if it gets too dry.

Basket sleds have a certain grace that toboggans lack. Miki and I
have always used them, and while I could say that it is because we

see a lot of knee-deep water on our trails, it actually is because we like their traditional beauty.

Toboggans. These are actually toboggan-sleds, not the traditional toboggans. The modern toboggan is wider and is set up on runners. The bed rides two inches above the surface to reduce drag, but in deep snow it rides on the snow and will not bog down, as will a basket sled. Some have stanchions, but most rely on a sled bag to hold in your gear.

Compared to basket sleds, toboggans are more durable and stable and are capable of carrying bigger loads. Depending on the build, they usually are considerably heavier and more rigid than basket sleds and are less maneuverable when empty. Loaded toboggans, however, are more maneuverable and stable than loaded basket sleds.

The toboggan is very popular among distance racers; you rarely see stanchion sleds in these races. Jeff King has rigged his with a gee pole for racing the Yukon Quest. *Photo by Ron Lambert.*

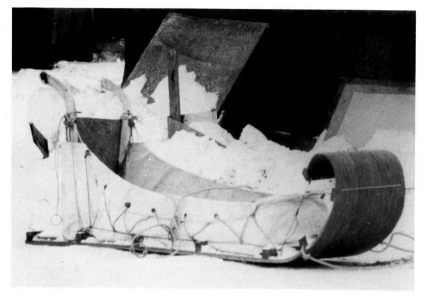

This toboggan at Old Crow, Yukon Territory, Canada, is styled after the sleds used earlier in the century. The flat bottom and enclosed basket serve well in the deep, soft snow found in forested areas of Canada and Alaska.

Other Sleds. Ingenuity has resulted in many sled designs. Sleds have been made from plywood, metal tubing, plastic, flattened oil drums, or boards hacked from the forest. Some innovative builders have put springs underneath the basket instead of stanchions, have improvised hinged stanchions for flexibility, have laminated wood with fiberglass or graphite for strength, or have added an emergency brake for that uncontrollable team. Some have combined the basket and toboggan sleds, keeping the plastic bed but adding a wooden basket with stanchions.

In parts of Canada and Alaska, the flat-bottomed toboggan is still used. These picturesque sleds are very narrow — sometimes only fifteen inches wide — to allow them to glide down snowshoe trails. The sides are made of stretched rawhide, canvas, or plywood. Traditionally, these sleds were used only with a few dogs in single file.

Skiers sometimes tow behind small sleds called pulks, which are discussed in the skijoring section in Chapter 15.

Figure 3-1
Basket Sled and Toboggan

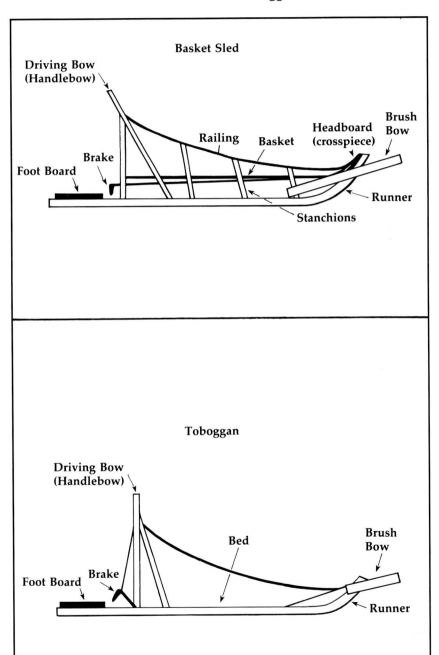

Sled Characteristics

Sleds must maneuver easily and track in a straight line. Longer runners track better but reduce maneuverability. Flexible runners allow the sled to bend during cornering and absorb shock if you hit something, but if they are *too* flexible, they make the sled sloppy. Narrow runners (less than two inches wide) drag less on hard snow, while wider ones — up to three inches wide — float better on soft surfaces.

A sled built a bit narrower in front, so that it is slightly wedge-shaped, will track better. The difference in width from front to back can be as little as one-fourth inch on a small sled to two inches on a long one.

Some sled builders put a slight rocker-type curve in the runner so that most of the weight rests on one point and the sled swivels more easily. A regular, flat runner has full contact with the trail and therefore trades maneuverability for straight tracking and stability. In rough country, a high upturn at the front takes the bumps better, as do longer runners.

The pieces of a wooden sled are held together with braided twine (twisted twine frays) or babiche (rawhide strips). Babiche has the advantage of shrinking tightly when it dries — but it also stretches when it gets wet. Twine is more readily available, does not rot, and is less tempting to dogs with itchy teeth. The metal parts of a sled should be bolted instead of welded. Bolts are easily replaced if they break, and they allow sled joints to flex. Welds that flex will eventually suffer metal fatigue and split.

The handlebow, or drive bow, may be square or rounded, vertical or nearly horizontal, and high or low, depending upon the design. Choose whichever you find most comfortable. If the handlebow is too high, it will be more difficult to control the sled, while a handlebow that is too low can cause back and shoulder fatigue. String, leather, or friction tape wrapped over the handlebow will increase your grip.

The brush bow can be made from one piece of steam-bent wood, laminated wood, plastic, steel, or some combination. Wood can be wrapped with rawhide for strength. We prefer half-inch plastic brush bows; although they can collapse in a hard collision, they are practically unbreakable and absorb shock better. Quarter-inch plastic is not rigid enough, even if two layers are put together.

Wood Types

Different sled woods vary in cost, availability, strength, flexibility, and bendability (the ease of shaping runners and other bent pieces). To resist breakage, the wood must have a straight grain, few knots, and no rot.

Hickory is strong and hard but heavy. Birch is much lighter and is shock-resistant if you hit a tree, but is likely to break under constant stress. It is also often hard to find. White ash is also lightweight and resistant to shock. White oak, although harder, is heavy and less resilient; its greatest asset is its natural resistance to decay. Hard maple combines the better traits of many woods. Since some sled parts must be bent, the bendability of a wood is important. White oak is the most bendable, followed by red oak, hickory, birch, ash, and maple. Green wood is often so bendable that it does not require steaming, while kiln-dried wood has so little moisture that it must be soaked and steamed before being bent.

Other Materials

Many new materials are being used in sleds. The new metals and plastics are hard, flexible, durable, and lightweight. Stainless steel, aircraft aluminum, and the recently introduced chrome-moly steel are all strong and lightweight. Plastics (see below) have revolutionized sleds. However, all materials have advantages and disadvantages. Wood flexes, but it will break. Metal is strong, but it does not spring back into shape and is inflexible. Plastic may be too flexible, but it is virtually unbreakable, except in severe cold, unless it is damaged by too much sunlight.

Runner Plastics

Runners used to go bare or were waxed, shod with steel, or glazed with ice. Now plastics are by far the most popular material for runner bases, followed only by steel. Plastic can be purchased in any width or length from many outfitters and mail-order catalogues, as well as from some hardware stores. Although nearly frictionless, plastic is not as abrasion-resistant as wood or steel, and a few miles on a gravel road will destroy plastic shoes. If not abused, plastic can last for years, although it is not as slippery once it has been abraded.

Runner plastic can be glued, bolted, or screwed onto the bottom of runners. Musher and sled designer Tim White of Grand Marais, Minnesota, developed the QCR, or Quick-Change Runner System, which involves sliding new plastic over aluminum rails attached to the runners. This saves tremendously over the time it takes to bolt on plastic and is particularly popular among racers. Unfortunately, it is not available for all kinds and sizes of plastic, and the initial installation is fairly expensive.

For the recreational musher, half-inch UHMW plastic is a good option. The extra-thick plastic might outlast the sled and is strong enough to hold up temporarily if the runner breaks. Scratches can be planed down, or the plastic can be removed and flipped for a fresh start. It does, however, cost twice as much as quarter-inch plastic.

Types of Plastic. Several kinds of plastic are available that vary in price, durability, slickness, and cold-weather performance. Although all are made of polyethylene, different manufacturing methods result in the varying characteristics. The following is a partial list of common plastics.

UHMW: This "ultra-high molecular weight" plastic is commonly used for runners and toboggan beds. It is economical, durable, popular, and available in many sizes.

P-Tex 2000: This is a very slick glue-on plastic that is popular among sprint racers. P-Tex can be hot-waxed for a super glide but unfortunately is not very durable.

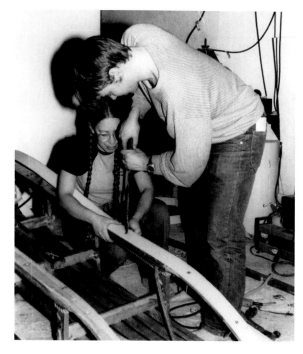

UHMW plastic is popular for reducing friction on sled runners and can be bolted and screwed on. Scratches that develop in the plastic can be shaved or planed smooth.

HM3: Similar to P-Tex, HM3 is a glue-on plastic — slick but not very durable.

UPX: Although expensive, this popular black plastic is durable and is used frequently in sheets for toboggan beds, as well as on runners. Some suppliers no longer offer this type.

XH (also HD): A softer plastic, XH is very slick and is popular among racers. It glides well in a wide range of temperatures, including colder snow (where most materials will drag like sandpaper). Although cheap and versatile, XH is not very durable.

Orange V: This is a very durable plastic that holds up even on bare ground. It is waxable and more flexible than other plastics and is a good plastic for temperature extremes — above freezing or below zero — but it is expensive.

UH 4000: Like UHMW, it is very durable, waxable, and moderately cheap. Unwaxed, it does well in moderate snow conditions.

Teflon formulas temporarily improve glide when used on sled plastics, but they last only a few miles. Hot-waxing, too, works only temporarily, but it does improve the slickness and is popular among sprint racers. Runners are hot-waxed like cross-country skis. Different waxes are available for different temperatures, but runners should not be waxed in extreme cold. The plastic must be smooth and finely sanded before the ski wax is melted and smoothed onto the warm plastic. There is an art to this technique that is best learned from ski masters who can also fill you in on the latest materials and methods.

Softer plastics can be easily shaved with a piece of cut glass to smooth out scratches. All plastics should be protected from excessive sunlight.

Steel Runners/Birch Runners

Steel is also popular as a runner shoe. Its main advantage is its durability in gravelly conditions. Its sharper edges will not skid as badly. Spring steel offers the best overall performance. Cold-rolled steel is very durable but drags harder, while stainless steel is faster but less durable.

A Canadian musher told us that in severe cold — fifty below zero (F.) — nothing glides better than green birch runners.

Snowless Rigs

Because of the pounding and jerking of wheeled rigs on snowless terrain, a good shock-absorber system between the vehicle and the dogs is essential with any snowless rig.

Dog Carts

Dog carts can be used in snowless conditions for training and racing smaller teams. Some aluminum carts weigh as little as thirty pounds, while larger models weigh two hundred pounds. Light carts have a free-swinging or a steerable front wheel; heavier, four-wheeled versions are more stable and have a handlebar for steering and hydraulic brakes to give you a semblance of control over the whims of the cart.

Carts should be low and wide for stability, with good suspension and a sturdy build to withstand vibrations. Good brakes that can be locked when you stop are essential. On smaller carts, you may have a drag brake (friction brake) or a "digger" on which you stand. Larger

Kathy Moulton drives a team of Siberian Huskies. During the summer, dog carts can replace sleds. Carts should be solid and stable to allow good control. *Photo by David Waguespack; courtesy Oregon Dune Mushers.*

carts require hydraulics. A hand brake/emergency brake can be used as a backup; however, no braking system short of a snub rope will hold a larger team. Deflective devices should protect all of the wheels.

Before using any wheeled rig, check the tires, the steering system, the towline linkage, and the brakes, including the hydraulic fluid level if applicable.

All-Terrain Vehicles

All-terrain vehicles (ATVs) are very popular for training larger teams. They are heavy and have good brakes and steering, yet they are more versatile than the lumbering car chassis. You can use the motor to encourage a speed-up command, to climb tough hills, or to help flagging pups. However, overuse of the motor encourages laziness, because the dogs begin to count on your help.

Some machines require the engine to be running when the vehicle is in motion, so check your owner's manual. Do not hook the dogs too close to the machine; you have plenty of control, so give the dogs some space. The speedometer is great for pinpointing speeds — the speed at which a dog breaks into a lope, or your team's average or top speed. The odometer can accurately measure your training trails — you might be surprised at the discrepancy between your educated guess and the real thing.

The Car Chassis

A stripped-down car chassis may be heavy, but it allows excellent control even with a large team (see the photograph in Chapter 11). You can even hook up two towlines to a chassis and run dogs four abreast (be sure to have good leaders). Being a sit-down vehicle, hopefully with good suspension, the chassis is more comfortable than a dog cart. Several people can come aboard to ride and to handle dogs. Chains on the tires will increase the braking effectiveness. The chassis is, however, limited to wide, smooth-surfaced trails or roads.

Dog Walkers

These are discussed in Chapter 11.

Rigging

Any strong rope that can be spliced can be used for towlines (ganglines). The popular polyethylene rope is hollow, easy to splice, durable, and inexpensive. Polypropylene rope is cheaper but tends

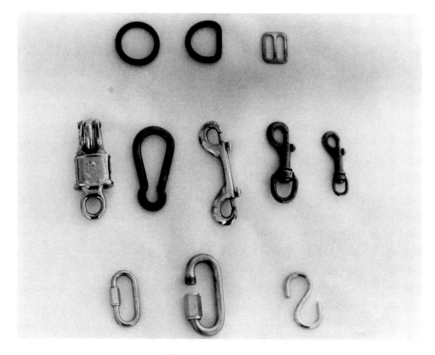

Mushing Hardware
Top: O-ring, D-ring, slider, used in harness, collars; larger O-rings are also used on dog chains and towlines. *Center:* Panic snap (quick-release snap) for snubs, skijoring; spring snaps for towlines and picket lines; double snap to quickly replace broken swivel snaps; ⅝-inch swivel snap for pickets and tugs; ⅜-inch swivel snap for puppies, necklines. *Bottom:* Small quick link, for picket chains (closed); large quick link, for towlines, picket lines (open); S-link, for fastening snaps to chains.

to fray and break more easily. For towlines, ½-inch or ⅜-inch rope is best, while ¼-inch and ³⁄₁₆-inch rope is good for tugs and necklines. Untangling dogs is easier if the tugs and necklines are of a different color than the towline.

Use ⅝-inch or ⅜-inch brass swivel snaps on tugs and necklines. An occasional musher uses short wooden toggles instead of snaps to secure tuglines, or he or she uses necklines with loops that fit over the dogs' heads. Both alternatives are slower than snaps but will not ice up and are less cold on the fingers.

The length of your towline sections depends upon what you do

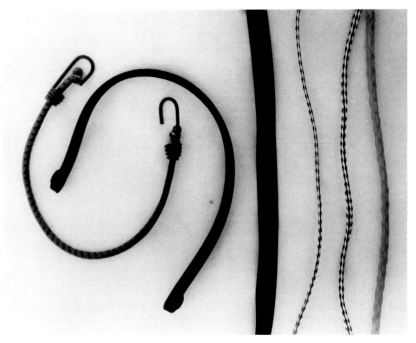

Left to right: Bungees, one of elastic (good for lashing loaded sleds); another of rubber (good for shock links and brake springs). One-inch flat nylon webbing, used for dog harnesses. Different thicknesses of poly rope, used for tugs, towlines, necklines, and other purposes. It comes in many weights and colors and is easily worked with a splicing tool.

with your dogs. Faster dogs need longer segments so that they have room to run in rhythm. Apparently, hounds can be run more closely together than huskies. Trotting dogs can be spaced more closely together to shorten the team length and get more power to the sled. This is important when freighting.

Most towline sections are 93 to 103 inches long. In freighting teams, sections can be as short as 85 inches. A smaller dog may not fit into a standard section of towline; the loop on the back of his harness must be lengthened so that he will fit.

Tuglines range from 55 inches on sprint teams down to 36 inches

A fid, which is a splicing tool used to make loops like the one pictured here, in hollow rope.

on some work teams. Tugs for wheel dogs are longer — usually 55 inches — to allow more maneuverability and to reduce jerks from the sled. If the wheelers' tugs are not long enough, at least lengthen the towline (perhaps by inserting a shock link) so that the dogs are not crowded by the sled. Lead dogs, too, need longer tugs.

Necklines hold the dogs in position and help balance them on corners. The necklines must not be so tight that the dogs are dragged by the neck, or so long that the dogs can get tangled in them. Most are 10 to 14 inches long, and angle back to the dogs' collars so they will not get a leg over it. Necklines between double leaders are about 14 inches long.

Some mushers insert a shock link in the towline between the sled and the team or put stretch cords (usually bungee) on individual tugs. The shock link normally should be tight, not springy; otherwise, it will not resist obstacles firmly enough. Shock links are especially needed on larger teams and on rough trails.

If you run pups or line-chewers, you can run aircraft cable through

Trapline dogs often haul heavy loads on poor trails. The short towline gives them more leverage and power. At faster speeds, a longer line is needed to prevent bunching and tangles.

the hollow towline so that a chewed rope will not separate. (Some mushers use chain instead of rope and cable.) A cable must have enough slack inside the towline so that the rope can stretch. If the tuglines and necklines are also made of cable, you *must* have a break-away point. Snap the cable neckline onto a twine loop or onto a split key ring on the dog's collar so that it will break before the dog does if he hits a tree.

Harnesses

For a harness to work, it must fit. The harness should lie smoothly over a dog without pinching, twisting, or bunching. (The new siwash-type harness, discussed shortly, does bunch along the back when the dog is not pulling.) The harness collar should not press into a dog's throat but should rest just below the notch where the windpipe dis-

This cross-back harness lies smoothly over Sky's back. Judging by the size of the neck and the length of the back, it is a bit large for him.

Arthur Walden, author of *A Dog-Puncher on the Yukon*, probably used leather freight harnesses like this one years ago.

appears. It should fit snugly into the groove in front of the dog's shoulders and not lie loosely over the shoulder blade. A race harness must end just above the base of the dog's tail. A tight harness can pinch or choke a dog; a badly fitting or poorly padded one can cause ugly sores in the armpits, and any of these problems can made a dog reluctant to pull.

Some small dogs have larger chests and require a bigger harness than narrow-chested dogs of the same weight. Others need harness adjustments as the season progresses: fat dogs slim down, others grow bulky with muscles, and heavy-furred dogs might need a harness size change as the coats grow thicker, or if they shed. On long-distance races, dogs may lose so much weight that they may require a smaller harness.

Harnesses may need to be specially fitted. Hound-type dogs have narrow chests; an open (wider) breast plate will not slip as much as a closed breast plate on these dogs. If the armpits are chafed, a longer breast plate may be needed.

Harnesses were once made of leather or cotton webbing, but now they are made from soft, flat, one-inch nylon webbing and are padded around the neck and sometimes along the sides with artifical fleece,

Figure 3-2
Harness Styles

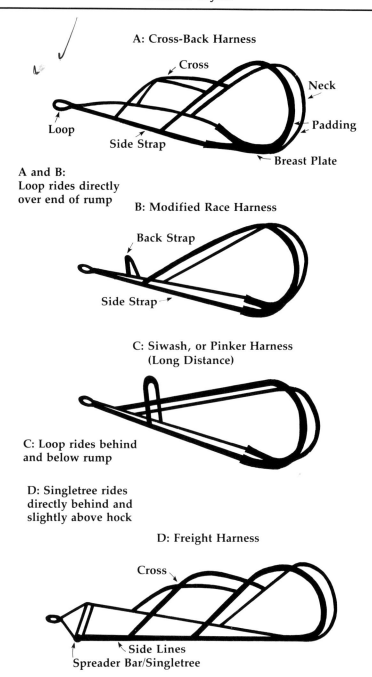

A: Cross-Back Harness

Cross

Neck

Padding

Loop

Side Strap

Breast Plate

A and B:
Loop rides directly
over end of rump

B: Modified Race Harness

Back Strap

Side Strap

C: Siwash, or Pinker Harness
(Long Distance)

C: Loop rides behind
and below rump

D: Singletree rides
directly behind and
slightly above hock

D: Freight Harness

Cross

Side Lines
Spreader Bar/Singletree

bunting, or similar material. Many have reflective tape for nighttime safety. While matched harnesses make a team look great for spectators, you will find that harnesses color-coded for size are easier to use. The tugline snaps onto a rope loop or a D-ring at the back of the harness. Rope loops are cheaper, lighter, and adjustable, while D-rings are easier to hit with snaps.

Race harnesses can be made of lightweight nylon or polypropylene, but these have not gained much popularity. Distance race dogs and freighting dogs require more padding on their harnesses than do sprint dogs and recreational dogs.

In days past when dogs often pulled a hundred pounds each, they wore freight harnesses with thick leather collars. Today, dogs rarely pull that much, and many different types of harnesses are available.

The cross-back or race harness is the most popular and comes in many styles. It allows free movement but lies snugly against the dog. Some modified race harnesses dispense with the cross-back. The side lines extend farther backward, to the last rib, allowing better chest expansion. A back band stabilizes this harness, but it is easier for dogs to back out of, and the harness will bunch up when the dog is not pulling. (A chronic harness-slipper can be discouraged by adding a belly band behind the rib cage.) This type of racing harness does not seem to have a definite name. Bob Lugo of Free Spirit Kennel & Outfitter calls his version the Pro. Tun-Dra® sells a heavier version called the Trail Harness.

Distance racers sometimes use another modified harness, called the siwash or Pinker harness (not to be confused with the old siwash, which has a spreader bar — see the photograph). This harness takes more weight off of the hips and allows better expansion of the rib cage and freer movement of the back, like the Pro harness.

Freight harnesses have side lines that connect directly to a spreader bar at the hock, instead of canting up to the hips. This prevents a downward pull on the hips, as is seen on the cross-back harness. Correct placement of the spreader bar is essential so that it will not interfere with the hind legs, or hang slack and tangle. These harnesses are heavy and awkward to use but are efficient for pulling loads.

Wheel dogs, especially, can suffer strains in the back and hind legs if the harness is pulling down on the hips. This problem can be relieved by using the siwash or freight harnesses, or by rotating wheelers frequently. Usually this is seen when the dogs are pulling heavy loads for long distances.

Oly models a Taiga Max Siwash Harness, designed by Taiga Mushing Supplies. This style allows good chest expansion, but the dogs sometimes slip out of them. The arched back strap should not put any pressure on the back; it merely keeps the back from pushing through the harness.

Only dogs pulling heavy loads, like this weight-puller, need heavy-duty harnesses that pull from the shoulder. A spreader bar in back holds the sidelines apart to keep the harness from pinching the hips. Bruce, a Malamute/ Labrador mix owned by Peryll Kyzer of Anchorage, Alaska, has pulled forty-eight times his own weight. Bruce's harness is an excellent example of a proper weight-pull harness. *Photo by Ken Bade; courtesy Sue Renkert.*

Collars

Nylon-web collars are cheap and durable. Styles include the semichoke and the adjustable collar. If you have collar-chewers, you can use chain collars that will *not* slip tight. (These are illegal in some races.) You can also run chain through hollow nylon webbing so that the dogs cannot chew it apart. Leather collars are used rarely simply due to the expense. Less durable collars are easily made with polyethylene rope, but these are more likely to cause chafing.

Puppy collars should be snug to discourage chewing but must be checked every two weeks and loosened as the pups grow.

Larger D-rings and O-rings are easier to hit with a snap when hooking up but are more likely to freeze to a dog's tongue.

Booties

These are discussed in Chapter 7.

Collars, left to right: semi-choke; adjustable (slider allows size adjustment); chain collar padded with hollow nylon, for the expert chewer; semi-choke collar made from hollow rope (cheap, but not durable). Easy to make with a fid.

Puppies' collars must be checked frequently to be sure that growth does not lead to choking. This collar is too long, tempting the pup to chew.

Miscellaneous Gear

Snow Hooks and Snub Ropes

The snow hook (or brush or ice hook) anchors the team when you stop. At hookup, a snub rope must be used to hold a big team (see below). The snow hook attaches directly to the towline, not to the sled, to prevent the dogs from pulling the sled apart. The hook can be anchored beside the sled or between the runners and behind the sled brake. Some hooks can be sharpened for pounding into the ice. Otherwise, you must chop a notch into the ice to set the hook.

A wider hook, or one with fins or a plate between the tines, is more effective in soft snow. A high handle, too, is easier to grab out of deep snow. Most hooks are made of steel, but lighter aluminum race hooks are also available. Single-prong hooks are light and work in brush but tend to fall sideways when you stomp them into the snow. All hooks should have curved prongs so that they dig deeper as the team pulls forward. For longer stops and at hookup, a second smaller, removable hook can be snapped to the towline directly behind the leaders to keep the team from swinging and to take the pressure off of the leaders.

Sometimes an uncontrollable team can be stopped by catching a tree with a hook, but this is risky. The line might snap, or you might get hurt if the sled stops suddenly. Unless you are headed for heavy traffic or an indignant moose, it is better to let the team run until they calm down; then stop and turn them around. I once tried to use my snow hook to stop my dogs from chasing a small dog. The hook rope broke and I lost control. Luckily, the ferocious little dog held my team at bay until I could pull them away.

For safety, a holster keeps the hook secure in the sled when it is not anchoring the dogs. Many types of holsters are available, including plastic, leather, or cloth. Snow hooks are dangerous. Be careful with them and be sure that they are secured when the sled is moving.

Many mushers use a snub rope in addition to, or instead of, the snow hook. It also is fastened to the towline; the other end is fastened to a tree with a quick-release knot or a "panic snap." Both of these release instantly with a quick jerk. (The knot should be made only after wrapping the rope several times around the tree or post, to prevent tension from jamming the knot.) Do not let the snub rope drag behind the sled. You or another team might get tangled in it, plus it is illegal in some races.

Whatever method you use to anchor your dogs, be sure that you can release the team while keeping one hand firmly on the handlebow.

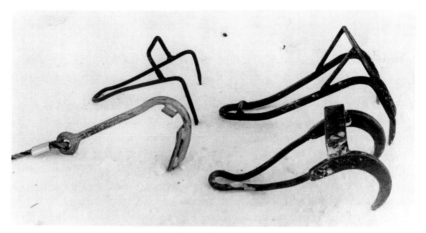

Snow Hooks

Top, left: Lighter hook, good only for holding leaders (attach to towline *behind* leaders, *not* to leader's collar) or for holding two or three dogs. *Top, right:* A bad hook; the straight prongs pulled out of the snow, resulting in a bad accident. *Bottom, left:* Single-prong hook; doesn't work well. *Bottom, right:* Standard hook; curved prongs bite snow.

A quick-release from RAMCO outfitters, attached to a snub rope. The panic snap opens instantly when the dark rope handle is jerked, thus releasing the dog team.

Skijoring Gear
This is discussed in the section on skijoring in Chapter 15.

Cable Pickets
We used to carry a thirty-pound picket chain to stake the dogs on camping trips, but now everyone uses cable picket lines with short drop lines for each dog. These weigh only a couple of pounds and have 12- or 14-inch drop lines with swivel snaps for individual dogs spaced five feet apart. The lengths vary and can be custom-ordered. These lines are intended only for temporarily staking the dogs in camp.

Pickets should be made of aircraft cable, not twisted cable that frays quickly. Plastic-coated cable resists fraying and is easier to untangle and stretch out. To lengthen the picket, stretch a rope between the end snap and the nearest post or tree.

Single-dog pickets are handy and can be purchased or made by clamping a large O-ring to one end of a length of cable and a swivel

Picket line for several dogs. May be of aircraft cable, or chain. These are good for temporarily staking dogs during hook-up, at races, and while camping.

snap to the other. Materials can be purchased from hardware stores or mail-ordered from hardware and trapping-supply catalogues.

Devices to Increase Control

Stabilizing Rudder. This attaches to the back of the runner and acts like a skate blade to reduce skidding. It is useful on ice in high wind when the sled is whipped around. It also controls skidding on sidehills.

Snow-Machine Track. Sixteen or twenty inches of snow-machine track can be dragged behind the sled brake and between the runners, upon which you can step to slow down the dogs. The track should be narrow, not wide, and you might need to cut and shape it to fit. Studded tracks give you more control. The track fastens to the back stanchions, not to the bridle.

Rough-locks. These are chains wrapped around the runners to create a drag that can tame steep, icy slopes. They can also control large or unruly teams. Additional wraps of chain increase the drag; so does having a load in the sled. The chain should be placed around the runner and back stanchion so that the front of the sled can swing unimpeded. If only one runner is rough-locked, you can step from one runner to the other to control the drag.

Dog Bags

Dog bags are used (often required) in sprint races to haul in dropped dogs. A dog can be lashed in the sled with spare necklines or stuffed in a sack tied around the neck, but a bag is easier and safer. It must be made of a tough, tear-resistant fabric, such as cordura, and have a wide mouth that closes firmly around the dog's neck.

Sled Bags

Full-length sled bags have replaced the old tarps once used by travelers. They come in many sizes to fit toboggans and basket sleds and are usually made of cordura. Some are simple, and others are loaded with compartments. New designs include a tentlike "bivvy-sack" conversion for sleeping more comfortably in the sled. Although handy, sled bags are not as versatile as tarps.

Dog Boxes

The dog box used for hauling dogs in a pickup should meet your own needs. It can be a single-decker, double-decker, or, on larger

A bit of cord keeps this rough lock from slipping so the snap does not drag under the runner. When not in use, the chain can be snapped under the sled rail, out of the way.

trucks, a double-decker walk-in type where compartments open to the inside.

Since many mushers drive thousands of miles a year to reach mushing trails and races, the box must be safe and comfortable for the dogs. This means having well-ventilated individual compartments large enough for the dog to turn around, but not much larger. The dogs need to brace themselves against the walls on rough roads; smaller boxes also hold heat better. Ventilation is especially important during warm weather.

The box must be bolted or strapped to the truck so that it will not bounce or blow off. Straw is a must in the winter but should be replaced in the spring. One musher's box almost burned up in the summer because of spontaneous combustion in the damp straw. If the compartment doors open to the outside, they must have locks so

Most serious mushers build a plywood box for carrying dogs on a pickup. The boxes can be two-tiered, like this one, to hold additional dogs. A shovel holder on the back keeps that tool available for clean-up.

that the doors will not fly open. A double system is safer; this usually means adding a chain or bar that drops or slides over all the doors.

If you do not have a pickup, or if you have too many dogs for one box, you can tow a dog box on a trailer. Or, the dogs can be transported in a van or in a larger car (preferably in kennels or tied down). These alternatives are particularly popular in Europe.

Sled Racks, Hooks, Tack Box

The sled rack on top should also be strong and capable of holding a sled against the wind. Other racks and hooks are useful for hanging shovels and gear. (The shovel is a must for cleaning up staging areas.)

A tack box and a method of picketing your dogs to the truck are also useful.

Winter Safety Gear

Winter mushing means icy roads. Driving carefully and carrying chains, a two-way radio, blankets, and other emergency gear will help keep you safer.

Little Plastic Sleds

A child's plastic sled is marvelously useful. Children use it with one or two dogs. You can haul wood, water, camp gear, or dog food with it. Distance racers can carry one for hauling feed at checkpoints. It is featherweight and easily fits inside a dogsled.

We often tow one of these sleds behind us to take fifty pounds of feed off of our freight sled. It is surprisingly durable; one towed behind our sled for several hundred miles on the rough ice of the Porcupine River and did not wear out until we hit the gravel-strewn Dempster Highway in Canada.

Headlamps

Headlamps have replaced flashlights for night use. They free the hands for working with the sled and the dogs. We have also used them in dim light for stitching up wounded dogs and peeking into dogs' throats for porcupine quills, bad teeth, or sore tonsils.

Distance racers and mushers who train at night need efficient, comfortable headlamps. Although expensive, krypton bulbs and lithium batteries add tremendously to the brightness and endurance of the light. Carry a penlight, too, for changing batteries and fixing loose wires.

The elastic headstrap is more comfortable if it is wide or partially replaced with leather or cloth. A hard hat with a headlamp might be more comfortable if it fits over your head gear.

Even if you do not need the light at night, keep it on to warn other travelers of your approach.

Camp Stoves

For years, the standard two-burner Coleman® white-gas stove was used universally by mushers who wanted more than an open fire. It is easy to operate and reliable except in extreme cold and high wind. Distance racers have searched for the ultimate stove that converts snow to boiling water in minutes. Many use a specially built camp stove that is enclosed to keep out wind. A variety of fuels have been tried, including alcohol, propane, charcoal, or coal. Many inventions have hit the trail, but only a few, like the Swenson Cooker sold by RAMCO, are marketed actively. Recently, alcohol stoves have surged in popularity. They light easily and burn hotly even in the wind. These stoves can be improvised by placing alcohol in a metal bucket with a roll of toilet paper for a wick and a grill underneath the cooking pan. Unfortunately, alcohol, like white gas, is expensive and unavailable in some remote areas.

While propane provides efficient heat, the bottles are too bulky to be popular. Charcoal cookers are fast, but the fuel is heavy and dirty and needs white gas for a quick start. For the average camper, a Coleman® stove or a campfire suffices nicely, but when the stakes are high, the stove must be perfect. Before taking a new stove to the Iditarod or the North Pole, trail-test it thoroughly and be familiar with operating it in wind, snow, cold, and rain.

Coolers

Available in many sizes, coolers keep dog food from freezing while on the trail. You can add hot water to frozen meat; later, when you stop to snack the dogs, the meat has thawed. A bucket with glue-on foam can be made to suffice as a cooler.

Do not get so caught up in buying space-age gear that you forget the most important things — the *dogs*. Without them, you would not be going anywhere.

CHAPTER 4

QUALITY FOOD EQUALS QUALITY PERFORMANCE

In George Attla's classic book, *Everything I Know About Training and Racing Sled Dogs,* he mentions feeding a commercial dog food in the 1973 Iditarod race. By the time he was a third of the way into the race, he knew that the diet was inadequate. Another musher told him to get some meat — how could he expect his dogs to run on "cornflakes"?

Since then, commercial feeds for working dogs have improved beyond comparison, but most top mushers still feed their dogs portions of meat for an extra edge of performance. High-quality diets are exceedingly expensive, but it is fruitless to have outstanding dogs if a mediocre diet is hampering their performance. "Eat to win" applies to the canine as well as to the human.

Water

The cheapest and single most important ingredient that your dogs need is water. Inactive dogs require one or two quarts a day, but certain conditions can double or triple these requirements: hot, cold, or windy weather; hard work; illness; and milk production in bitches. In extreme conditions, a dog may need up to six quarts of water a day.

Professional mushers recognize the value of watering dogs throughout the snow season. Many people think that their dogs function well by eating snow, but while a dog can survive *if* snow is available, this is a poor policy. Dehydration develops in stages, and the early signs can go unnoticed or be attributed to other factors. Performance drops, and the dogs overheat and are less alert and responsive. They may not eat as well, utilize food as efficiently, or cope with the cold as easily.

A dog that eats snow wastes a tremendous amount of energy melting the snow. It takes three to eight quarts of snow to make one quart of water. A hard-working dog will be too tired to eat that much snow. Some dogs do not even have access to snow or water if the ground is frozen or glazed with ice.

In freezing temperatures, offer the dogs a quart of water each once or twice a day. If the dogs refuse to drink clean water, bait it lightly with meat broth, melted tallow, or a little commercial dog food. Do not feed them soups. A watery slurry passes through the digestive system too quickly and can cause gas and digestive upsets. Dogs drink best after a meal or after a run, but drinking heavily at these times can also cause upsets. Dogs sometimes refuse to drink water that is too warm, too cold, bad-tasting, or foreign (as on trips). Flavoring will help overcome this reluctance.

On camping trips, you might have to melt snow for water. Find a clean source, such as from a cabin roof, laden tree branches, or river ice. Snow from roadsides and forest floors might be contaminated with seeds, spores, animal droppings, soot, and chemicals.

A well-hydrated dog has tight, springy skin, wet gums, and bright eyes. Pale urine means that the dog is drinking enough; a dark yellow or orange urine means that he definitely needs more water. Dehydration is discussed in Chapter 6.

Feed

Feeding can be as simple or complex as you care to make it. To compare a dog to an engine (a risky proposal), the animal is only as good as the fuel that he burns. However, a good feed can only help the dog to realize his full potential. If he has no potential, a good feed will not help him any more than high-octane gas will turn a station wagon into a race car.

The recreational musher who runs dogs under fifty miles a week needs no more than a commercial feed of reasonably good quality, plus a little extra fat in cold weather. Hard-working or racing dogs require a higher-quality feed to keep them in top form. These dogs require so much energy that they would have to eat four to six full-size meals a day of low-quality food — and their systems cannot handle that much food. (Supermarkets rarely sell top-quality feeds; they must be purchased from feed stores.)

An inactive dog requires perhaps 800 calories a day. This increases if a dog is pregnant, nursing, growing, working, stressed, or exposed to weather extremes. A dog in serious training might need 3,600 calories a day, while a dog with a long, hard pull in cold weather can use 8,000 calories. Some authorities believe that a dog can burn up to 10,000 calories a day in a long-distance race. These calories can be obtained only if the dog is fed a calorie-dense diet of the highest quality possible.

Commercial Feeds: Read the Label

Commercial feeds range in quality from "cornflakes" to "high octane." A high-quality feed contains 30 to 35 percent *quality* protein and more than 15 percent *quality* fat. The ingredients are listed on the bag in decreasing order of content, starting with the main ingredient. The list should begin with a good protein source like chicken, followed by a second source of protein or a good carbohydrate source like corn, rice, or wheat middlings.

Look for that protein source to be in first or second place, and

This small feed manufacturer in Fairbanks, Alaska, produces its own feed and tests it in this kennel and on the race teams that it sponsors.

consider the quality of that source, because different types will differ in quality. For instance, chicken is better than meat by-products (this is discussed below). Look also for specifics on the label. "Animal fat" is ambiguous and could come from chicken, pork, or beef—whichever is available or cheapest at the time of manufacture. This feed may not consistently have the same ingredients, and your dogs therefore will not perform consistently on it.

Nutritional Requirements

A casual musher does not need to know a dog's basic nutritional requirements, but in fierce competition or polar journeys, understanding diet plays a major role in pushing a team to its peak potential. (I say "potential" because breeding, selection, and training are also critical in developing a team.)

Proteins

Proteins aid in combatting stress; they build and repair body tissues and serve in blood, hormones, the immune system, and body processes. Although they can be burned as energy, they are less efficient than fat or carbohydrates. A high-protein diet is desirable for hardworking dogs to build and repair muscles. Puppies also require high levels of protein. Older dogs, however, sometimes suffer from kidney disease, which is exacerbated by too much poor-quality protein.

Proteins come from animal or plant sources; some are highly digestible, and others are virtually indigestible. The percentage of protein indicated on a feed bag reflects only the amount in the bag, not the amount that a dog can ultimately use. This means that the protein source must be both highly digestible and balanced in amino acids to live up to these percentages.

Of the twenty-five amino acids that combine to form different proteins, fifteen are produced in the body, while the others — the "essential amino acids" — must come from the diet. These essential amino acids must be balanced according to the ratios by which the body uses them, like the ingredients in biscuit dough. Too much baking powder makes the batter sour; too little leaves it tough and hard. Similarly, a deficiency in one amino acid causes underutilization of the others, while an excess actually increases the requirements of the others. If the amino acids are not balanced, as in low-quality proteins, even a digestible protein can be of low "biological value" (the amount of consumed protein that is actually used). The ratio is filled only until the most limited amino acid is used up; then the protein-building process stops. If you have a hundred pounds of flour and one small can of baking powder, you can't make very many biscuits!

In other words, a good protein must be easily digested *and* properly balanced with amino acids. Cooked eggs have the best natural balance of amino acids. Other good proteins include chicken, fish, meat, milk protein, and some meat by-products. Low-quality proteins include meat-and-bone meal, some animal by-products (skin, connective tissue), and most vegetable proteins.

Some dog foods contain soy protein. Many mushers shun this source of protein, because rumors, as yet unproven, charge that it causes diarrhea in working dogs, that it affects the thyroid gland, and that dogs lack the digestive enzymes required to break it down.

When a label reads "meat by-products," you should ask exactly what products are used. The term includes many miscellaneous products, from chicken parts to cheap protein that is hardly digestible; or it could mean that the manufacturer buys whatever is cheapest that month.

Fat

Fat provides an intensely concentrated energy source for long periods of hard work, and it helps to keep the animals warm in the winter. Fat increases the palatability of food so that dogs eat more readily; it also contains essential fatty acids and aids in the absorption of fat-soluble vitamins, including A, D, E, and K. It is essential for maintaining a healthy skin, coat, and feet. Feeding extra fat to your dogs might help if they all have bad feet for no apparent reason.

Chicken fat and corn oil are popular among mushers; fish oil is also good. Mutton, pork fat (lard) and beef fat (tallow) are lower quality but more economical. It is believed that coconut and palm oil can't be stored in the body, but they increase the digestibility of other fats.

Never feed rancid fat to your dogs. It causes digestive upsets that lead to lines of diarrhea stringing down the trail. It also destroys vitamins A, D, E, and K and linoleic acid. Rancid fat comes not only from sun-stroked tallow, but also from old dog food and spoiled or partly spoiled meats.

Fat provides more than twice as much energy as proteins or carbohydrates. When increasing the fat in your team's diet to meet higher energy needs, do so slowly, watching for signs of intolerance such as diarrhea. Dogs working in cold weather can adapt to diets of more than 50 percent fat. However, fat provides few nutrients — only energy. Excessive fat can actually reduce the digestibility of some

Dogs like to eat, but when they are stressed in heavy training or hard racing, palatability is important. Fats and meats increase palatability; dogs also prefer food that they can sink their teeth into and chew over soups and mush.

nutrients like calcium and magnesium, so do not overdo it. Too much fat can satiate the dogs before they meet their nutritional needs, and it can cause diarrhea in warm weather or if fed with insufficient protein.

Carbohydrates

Carbohydrates (starches) provide a cheap, easily utilized source of energy. Properly prepared, they also aid in intestinal functions, in promoting stool consistency, and in metabolism. Although carbohydrates include sugars and fiber, starches are the most common in dog food. These must be cooked to be digestible. Good sources include corn, wheat, or rice; other sources are dehulled barley, oats, and potatoes.

Other Additives

Proteins, fat, and carbohydrates make up the bulk of any dog food. Other additives include micronutrients (vitamins and minerals) and stool hardeners, fiber, artificial flavors, and artificial colors (for the dog owner, not for the dog).

Vitamins and minerals keep life processes running on the chemical level. The B-vitamins, vitamin E, choline, and vitamin C are all particularly important to working dogs. Vitamin B-12 is thought to increase resistance to stress and to stimulate the appetite.

The value of vitamin C has been disputed. Unlike humans, dogs produce it within their bodies so that it is not an essential ingredient. Some manufacturers claim to provide vitamin C, but the vitamin oxidizes rapidly. Studies have shown that three months after manufacture, the usable vitamin C in the feed approaches zero.

Minerals must also be balanced correctly. Phosphorus works in combination with many minerals, but any excess will bind with minerals like calcium in the digestive tract. Too much phosphorus results in calcium deficiencies, and perhaps in zinc and magnesium deficiencies. Dogs fed a straight meat diet are especially likely to get too much phosphorus. Among other things, a calcium deficiency can predispose a dog to metacarpal fractures. Dogs require 1.2 parts calcium to 1 part phosphorus. Excessive phosphorus actually reduces the available calcium. Most meats and grains provide too much phosphorus; the few foods that provide more calcium include bones, finely ground bone meal, milk, and beet pulp.

Other minerals, including trace minerals, are important even though they are poorly understood. Iron and magnesium, along with vitamin B-12, help to prevent anemia. Zinc, in which some huskies are deficient, helps to prevent skin and feet problems and may help to combat fatigue. Iodine is required by the thyroid gland, which controls body temperature and metabolism. Selenium works with vitamin E to maintain muscle integrity.

Vitamin/mineral supplements are discussed in the next section.

Finally, the fiber content of commercial food should be about 3.5 percent. Fiber provides no nutrients, but it benefits the digestive system and helps to regulate water absorption, thus combatting diarrhea and maintaining stool consistency. Too much fiber displaces other nutrients and increases stool size. Beet pulp is a good fiber source.

Some manufacturers add a chemical stool hardener, but this should be avoided. It makes the stool harder without regulating consistency. If a dog food causes such loose stools that a hardener is required, it probably is not suitable for working dogs anyway.

Supplementing Commercial Feeds

Despite the great advances made by manufacturers, most professional dog drivers supplement the commercial feed, hoping to improve performance, health, and palatability. However, when deciding what and how much to add, remember that you are tampering with a quality product packed with balanced nutrients. More may not be better; a vitamin deficiency is far less damaging than a vitamin overdose. The first rule of nutrition is: You want to provide your dogs with the *optimum* amount of nutrients, *not* the maximum.

Serious mushers everywhere add meat to their rations, and this is discussed in the next section. A number of other supplements also can be added to specialize the diet. Small, high-calorie snacks can put weight on a thin dog or give him a boost of energy. These include chunks of high-fat meat, cottage cheese, honey, tallow (or other fats), wheat germ oil, cooked egg, or milk (although some adult dogs cannot digest milk).

Dogs on a good commercial feed will not need vitamin supplements. If you do use supplements, be very careful not to give an overdose. Some supplements, such as Red Cell® or Kzyme®, contain additives like hematinics or enzymes, which manufacturers claim will supposedly boost a dog's aerobic endurance or his digestion. They are popular among some mushers.

Raw liver is an excellent supplement if used in moderation (two to four ounces a day). It provides a compact, rich source of fat and nutrients. Some hazards associated with liver are presented in the next section.

Electrolytes are probably overused on dogs by some mushers. Excessive salts are flushed out by the kidneys, resulting in (as they say in some circles) expensive urine. The applicability and hazards of electrolytes are discussed in Chapter 6.

The B-complex vitamins are also popular among racers, especially long-distance racers who think that the injections stimulate tired dogs to eat. Vitamin C is sometimes used, too. Some professionals feel that one-half to one gram daily benefits a dog under stress or on a high-fat diet. Although the kidneys do remove excess vitamin C supplements, high levels can affect the metabolism of copper, iron, and some vita-mins.

These and other supplements can be purchased from veterinarians, feed stores, and mail-order outlets.

Supplementing with Meat

Today's winning teams eat meat. A diet of up to two-thirds meat, fed with a commercial feed, is potent and more economical than it sounds, because smaller portions are required. Meat is very palatable. Dogs eat it readily and gain weight easily on it; they have smaller stools, and they perform better. Meat is an excellent source of water, protein, and sometimes fat. Many racers, including Charlie Cham-paine and Jim Welch of Alaska, and Harris Dunlap of New York, absolutely swear by it. Distance racers often find that their tired dogs eat nothing except meat.

However, you should be aware of the problems associated with feeding large amounts of meat. Meat is often of variable quality (chicken meat ranges from 15 to 32 percent fat). Frozen meats can be hard to find and store, and canned meats are expensive. Fed alone, meat *cannot* provide a balance of nutrients, and the high levels of phosphorus can cause calcium deficiencies. This imbalance can be offset by supplementing each 8 pounds of meat with ¼ to ⅓ cup of finely ground, steamed bone meal. To quote a more precise source, use 1.8 pounds of bone meal for every 98.2 pounds of turkey meat (Dr. F. M. Husby, University of Alaska, Fairbanks). The *Merck Veteri-nary Manual* advises supplementing each pound of meat with two or three grams of calcium carbonate. Recently, new feeds such as Kobuk's Meat Balancer® have been developed that can be added to meat to balance its nutritional deficiencies.

Frozen meat is available in most areas where mushers have created a demand for it. In some sections of Canada, Europe, and the lower forty-eight states, you may have to search for a reliable meat source. Meat usually is available in areas where fur farming is done. Chicken farms and ranches may also have meat for sale. Feed stores that cater to mushers often sell blocks of frozen meat; commercial fisheries sell waste fish; butchers may have trim; manufacturers like Alpo® sell canned meat; dried salmon, seal, and whale meat is sometimes avail-able in the north; and occasionally, wild game like deer or beaver may be available. Trappers often cook meat from lynx, otter, muskrats, and other fur-bearing animals for their dogs.

Whatever the source, make sure that it is reputable. Meat pur-chased "on sale" from a disreputable dealer can be spoiled (it does

Frozen meats can be cut up and fed in lumps, or it can be stirred and thawed in hot feed. We like feeding it as snacks in the morning.

not have to thaw to spoil). To prevent human consumption, commercial meats are often dyed or charred.

Smell your dog meat for spoilage and rancidity; frying a bit of the meat brings out suspicious odors more sharply. Check the thawed meat for bone chips, rocks, and other contaminants.

Most dealers *will* give you an honest deal, but if you buy a cheap meat, you will probably get a low-quality food with excessive amounts of indigestible protein, labeled with the otherwise-legitimate title, "by-products." This meat can contain indigestible hair, skin, feathers, beaks, claws, crop contents, tendons, connective tissue, blood vessels, and tracheas. Meat from really poor sources can also contain cancerous tissue, pollutants, feed additives, drugs, bone chips, or excessive hormones from glands, or it may have come from diseased or parasitized animals.

According to one source, chicken and eggs are most likely to harbor bacteria, while horse meat and liver are more likely to contain drugs.

Dried fish is a good source of protein. If you cannot catch and dry your own, you can occasionally purchase it.

We feed our dogs whitefish with supplements. During the fall fish run we catch and freeze them as "greenfish" for winter use.

Consider the meat source — chickens frequently carry the *Salmonella* bacteria, and cattle are fed hormones and feed additives. Pigs, bears, and seals are known to carry trichinosis. Valuable horses are often put down only after being unsuccessfully treated with numerous drugs. The liver is where many noxious chemicals build up until they can be broken down. One Iditarod racer's dogs reportedly tested positive in the drug check because of the contaminated horse liver that he fed them. Dogs have died after eating meat from euthanized horses. It makes you stop and think. It behooves you to research your supplier.

If you use wild game, *it must be cooked!* Cooking only slightly reduces the nutrient levels, and almost all wild game harbors tapeworm cysts that can be transmitted to dogs and in some cases to humans. (See the discussion of the *Echinococcus* tapeworm in Chapter 6.) Rabbits, hares, and other rodents can also transmit tularemia. Some authorities claim that freezing meat for three months will kill parasites, but others dispute this. Cooking is more reliable. We boil our moose scraps for hours to be sure that they are well cooked.

Beaver meat has few parasites and may be fed raw, although the fresh unfrozen meat can transmit the *Giardia* intestinal parasite. De-boning beaver meat will prevent the bones from blocking the gut. Otherwise, feed it with commercial food, whose bulk will surround and pad the bones as they pass through the digestive tract. Beaver meat is popular because of its high fat content and palatability. Frequently, a dog will eat beaver after refusing all other food. In Alaska, beaver carcasses are so popular that trappers charge twenty-five dollars each for them. Beaver meat is also available in Canada and in many northern states where beavers are trapped, and they are occasionally sold in feed stores. However, the dogs need time to adjust to a beaver diet, and it is too rich to serve well in temperatures over 20° F.

In spite of the pitfalls of feeding meat, a *good* meat is the best supplement that you can offer your dogs if the nutritional intake is balanced. When comparing meat to dry feed, remember that meat is more than two-thirds water. When the dry weight of meat is compared to dry food, it contains 30 to 80 percent protein and 20 to 30 percent fat — much more than dry food. The high percentage of water is not a drawback except when price per pound is concerned, or when you are carrying the food in your sled. The extra water can help dogs muddle through a long race even if they are refusing to drink.

Home Brew

Before commercial food was available, mushers cooked a home brew of whatever meat or fish they had on hand, along with rice or oatmeal. Mushers in remote areas of the north, and even some stateside mushers, still use this old formula. We feed our dogs whitefish cooked with rice and tallow, filled out with meat powder and commercial feed if there are not enough fish. One year our commercial feed order was delayed, and we spent many long days sneaking through the forest shooting rabbits so that our dogs could eat. Although cheaper than commercial feeds, this system has some drawbacks. Protein sources vary in availability, considerable time goes into preparation, and you cannot be assured of an optimal nutrient balance.

Most mushers work out a diet for their own teams, taking into account what is available to them, how the dogs perform on it, and how much it costs. A basic trapline diet, such as the one that Miki is preparing here of fish cooked with rice, is cheap and economical. Other ingredients such as meat, liver, tallow, and vitamins may be added.

If you mix foods from the three basic groups — proteins, carbohydrates, and fats — your improvised diet will be roughly balanced. Protein may come from commercial sources such as meat meal, fish meal, or frozen meat, or from fish or wild game scraps. (Feeding edible game meat to dogs usually is illegal.) Meals are easy to use but are less palatable and can spoil in the summer. They vary in quality, so find a reliable supplier. Meat-and-bone meal has a lower digestibility due to the bone, but it reduces calcium-phosphorus imbalances.

Fish and fish meals provide excellent protein, although it has been suggested that certain sea fish and fish oils contain excessive vitamins A and D and that some fish lack the necessary fats. Fish may be cooked whole, and bones are rarely a problem. You can remove the larger bones of the jaw and head, but most dogs digest the smaller bones whether raw or cooked. Dried fish may replace cooked protein but may contain parasites.

Eggs have a higher biological value than any other protein source, but they should be cooked because the raw egg white ties up biotin. Eggs can be purchased in powdered or frozen block form; the frozen kind is dyed to prevent human consumption.

Add to your meat a cooked starch such as rice, barley, wheat, cornmeal, or oatmeal. Finely ground grains cook faster and are more digestible. Barley and oats should be hulled, and rice should be polished, to increase digestibility. Flaked maize (corn) is better than maize grits. We have tried other grains but always come back to rice. Oatmeal burns easily, and flours come out lumpy, like dumplings.

Add a fat source such as corn or fish oil, lard, tallow, or blubber. Fats specially blended for dogs are now available but are expensive. Fat is critical in the winter and should be adjusted according to the need, which usually is 20 to 30 percent; in the summer, dogs need at least 10 percent fat.

Cook the grain plus any raw meat together (meat and fish meals can be added after cooking), along with the fat and roughly one gallon of water to each pound of grain. The protein-to-carbohydrate ratio can vary from one part protein to one part carbohydrate, up to three-to-one for a better diet. The food is cooked over a slow fire (wood or propane) or in a double boiler, at a slow simmer to avoid burning. Grain is soft and translucent when done, and flour will thicken. Poorly cooked grain will pass right through the digestive tract and can cause diarrhea.

Some drivers mix commercial feeds or other supplements with the cooked ration to ensure a more complete diet. A highly concentrated feed like Iams Eukanuba® or Purina Pro Plan® is best.

Feeding

Do not mix too much water with your feed, because soups are digested poorly. Also, do not let food stand in buckets for over an hour, because it ferments rapidly if the buckets are dirty. Remnants

Buckets of feed left by a heat source can ferment and give the dogs diarrhea.

of food in dirty dishes, too, can harbor *Salmonella*, which will rapidly contaminate the next batch of food.

Although you can feed your dogs a lower-cost maintenance diet during the summer, you must feed them the best year-round if you want them to reach their peak potential. At least feed them a quality diet through May to ensure complete healing of any work-related injuries, and start up the good diet a few weeks before training begins. Although you may switch to a feed with *less* protein and fat in the summer, you still must feed *quality* protein. If you are with a good brand of feed, stay with it, but buy the "maintenance diet" instead of the "working diet" or "stress diet."

The digestive enzymes in a dog's intestine vary according to the food that the dog eats, and it takes a dog six weeks to fully adjust to

Curtis Erhart dishes out dog food. Large kennels require a considerable amount of food, and top racers understand the need to feed a quality diet. Still, economics plays a role in your decisions. *Courtesy* Fairbanks Daily News-Miner.

a diet change. If you plan a special race diet, start it six weeks early to allow for this adjustment.

Working dogs are kept thinner than most pets. Check the weights of your dogs once a week, or preferably every day. Feel the body underneath the fur by digging through thicker coats. The ribs, the backbone, and the pelvis should be easily palpable but should not jump out at you. Feel the whole body, because some dogs feel thin at the ribs and fat over the pelvis. Sprinting dogs are kept thinner than other sled dogs.

Keeping your dogs too thin reduces their stamina and may result in nutritional deficiencies. Keeping them too fat slows them down and contributes to overheating, cardiac diseases, and other ailments — not to mention the extra weight that they have to carry.

This dog has dense fur, which makes her look fat. You must feel through the fur to make sure that the dog is the correct weight.

Dogs in chronic poor condition can be tested for worms, digestive enzyme deficiencies, hypothyroidism, and other diseases affecting digestion and metabolism (see Chapter 6). If all of your dogs have the same problem, they might need more food, better food, or extra fat.

Some dogs are lean and bony and never get fat. Our skinny Rusty eats much more than his chunky daughter, Amber, although she is only five pounds lighter and more active.

Evaluating the Diet

First evaluate the information of different feeds before choosing a product, then determine how your dogs respond to the diet. Shift gradually to the new diet over a five-day period, and give the dogs a few weeks to adjust before calculating how much of the new food they require to maintain good weight. This calculation, combined with changes in performance, is the best way to evaluate food quality. A dog might need half as much food when he switches to a high-quality diet; this food might cost more per pound, but it may cost less per dog if he needs only a little of it.

With a better diet, stool size and quantity should decrease, while consistency and firmness should improve. On the other hand, if you shovel up more than you shovel in, you might have a digestibility problem. Examining stool quantity is not as reliable as examining food intake and performance, because droppings can be swollen by excess water (usually due to the type or amount of fiber in the food).

A top racer who endorses a brand of food in return for its sponsorship does not necessarily feed that brand during competition. Just because your hero's lead dog is sitting by a bag of it does not *necessarily* mean that the dog eats it. When choosing a dog food, do not go for the hype. Go for the facts.

CHAPTER 5

PAY ATTENTION TO DETAILS: MAINTENANCE

Maintenance involves both a daily and a yearly routine to keep your dogs healthy. Taking shortcuts will gradually weaken your team's condition and performance. The prevention of many ills (and bills) lies in caring for your dogs with responsibility and understanding.

Some state and local governments require mushers to have kennel permits and to adhere to other regulations, logical or otherwise. Failure to obey these laws could cost you your team. Books offering legal advice for dog owners are available.

Confining

Very few mushers allow their dogs to run loose. Even in sparsely populated areas, this is irresponsible. Huskies in particular enjoy ranging, and this interferes with training schedules. We have had more than one dog that would disappear in a snap if he was released. These dogs usually would be gone until the next day and would return exhausted and filthy with swamp water after a long search for game. One dog ran off with a yearling; apparently, the two were separated and the inexperienced yearling got lost. The older dog returned in the morning; the younger one was lost for about five days. We almost never turn our dogs loose without supervision.

Chains

Except for parts of Europe where chaining dogs is illegal, the majority of mushers picket dogs on chains. The dogs are restrained but are

Running a large kennel requires not only a great deal of work with the dogs, but also knowledge of legal considerations. Local governments often restrict the number of dogs that you can keep on your property, or require kennel permits. Joe Runyan's dog yard at Nenana, Alaska.

easy to reach and touch. Chains are inexpensive and can be moved readily. Dogs learn to keep their chains untangled and extend this skill to the towline.

Chains can be four to eight feet long. A loop, ring, or swivel at one end of the chain attaches to a picket post or underground anchor; a ⅝-inch brass swivel snap at the other end allows the dog to be released quickly. Additional swivels can be inserted to prevent the chain from twisting. Oiling the snaps occasionally reduces corrosion, stiffness, and icing.

You can stake chains on wooden or metal posts, trees, or car-axle posts. Mushers short on space sometimes use a heavy chain or cable line securely anchored at either end. A dozen or more individual picket lines are then attached to it. These gang pickets use space efficiently and also work well in permafrost or soft, sandy soil where it is difficult to sink individual posts. Chaining dogs too close together can result in accidental breedings and dog fights.

Kennels

Kenneled dogs can move more freely than chained dogs, and there is less concern over loose or stray dogs causing trouble. Pups and bitches in season are safer. However, pens are expensive, difficult to move, and inconvenient for frequent socializing and cleaning. In areas of heavy snows, the door base must be elevated so that the door will not jam against the snow. Most mushers keep only a couple of pens for pups and breeding females.

Barns

Mushers occasionally keep their dogs in barns; this was more common in the "old" days. Dogs kept in barns need less food; they have shelter from the weather and stay warmer and will not grow such thick coats, which means that they will not overheat as much. If the barn is heated, winter watering chores are much easier because the water does not freeze. However, the dogs will not be acclimated if you take them on overnight trips to distant races or on camping trips. Heating and lighting the building might be costly. If the floor is made

Chains Commonly Used for Picketing Sled Dogs
Top: 3/0 zinc-plated lock-link (weldless). *Center:* 3/0 zinc-plated tenso chain (twisted, weldless chain). *Bottom:* 2/0 straight link coil chain.

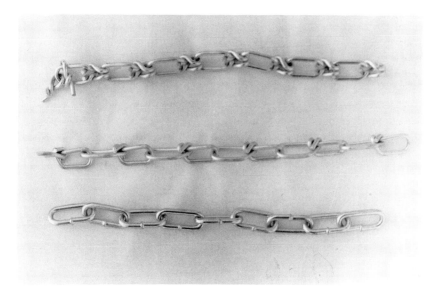

Dogs tied this close might tangle in their chains and choke, or they might fight. These two, however, are merely sharing their warmth on a nippy day.

of dirt, parasites might be more of a problem because the eggs will not freeze. A cement floor is easier to hose down.

House Dogs

Contrary to some rumors, it is all right to let your dogs inside the house during the winter as long as they do not get too hot, and as long as you let all of the frost and any ice melt and dry completely before turning them outside again. We frequently bring our whole team inside after a hard run, especially when it is thirty below outside. They can dry off and rest more easily inside, and you can water them with less trouble.

Fencing

A chain-link fence around the perimeter of your yard is costly to put up but effectively protects your dogs from strays and intruders and keeps escapees confined. (You do not want to get sued because some unattended child wanders into your dog yard and gets bitten.

The fence reduces that possibility.) A fence does limit your ability to move your yard to fresh ground, and it can be inconvenient for entering or leaving with a team. But in densely populated areas, the fence can be invaluable.

Substrate

Most drivers park their dogs on dirt because it costs nothing (its one great attribute). Unfortunately, worm eggs thrive in dirt. Plowing the area regularly will reduce the eggs in the dirt. Mud is a real problem during rainy spells, and dust plagues you during dry spells. Seeding the yard with a hardy grass helps both problems, at least a little.

Sand or gravel will keep dust and mud down, will drain better,

One problem with tying dogs on dirt is the mud that you must contend with during breakup. Moving dogs to a drier spot minimizes the problem. These dogs take refuge on their dog houses.

will help toughen feet, and will make manure removal easier. It is expensive, though, and must be refilled once or twice a year. And — some dogs like to eat rocks! Sawdust is absorbent and cleans up easily, making it a good base for puppies if it is not too dusty. It can be purchased cheaply from local lumber mills.

Dogs parked in heavy shade are protected from the sun and wind, but in some areas they might be troubled by insects and fungal infections due to dampness. Light shade, if you have a choice, is better than exposed yards or densely overgrown yards. In the southern states, shade is far more important; in the north, when mosquitoes are fierce, an open, windy area is preferable. If you live in a populated area, try to plant your dogs downwind of your neighbors, and be sure that the yard does not drain into any creeks.

Housing

Every dog needs a house. It shelters him from weather and insects and provides a comfortable bed and a sense of security. Plywood houses are cheap and easy to build, which is lucky, because many athletic dogs chew up their houses. You can also build inexpensive houses from scrap lumber, short logs, discarded crates, oil drums, or large, discarded wooden spools once used for cable and heavy wires. In the "old" days, some dog drivers built long log houses with several doors so that the dogs could share their warmth. Even today, some dogs share a single long house or open shed.

In the north, especially, houses must not be too big or body heat will dissipate. A small doorway helps to retain both heat and straw. A good house has a floor, a short "rain porch" overhang, and plenty of clean straw. Elevating the house on legs keeps the floor from rotting, and a hinged roof allows you to clean the house or add straw, and to reach puppies or sulky dogs. A burlap sack tacked over the door holds in heat and keeps out bugs, but you may need to teach the dogs to push through it (or, just hang it halfway down so that they can push underneath it). According to one observation, two sixty-pound hounds in one dog house with a burlap door maintained an inside temperature of 70° F. while the outside temperature fell to 10° F.

A coat of latex paint (**not** a lead-base paint) looks nice and prevents rot but is not essential. "Uncle Elmer" of Team & Trail Publications suggests that blue paint might discourage flies but that white paint is cooler and cheaper.

A nice home, good bedding, clean yard — Tish has it made.

Kenneling dogs in these long houses shelters a number of Joe Runyan's dogs with a minimum investment.

Clean-Up

Picking up your dog yard is a daily chore. It decreases the number of parasites, reduces the contact of your dogs' feet with noxious waste chemicals, allows you to analyze each dog's intestinal health (by examining stool quantity and consistency), and prevents bacterial infections. You can also spot developing health problems, work with spooky dogs, and play with pups just because you are in the yard anyway. My sister and I frequently go to the yard to do chores and end up sitting on dog houses, socializing with the dogs and planning our next year's sledding adventures. It is a leisurely time, a time to enjoy our dogs.

Pick up droppings with a light, square-ended shovel and a scraper such as a slender board or a cut-off hoe. In the winter, a pointed shovel works better for breaking loose frozen droppings. Many garbage disposal sites do not allow the dumping of animal wastes, and if you cannot find one that does, you might have to bury or compost the manure. Do not dump it on river ice or tie your dogs on a frozen river.

Shedding

Huskies shed heavily once or twice a year, usually in the spring or summer. Some shed at any time, regardless of the weather. A winter whelping often causes a bitch to shed. Winter shedders do not seem to have much trouble keeping warm, but they should be given extra straw and watched for weight loss. Harris Dunlap, a successful East Coast sprint racer, has said that the shedding period is stressful to dogs.

Brushing huskies when they blow their coats is not necessary, but it does make them cooler and more comfortable and can reduce the chances of their developing eczema. Husky fur can be spun into a warm yarn similar to wool. Contacting a local weaver's guild might bring an artisan to brush your dogs for free, and you might even get a knit hat from your own dogs' fur.

Spinning dog fur is a unique craft that dog mushers can support with the voluminous quantities of fur that their dogs shed each year.

Insect Control

Mosquitoes and other insects can be kept down by cutting grass and shrubs around the dog yard and by keeping the area clean. (One year, our dog yard was overgrown with stinging nettles, and Miki declared war on them by chopping them up with a hoe while chanting, "Death to the nettles! Death to the nettles!" She apparently scattered seeds while chopping the nettles, because the next year we had twice as many.)

Anyway, most huskies do not mind mosquitoes, but some dogs do have nervous reactions to clouds of insects. Only in old-time books have I read of dogs being pestered to death by mosquitoes. You can use insect repellent sparingly if necessary but only on the muzzle, ear tips, and lower legs where the fur is thin. Spraying the yard with

This dog yard on the coast of the Bering Sea, at Unalakleet, Alaska, is open to the wind, which will cut down on insects and keep the dogs cool in the summer. However, this can be hard on the dogs during the winter unless they have good houses and straw.

insect retardant or building smoke smudges (where legal) will keep insects down when they get really bad.

Horseflies are maddening to the dogs and bite until they make small bloody wounds, but if the dogs have houses, they can usually escape the insects.

Canadian black flies can get so thick that they practically choke a panting dog. They bite around the eyes and ears until scabs form. Minor eye infections can result, especially in old dogs. We stumbled across a few repellents that work as well or better than mosquito dope: Noxema Skin Cream ®, Avon's Skin So Soft®, and citronella spray. Bag Balm® and povidone-iodine (Betadine®) are also reported to work.

Cart-training the dogs or running them loose can be a real relief, no matter how temporary, for insect-tormented dogs.

Noise Control

Dogs naturally bark when excited by hookup, dinner time, or strangers, and they get in the habit of barking when they are bored or unhappy. Barking can spread throughout your yard and to your neighbors' dogs. For the sake of your neighborhood and your own peace, discourage excessive barking. Most mushers tolerate some noise during harnessing and feeding, but the dogs should not be allowed to bark all the time for no reason.

Reduce noise by keeping your dogs happy and occupied. A dry, comfortable house, fresh water, regular feeding and exercise, and protection from insects are basic requirements. A large bone, rawhide, or some durable toy will help to distract boredom barkers.

Persistent and consistent discipline for the worst offenders usually produces results, and the other dogs, seeing your efforts, quickly realize that excessive noise is bad. Sled dogs *can* be trained to obey the command "Quiet!" Once your dogs accept a limit to their barking, new additions and pups develop restraint more easily. Dogs often bark and howl when you are away, especially if you are running a team. You might need to sneak back to discipline these dogs, or leave a handler at home to enforce the rules. This is especially important if you are running dogs at night, when your neighbors are trying to sleep. Avoid electronic devices that might be triggered by other nearby barkers.

Records

Chores, including those listed on Table 5-1, must be performed regularly. To avoid missing important dates such as vaccination times, you should keep records on your dogs. Include dates of birth, purchase, sale, worming, vaccinating, heat cycles, breeding, and medical problems or operations such as neutering. (It would be embarrassing to sell a neutered dog and forget to tell the new owner!) A dog's pedigree, identifying marks, or tattoos can be entered, as well as information on previous owners, race records, and offspring. When you purchase a dog, or when your pups reach adult weight, weigh them on a scale and record the information for future reference. Dogs can be weighed seasonally if you want to keep accurate records on them; this is especially useful when you sell a dog or if he requires medication administered by weight.

You can also log each training run, noting the number of dogs taken, miles travelled, trail conditions, and so on. An estimation of a dog's mileage can increase his value.

Records offer resale advantages, they can help your veterinarian, and they can help you plan worming and vaccination schedules, breedings, and other activities.

Parasite Control

Internal parasites are found from the Arctic to the tropics, and dogs can get worms even in the cleanest yard. Because dogs with worms lose vitality, almost all mushers are concerned with parasite control. Hookworms and roundworms, which dogs pick up from droppings, might be less of a problem in the north where droppings are frozen much of the year. However, tapeworms will be a bigger problem when wild game and fish are fed improperly.

Dogs with worms are susceptible to diarrhea, disease, and vitamin deficiencies. Worms reduce a dog's overall health, performance, and attitude, and in pups, a bad case of worms can prove fatal. The first step in parasite control is keeping a clean dog yard so that worm eggs do not have a chance to mature. The second step is to avoid feeding food that might be contaminated with tapeworm cysts (raw meat). Do not let the dogs eat horse manure or other animal droppings. Wash your hands after working the dog yard to avoid the possibility of ingesting eggs yourself. Although these steps will help to control

Table 5-1
Dog Yard Chores

Frequency	Chore	Notes
Twice daily	Water	See Chapter 4 for the effects of mild chronic dehydration
Daily	Feed	Dogs with high caloric requirements should be fed twice daily
	Pick up yard	
	Check weights	If dogs are racing
Weekly	Check weights	By look and feel (see Chapter 4)
Spring/fall	Move dog yard to clean site	If possible
	Worm and vaccinate	As required
Pre-race (December or January)	Corona and kennel cough vaccinations	If recommended by veterinarian
	Worm	As required
Regularly	Clip toenails	
	Worm, vaccinate pups	As recommended by veterinarian
	Replace bedding (straw)	
	Replace worn gear (houses, chains, collars, etc.)	
	Replenish substrate (gravel, sand)	

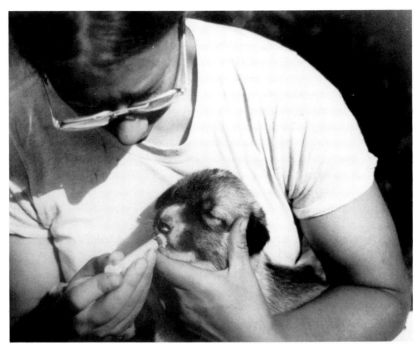

Accurate dosages of liquid wormers can be administered to puppies by measuring the wormer in a 3cc or 10cc syringe, with needle removed, and squirting the medication into the puppy's mouth.

parasite populations, they will not eliminate them. And while wormers will eliminate adult worms in the digestive tract, they will not prevent dogs from picking up more worms.

Most mushers conscientiously worm their dogs on a regular basis — every two months or twice a year, as they feel necessary — to assure that the dogs are relatively worm-free. However, some veterinarians contend that stool samples should be examined for parasites periodically, and that each dog should be wormed *only* if he has parasites, and then *only* for the parasite with which he is infected. This is because wormers are poisons that each dog must handle in his body. Stressing a dog by repeatedly worming him does not make much sense if he does not have worms! Another advantage to fecal exams is that you can then pick the wormer most effective against your dog's infection. (Many wormers do not kill tapeworms, for instance, and others, like piperazine, only knock out one specific worm species.)

Unfortunately, you would have to be independently wealthy or have a good sponsor to pay for regular fecals if you have sixty-four dozen dogs. You have two other alternatives: stick with a regular worming schedule, or invest in a fifty- to one-hundred-power microscope and learn to identify parasite eggs yourself.

When you worm regularly, rotate wormers using a different drug each time, because parasites can build an immunity to one drug if they are repeatedly exposed to it. (Make sure that it *is* a different drug, not just a different brand. Strongid T® and Nemex II® are both pyrantel pamoate, just as Bayer® and Anacin® are both aspirin.) Follow the instructions given with each wormer. Some require fasting, others are mixed with food, and still others can be given regardless of meals. Puppies, pregnant or nursing bitches, old dogs, and debilitated dogs should be wormed on a veterinarian's advice and only with a mild wormer. Puppies in particular need to be wormed regularly with a mild wormer. Some wormers are very harsh, even those found in pet stores. We purchase ours from a veterinarian; they are also available through some musher's and pet-supply catalogues.

A horse wormer, Ivermectin, has been used by some mushers recently, but it is not approved for dogs. It is reportedly ineffective against roundworms and has proven toxic to some dogs.

Tapeworms are especially hard to eradicate, and the only effective wormers are expensive. Droncit®, a fairly new wormer, is especially effective against the tapeworm *Echinococcus.* The human health hazards of this parasite are discussed in Chapter 6.

In some areas, especially along the East Coast, heartworms can be a problem. If you live in the lower forty-eight states or in southern Canada, contact your veterinarian to see if your dogs are in a high-risk area.

Moving your dog yard twice a year, and worming at this time, is an effective tactic. We move our dogs during the spring thaw in May and after freeze-up in October. Moving the dogs gives them a change of scenery, too, and provides a good time to replace the straw in the house.

If you cannot move the dogs, consider disinfecting your yard. Your veterinarian can recommend an effective solution. Some insecticides will hurt their feet. Tilling the yard will plow under and disperse worm eggs. (Roundworm and hookworm eggs are extremely resistent and can live for years in the soil.)

Keeping worms under control is a constant battle. To do it effectively, you must study the life cycles of common worms and learn how to break the cycles. If you know how they reproduce, where

Table 5-2
Common Wormers

Wormer	Effective Against: Round	Hook	Tape	Whip	Notes
Pyrantel pamoate (Imathal®, Strongid T®, Nemex II®, Pyrominth®)	●	●			Inexpensive. Repeat in two weeks or as recommended by a veterinarian. Very nontoxic, safe for pups.
Disophenol (D.N.P.®)		●			Repeat in two weeks or as recommended. Injected subcutaneously. Low safety margin; inexpensive.
Fenbendazole and Mebendazole (Panacur®, Telmintic®)	●	●	●	●	Requires three consecutive daily doses. Not effective against *Dipylidium* tapes; effective against *Echinococcus* at increased doses. Relatively expensive.
Praziquantel (Droncit®)			●		The best for *Echinococcus*; relatively safe, very expensive.
Ivermectin (Heartgard®, Ivomec®)					Toxic to some breeds. Except Heartgard®, it is not approved for dogs but reputedly is effective against hook, and whipworms.
Piperazine®	●				Safe for pups unless overdosed. Repeat in two weeks or as recommended. Very inexpensive.
Diclorvos (Task®)	●	●		●	Relatively toxic — observe contraindications.
Bunamisole HCL (Scoloban®)			●		Effective against *Echinococcus* and *Taenia*; less effective against *Dipylidium*. Expensive.

Table 5-2 (Continued)
Common Wormers

Wormer	Effective Against: Round	Hook	Tape	Whip	Notes
Butamisole HCL (Styquin®)	●	●		●	Injected subcutaneously.
Febantel & praziquantel (Vercom®)	●	●	●	●	Requires three consecutive daily doses. Not effective against all tapes. Observe contraindications. Expensive.
Diphenthan-70 & methyl-benzine (Vermiplex®)	●	●	●		Fasting required. Relatively toxic for liver and kidneys. Does not get all tapes. Expensive.
Toluene & Dichlorophene	●	●	●		Fasting required. Toxic for liver and kidneys. Inexpensive.
DEC styryl-pyridinium chloride (Styrid-Caricide®)	●	●			Daily dosing to control worms.
Sulfadimethoxine (Albon®); also Amprolium (Corid®)					These drugs are effective against the intestinal protozoal parasite, *Coccidia*.

Notes: Some wormers cause fatal reactions if given to a dog with heartworms. Prices vary considerably. Consult your veterinarian. Some wormers are not effective against all tapes. *Echinococcus* and *Taenia* tapeworms come from wild game; *Dipylidium* is transmitted by fleas; *Diphyllobothrium* tapeworms come from fish.

they live, and how they infect dogs, as well as how to interrupt the cycles in different stages, your battle against parasites will not be limited to the use of toxic wormers.

Vaccinations

Vaccinate every dog once a year with the seven-way combination shot that covers distemper, hepatitis, leptospirosis, parainfluenza, two types of adenovirus, and parvovirus. In addition, each dog must have a rabies shot every one to three years, depending on the vaccine and applicable state laws. You can also consult a veterinarian about vaccinating against kennel cough and coronavirus, diseases that spread primarily through kennels and in races, where many dogs

To give an injection, lift the loose skin on the back of the neck and push the needle into the flap of skin. Most shots are given subcutaneously like this; only a few shots, like rabies, are given into the muscle of the back leg.

A large yard like Joe Runyan's in Nenana requires a tremendous effort to maintain, especially when you start looking at the financial aspects. It takes a real commitment to keep the yard organized and well maintained.

come in close contact. Do not vaccinate your dogs with the nasal form of the kennel cough vaccine right before a race, because it can cause a mild but contagious infection; this is best done before training. Although kennel cough is rarely fatal itself, it leaves the body susceptible to more serious diseases like pneumonia. Dogs that are stressed, such as those with a tough racing schedule, will be particularly vulnerable to these secondary infections. Most dogs should be vaccinated against coronavirus before race season, because the virus can lie dormant in a dog until he is stressed and then erupt as a full-blown intestinal infection.

Vaccinating puppies is covered in Chapter 8.

How can you vaccinate your dogs without paying a phenomenal veterinarian bill? Do it yourself. The procedure is simple and certainly less stressful on the dogs. Have a veterinarian show you how if you are uncertain about it. Some veterinarians are reluctant to sell vaccines and syringes, or they charge excessive prices. A veterinarian who caters to dog drivers will be more sympathetic to your needs. Rabies vaccines are more controlled, but many states offer rabies vaccinations free or for a nominal charge. Huge rabies clinics are staged for dog mushers in Alaska. In remote villages, a lay vaccinator can be certified by the state to vaccinate the animals in a village.

Miscellaneous Chores

Check each of your dogs at least once a week to see that all is well and that his weight is correct. Clip toenails as needed; some dogs keep their nails worn to stubs, while other dogs' nails grow at phenomenal rates (nails are covered in Chapter 7).

Check underneath each dog's collar occasionally. Some dogs get sores here, especially when they are shedding or when the collar is made of nylon web and is too tight or weighed down by a heavy chain. Shifting the collar now and then helps to keep it from wearing through the fur and then through the skin. Once the sores appear, the best treatment is to clip and wash the area and switch to a chain-link collar (*not* a choke collar) until the sores heal. You can keep this dog in a pen instead of on a chain for awhile.

Change straw occasionally, especially if it is damp, and add extra straw as needed. Females in season should be isolated to prevent unwanted litters; dogs with medical problems must be watched closely; and, of course, puppies create many additional chores that are covered in Chapter 8.

If you race your dogs, you will find that paying attention to details is the only way to build an outstanding team. This care starts in the dog yard with regular and responsible maintenance.

CHAPTER 6

MUSHER'S MEDICAL MANUAL

Although naturally hardy, sled dogs do get injured and sick as a result of their strenuous life-style. We will cover some common problems, but *this information is not a substitute for professional advice.* Many conditions cannot be diagnosed by a layman, and even veterinarians must rely heavily on X-rays, cultures, and laboratory tests. Neither we nor our publisher can be responsible for the results obtained from the advice herein. Do not give any drug to your dogs without first discussing its effects and side effects with your veterinarian. Common beneficial drugs such as aspirin and antibiotics can be harmful or fatal *even when used as directed.* While this chapter has been written with the help of several veterinarians, you should consult your own veterinarian if you have a problem.

In addition to understanding canine health care, every musher should know first aid. Because that information is readily available elsewhere, and because most of it can be applied to dogs as well as to humans, it is not covered here. Parasite and disease control are discussed in Chapter 5, while foot problems are covered in Chapter 7.

Lameness

Lameness can be caused by sprains, strains, cuts, sore feet, arthritis, bursitis, tendonitis, osteomyelitis, bone cancer, broken bones, toenail injuries, and countless other problems. If lameness persists over a day or two, if obvious swelling or deformity is seen, or if the dog puts no weight on the limb, seek professional help.

At a trot, a dog's head bobs upward when an injured foreleg strikes the ground, and as the sound leg strikes, his head drops. In a hind-leg injury, the pelvis on the lame side may be carried higher, with the

Breaking trail for long hours can wear away the fur behind the pasterns and up the legs, sometimes exposing the skin to frostbite or abrading it enough to draw blood. It is seen most often in older dogs, or in dogs with chronic, mild medical problems that cause skin, hair, and foot ailments.

Some injuries, such as a broken leg, require a long period of R & R and sometimes special housing to prevent wetness.

hip of the sound leg dropping lower. The head drops as the dog's weight falls on the *unsound* leg. As he favors an injury in one leg, he may overwork and strain the opposite one.

A few guidelines can help pinpoint the type of lameness. A dog that is reluctant to touch his foot to the ground may have a broken leg, a dislocation, a severe sprain, or simply a badly lacerated foot. One that is reluctant to swing the leg forward is more likely to be suffering from nerve, ligament, or tendon damage, from muscle soreness, or from other damage in the leg and shoulder. Unfortunately, the dogs have not read the literature and do not always follow the rules.

Sprains

Wrist sprains are strained or torn ligaments. We see them more often when our dogs are run on hard trails, down steep hills, or over "moose holes." Swelling and heat in the wrist are accompanied by lameness. (These signs can also indicate a more serious problem.)

A dog with a shoulder sprain is usually reluctant to extend his leg forward; the stride is shortened, and you may feel a swelling at the anterior (front) point of the shoulder. Shoulder injuries are common in sprint dogs and are often slow in healing, serious, or chronic.

For any sprain (tendon or ligament injury) or strain (pulled muscle), rest is the best treatment. A veterinarian may prescribe an anti-inflammatory agent to reduce pain and swelling, but many races ban these compounds. A dog can often recover from a mild sprain even while running a distance race.

Hind-Leg Injuries

Although less common, injuries to the hind leg are harder to diagnose. Torn knee ligaments cause severe lameness, and the dog may refuse to put any weight on his leg. If a dog loses control over his lower hind leg, he may have damaged the Achilles tendon or torn the large muscle leading into the tendon. Surgical repair is usually required to correct these problems, and complete recovery is rare.

Metacarpal and Metatarsal Fractures

Fractures of one of these small bones in the pastern (lower front and hind legs) can occur, especially when the dog is running on hard-packed trails or punchy snow, or over holes made by the tracks of horses or moose. Long-toed or light-boned dogs seem more susceptible. Malnutrition (including a high-meat diet without proper calcium supplements, or a high-carbohydrate diet) is also believed to contribute to the likelihood of these fractures occurring. Swelling, heat, and pain, along with a grating in the wrist, may be noted, and resulting lameness can be minor or severe. X-rays are needed to confirm the diagnosis, and a cast or surgery is sometimes required to prevent permanent lameness or stiffness. A limp that does not improve within twenty-four hours should be X-rayed to determine the possibility of a fracture.

Sesamoid Bone Fractures

A fracture involved one of these tiny bones in the foot causes lameness when the dog is running. However, the lameness may disappear when the dog is at rest, only to recur during exercise. Palpation produces pain. Surgical removal of the chip resolves the problem.

Lacerations

Lacerations frequently occur on the feet, legs, and face. Stop severe bleeding by applying direct pressure on a dressing placed over the injury or by using a compression bandage. Most simple lacerations heal well if they are kept clean. Diluted povidone-iodine (Betadine®) surgical scrub is a good choice for washing most open wounds. Clipping back the fur decreases the risk of contamination. We prefer an antibiotic powder (nitrofurazone) over ointment, because it sticks to the wound better and will not seal in bacteria. (Unfortunately, nitrofurazone [Furacin®] is believed to cause irritation, allergies, and skin cancer in humans.) Bandaging is usually unnecessary except when the underside of the foot must be protected.

Large gaping cuts require suturing, which is best left to a veterinarian who can determine and repair any underlying damage. However, if you live in or travel into an area where you have no access to professional help, you might ask a veterinarian to show you how to suture simple lacerations. He may also recommend that the dog be placed on antibiotics after stitching.

Dog-Fight Injuries

Lacerations and punctures occur frequently in dog fights, and often severe bruising is hidden underneath the fur. After any fight, examine the combatants carefully. We once found a five-inch, three-cornered tear completely hidden by fur after a fight. Ears, eyelids, gums, feet, and lower legs are frequently involved. Prompt, thorough washing

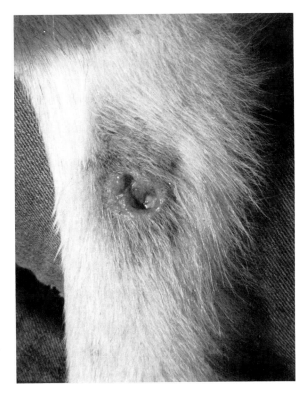

A gaping leg wound is a common result of dog fights. A couple of stitches will hold the edges together and speed healing if appropriate action is taken to prevent infection.

and packing with nitrofurazone powder helps to prevent infections. Severe wounds require veterinary attention. (Fighting is discussed further in Chapter 2.)

Common Medical Problems

Heat Stroke

In warm weather, especially with high humidity, hard-working dogs overheat quickly, leading to heat stroke and heat prostration. Overheating also occurs at colder temperatures (even 0° F.) but is most common during summer and fall training. Obesity, poor condition, thick fur, larger size, hereditary factors, or a large meal can all predispose a dog to overheating. Heat stroke can permanently damage the hypothalamus, which controls body temperature, and can also harm muscles and some internal organs.

Signs. Signs of heat stroke are rapid panting, weakness, a wobbly rear end, muscle tremors, excessive salivation, cyanosis (bluish gums), then collapse. Death can follow.

Prevention. Take advantage of cooler weather and run in the early morning or late evening. Avoid exercise at 60° F. or higher. (Gig races are usually cancelled if the temperature exceeds 60° or if the humidity is high.) Stop frequently to let the dogs cool down, especially in puddles so that they can drink a little, and do not ask for a lot of speed or power. Control obesity and other factors. When overheating is a real possibility, wet the dogs to the skin before and during training, and run through water when possible. Some people even carry water along for frequent wetting. Rest the dogs when they pant heavily, *before* other symptoms occur. An acclimated dog can stand heat better than one who has not been exposed to it recently. According to one source, dogs need one to three weeks to become acclimated to a warmer climate.

Stopping your team in water during summer and fall runs gives them the opportunity to cool off both by getting wet and drinking cold water. Joe Runyan's team out for a training run.

An overheated dog can be almost completely submerged in cool water. He may do this on his own if he gets a chance.

Cool an overheated dog by packing him with snow (especially the head, groin, and armpit areas) or *thoroughly* wetting him or dunking him (except the head) in cool water. Any dog that collapses from heat stroke should be carried home after being cooled and revived. Veterinary care may be required, and fatalities or permanent damage can occur!

Proper management can prevent heat stroke, as dog drivers in Arizona, Texas, and Florida have proven. Breeding for heat tolerance can help reduce the problem.

Frostbite

Frostbite rarely occurs unless something interferes with circulation. Tight booties, especially if they are wet, can cause frostbitten feet. A dog's leg can freeze if it is tightly tangled in his picket. If freezing is more than superficial, the foot or limb is hard and cold. Frozen skin often appears normal after thawing, only to break open in sores after a few days. A veterinarian should treat severe cases. Home treatment consists of thawing the part in warm water (*without* rubbing) and, if the skin breaks open, cleaning and applying antibiotic ointment. A veterinarian may recommend antibiotics to prevent infection.

Males often frostbite the scrotum. The skin becomes inflamed and may form scabs that slough off, exposing tender, pink new skin. Once frozen, reinjury is likely to occur, and the problem may not clear up until warmer weather comes unless the dog is kept inside. A protective diaper-type arrangement will protect the area. Lactating bitches can freeze their nipples in cold or windy weather and should not be exercised under these conditions. RAMCO makes a "tit guard" for their protection.

Diarrhea

Diarrhea can be caused by stress, disease, food poisoning, dietary changes, parasites, low-quality diets, and other problems. When the diarrhea appears orange or chalky, has a strong or unusual odor, or shows bloody streaks, it may be due to parvovirus, coronavirus, or other serious diseases requiring immediate veterinary attention. Stress diarrhea caused by excitement or hard work is usually temporary, and genetics appears to play a role in its frequency. On long hauls or long-distance races, diarrhea causes major problems, including weight loss, dehydration, and electrolyte imbalances. Because of the number of dogs involved in some events, epidemics of flu-like diseases often run through teams.

Food poisoning is probably more frequent than mushers realize. Meat (especially chicken) spoils easily, even without thawing. Some "flu epidemics" are probably actually due to food poisoning when racers feed meat that has spoiled in warmer temperatures.

You can obtain a mild antidiarrheal drug such as Kaopectate® from your veterinarian and follow his or her instructions for its use. Avoid stronger medications unless advised by a veterinarian. Diarrhea is sometimes a cleansing process to rid the digestive system of harmful bacteria or other problems, and stopping it too soon can cause further complications. Antidiarrheal drugs should not be used if intestinal obstruction is a possibility. Withholding food for twenty-four hours and then feeding a light, mild diet (such as cooked rice and broth) is beneficial. Treatment for dehydration and electrolyte replacement may be needed. Dogs with severe or prolonged diarrhea require hospitalization and intravenous fluids.

Some dogs develop a bloody diarrhea while running that clears up spontaneously. This is believed to be caused by too much carbohydrate or fiber and too little fat and protein in the diet. (Do not overlook the possibility that bloody diarrhea may indicate a much more serious problem.)

Dehydration

Water is the single most important requirement for life. It is instrumental in removing metabolic wastes and transporting nutrients to the cells. It aids in digestion, maintains body temperature, and affects the muscular and nervous systems. A shortage of fluid causes effects ranging from a slight loss of stamina, to loss of kidney function and digestion, to death.

Encourage your dogs to drink during the winter to avoid chronic, mild dehydration (see Chapter 4). A well-hydrated dog has 75 percent more endurance than a dehydrated animal; even a 3 percent loss can cause a 20 percent drop in performance. Unfortunately, the desire to drink does *not* reliably increase with dehydration, and a lack of thirst does *not* mean that the dog is well hydrated.

Large amounts of water can be lost from evaporation (especially from panting), and also from diarrhea and vomiting. Loss due to evaporation is greatest during temperature extremes. Cold air is very dry and sucks up moisture, while warm weather exaggerates the loss from salivation and panting. If the dogs eat a lot of snow in warm weather, the loss is offset. Wind also greatly increases evaporation.

Prevent dehydration by watering your dogs at every opportunity, especially during long races; frequent, small amounts of water are best. Let the dogs bite snow or drink from overflow along the way (unless you are sprint racing). When running in warm winter weather, the dogs will take advantage of short, frequent breaks to eat snow, which also cools them down and decreases panting. When running in a snowless area, stop in any water that you cross to allow your dogs to drink and cool off.

Signs. A loss of skin elasticity is a classical sign of dehydration. If the skin does not snap back when pinched, the dog is dehydrated. Gums feel dry instead of slippery, and the eyes can become sunken. At 10 to 12 percent dehydration, signs become more pronounced, with involuntary twitching. Shock followed by death occurs when dehydration reaches about 15 percent. In comparison, a dog can lose 50 percent of its protein and 100 percent of its fat before dying.

Treatment. Treat simple dehydration by replacing water in the diet, encouraging the consumption of snow and water, and resting the dog. You can force-feed water with a squirt bottle, giving only a sip at a time. If dehydration is due to vomiting, diarrhea, or blood loss, electrolyte replacement may be necessary.

In simple dehydration, the value of electrolyte replacement in hard-working sled dogs is still being debated. Some people advocate the use of electrolytes as a preventative measure. Others avoid their use altogether. An excess of electrolytes has a dehydrating effect as the body attempts to flush them out in the urine; therefore, injudicious use actually can increase dehydration. Use of electrolytes in dogs is not comparable to their use in human athletes, because humans lose salts in sweat, while dogs sweat very little.

When dehydration is severe or due to repeated vomiting or diarrhea that interferes with water replacement, an intravenous solution may be required to save the dog's life. This should be done by a veterinarian.

Arthritis

Arthritis causes stiffness and pain, especially after rest. It commonly afflicts older dogs. Exercising the dog on a leash prior to running him in the team loosens him up. The prudent use of anti-inflammatory analgesics as recommended by a veterinarian often extends the dog's working life by controlling pain, but arthritis has no permanent cure. (Beware of using banned drugs in races.)

Fainting or Collapse

Sometimes a sled dog will faint or collapse while running in the team. This can occur without warning, or the dog may be staggering, wobbling, or in distress beforehand. A number of problems can cause this condition, including choking (usually from tangled lines), heat stress, epilepsy, hypothermia, exhaustion, hypoglycemia, or shock due to illness or injury. If you think that a dog is on the verge of collapse, stop the team and carry him home in the sled basket.

If a dog faints, *immediately* check his breathing and remove his neckline if it is tight. If he is not breathing, quickly seal his mouth with your hand and blow into his nose just until the chest rises, repeating the breaths about twelve times per minute until the dog breathes on his own or his heart stops. If he has choked on an object, you may have to remove it before giving a breath. You may also need to pull the tongue forward and extend the neck in order to allow for free air passage.

If the heart stops, the chances of revival are slim. But if the dog has stopped breathing because he was choked by tangled lines, prompt artificial respiration can save his life. During the 1987 Yukon Quest, one of Jeff King's dogs was choked into unconsciousness by tangled lines while Jeff was snowshoeing out the trail. The dog was limp with unreactive, staring eyes and was not breathing, but fellow musher Rick Atkinson's quick action saved the dog's life. Several moments of artificial respiration revived the dog completely.

Heat stress and other obvious causes should be treated immediately, and the dog should be carried home. Unfortunately, the cause of collapse often is not apparent. (A seemingly healthy dog of ours fainted when he had a partial gut impaction.) Diagnosis must often be left to a veterinarian, and even then it may be impossible unless the dog can be examined during the fainting spell.

Dogs With Decreased Ability

Numerous conditions can cause a dog to lose his working ability, and we can only mention some of the more common ones. Most require diagnosis and treatment by a veterinarian.

Middle-aged and older males commonly suffer from chronic kidney disease. These dogs are reluctant to stretch out when running, may not want to lope, and may lag or show signs of back pain. Two of our affected dogs paced rather than trotted to reduce back movement. The problem requires veterinary diagnosis and can be treated with antibiotics, but it frequently recurs. Prostate trouble has similar symptoms; neutering helps these dogs.

Hypothyroidism often affects sled dogs and is discussed under hereditary conditions. A painful bone spur in the back discourages dogs from pulling; these dogs usually show signs of back pain when the backbone is squeezed between the thumb and fingers over the spur. X-rays provide a definitive diagnosis.

Anemia (low hemoglobin or red blood cell count) slows dogs down. It has many causes, including nutritional deficiencies, malabsorption, parasites, infections, and stress. According to Dr. David Kronfeld, a canine nutritional specialist at Virginia Technical Institute, stressed dogs release cortisol, a hormone that decreases red blood cell production and interferes with the immune system. His studies show that a diet high in protein (at least 32 percent protein) reduces this problem (*Mushing Magazine*, June/July 1989, p. 16).

Malnutrition decreases a dog's abilities. If your whole team is involved, diet is the probable cause. If only one dog is affected, he may have a malabsorption problem. When malabsorption is due to insufficient digestive enzymes, replacement therapy, as recommended by a veterinarian, often helps.

Sled dogs are amazingly stoic, and you might not be aware that they are in pain when they show no obvious signs. An obscure infection, such as an abscessed tooth, will produce toxins that affect the whole body. One of our dogs once went off his feed and seemed a little depressed. When a veterinarian X-rayed his chest, we learned that three-quarters of his lungs were compromised by pneumonia and that his life was actually in great danger. Problems like this are impossible for you to diagnose without professional help. Blood, urine, enzyme, and hormone tests, as well as X-rays, are often necessary to pinpoint a problem.

Hereditary Conditions

Because of the years of selection for healthy, hard-working dogs, most lines of huskies remain relatively free from hereditary problems. It is up to the breeders to ensure that this trend continues. Some people feel that Alaskan huskies and other non-purebreds have fewer hereditary disorders than pure breeds. If this is true, it could be due to inbreeding within pure breeds. Or, perhaps the intensive selection that sled dogs undergo has eliminated many of the hereditary disorders affecting performance. However, because less research has been done on huskies than on many other breeds, some hereditary diseases in huskies may simply be undocumented. Some purebreds have their own set of genetic problems; information on disorders of your special breed can be obtained from breed books or from a veterinarian.

Wheezers

This hereditary condition causes an incorrect development of the trachea, restricting the flow of air. It is most common among blue-eyed, white-faced huskies. At ten to eleven weeks of age, pups develop a distinctive wheeze on inspiration, and exercise can lead to collapse due to a lack of oxygen. Pneumonia often occurs. Bronchodilators relieve the distress, but dogs with this condition rarely mature, and those that do are stunted. Accurate diagnosis by a veterinarian is necessary to differentiate this problem from other respiratory and heart conditions. The problem is not widely known, and some veterinarians may not be familiar with it.

Hypothyroidism

A surprisingly large number of sled dogs have abnormally low levels of thyroid hormone. Hypothyroidism is believed to have a genetic cause in some cases. Short daylight hours (in northern latitudes), diet, and stress may also be contributing factors. It is possible that the causes and effects of hypothyroidism are somewhat different in sled dogs than in the general canine population.

Signs. Often the only sign is a slowing down or lack of stamina, which can have innumerable other causes. In more severe cases, the dog's abilities decline drastically, and his coat may become greasy and thin and may fail to shed properly. The dog may either gain or lose weight, and he may shiver easily. Affected females often have irregular heat cycles. Some dogs develop skin problems that also affect the feet. Because signs are so indefinite and variable, the condition frequently goes unrecognized. Since these dogs are often less aggressive, breeders may inadvertently select *for* the trait in an effort to eliminate fighting problems. Because hypothyroidism frequently does not appear until later in life, the dog may be bred before the condition is diagnosed, thus passing on the tendency.

In our affected dogs, we noticed an apparent inability to regulate heat efficiently (leading to frequent overheating or shivering) and a *loss* of weight (rather than the weight *gain* normally seen in cases of lowered metabolism).

Treatment. Only a blood test can confirm the disease. Although hypothyroidism is incurable, its symptoms can be alleviated by administering thyroid hormone pills as recommended by your veterinarian (usually once or twice a day) for the rest of the dog's life. Several weeks of treatment are required for the desired effects to appear.

Some mushers reputedly give the replacement hormone to healthy dogs to boost activity during competition. This is not only against race rules but is also harmful to the dog. Abnormally increased energy levels deplete the dog's resources, and he can "burn up." The musher essentially induces another disorder — *hyper*thyroidism. Also, when given to a normal dog, the hormone can retard the natural functioning of the thyroid gland.

Progressive Retinal Atrophy (PRA)

PRA is a hereditary disease affecting the retina of the eye. Night vision and visual acuity decline over a period of months or years, eventually resulting in blindness. You may first notice that the dog has trouble running at night, and later he may stumble during the day. The pupil of the eye widens as blindness increases. PRA is seen in some lines of sled dogs, and inbreeding increases the chances of its occurrence. Dogs with this condition should not be bred. Unfortunately, because PRA does not show up until adulthood or later, the dogs can produce litters and pass on the trait before you find out that they should not be bred.

Neutering

Mushers once thought that neutering a sled dog decreased his desire to work. This view is changing, and some mushers are neutering many of their males to reduce distractions and fighting. Neutering also prevents testicular and prostate problems from developing. Spaying eliminates the problems of running a female in season as well as the difficulties that she might develop with the reproductive tract (including pyometritis and cystic ovaries). It also reduces the likelihood of breast cancer developing. Spaying or neutering dogs with genetic faults prevents these traits from being passed on, and it eliminates unwanted pregnancies. Of course, it also eliminates the possibility of ever breeding a dog.

We have quite a few neutered and spayed dogs and never have had problems with them. Do not let these dogs gain weight, however. Some eat about the same; others require much less food. We see this as an asset, because it saves on feed bills. Also, these dogs do not seem to lose weight as quickly when stressed.

The major objection to neutering in large kennels is the expense of the operation, which adds up fast when a large number of dogs are done.

Blood Testing

Some blood tests can help to determine the level of a dog's fitness. The Packed Cell Volume (PCV), the most popular, measures the percentage of cells (mostly red blood cells) in the blood. Normal PCV levels range from 35 to 55 percent. Inactive sled dogs generally range

This recently spayed dog is certainly not suffering from lack of enthusiasm! She was spayed because she had hypothyroidism, a hereditary problem.

from 40 to 50 percent, while active sled dogs have ranges of 45 to 55 percent. Unfortunately, variation can occur between animals with the same levels of fitness and health, and may even vary in one animal depending on the time of day, the dog's diet, the amount of exercise, the level of excitement, whether the dog is hydrated (dehydration causes a higher percentage of solids in the blood), and whether lab error has occurred.

Because of these variables, blood testing is not an accurate way to compare two dogs or two teams. Its value lies in testing one dog or one team and then retesting later to see if an improvement has been achieved through training, diet, or medical treatment. If a dog's performance decreases for an unknown reason, a PCV blood test can be compared to one done previously. Decreased PCV values can indicate a medical problem. While PCV tests give an unbiased indication of a dog's fitness, they should be only a small part of an overall assessment. As a fitness test, the uncertain results may not justify the cost.

Drugs

Consult with a veterinarian before using drugs on your dog, and be sure to ask about potential side effects. Unfortunately, many veterinarians do not routinely discuss the problems that drugs can cause. The following drugs are of importance to mushers. Some are commonly used. Others are abused drugs, and all racers should be aware of them (see Table 6-1).

Antibiotics

Most mushers rely on broad-spectrum oral antibiotics; amoxicillin is one of the most popular. Most are prescription drugs. They are often effective against skin infections (including cuts) and infections of the gut, ear, eye, and urinary tract. They are not effective against viral infections (including parvovirus and other intestinal viruses), or against an infection that the bloodstream cannot reach, such as a walled-off abscess.

Always administer oral antibiotics for the prescribed time (often two or three weeks), even if symptoms clear up quickly. Otherwise, hardy bacteria can regain strength and reestablish the infection with strains more resistant to the antibiotics. Overuse and improper use are detrimental. Resistant strains of bacteria are harder to eradicate. Antibiotics can destroy the bacteria found naturally in the dog's intestinal tract, causing digestive problems. Secondary infections (such as yeasts) can move in when the normal "flora and fauna" are eliminated. Rarely, a dog will have a potentially fatal reaction to an antibiotic.

Although best used on the advice of a veterinarian, antibiotics should be carried on the trail any time professional help is more than a day or two away. If a severe cut or other injury looks prone to infection, start antibiotic treatment immediately, and give it for the full recommended time. Consult with a veterinarian as soon as possible, because he or she may have other recommendations. An invisible, low-grade infection slows healing, and a severely infected wound will

Table 6-1
Banned Drugs

Many races ban drugs that affect the performance of a dog, that can mask injuries, or that can be harmful to dogs. The following list is of drugs that are commonly banned, but not all races ban all of these, and some races may ban additional drugs. Therefore, be sure to check race rules. Some races do test for banned drugs, usually with a blood or urine test, and mushers may be subjected to testing, too. If a dog or team tests positive, the team and driver may be disqualified, or other penalties may be invoked.

Anabolic steroids
Analgesics (prescription and nonprescription)
Anesthetics
Anti-anxiety drugs
Antihistamines
Anti-inflammatory agents (including corticosteroids, anti-prostaglandins, and aspirin)
Cough suppressants
Depressants
Diet pills
Diuretics
DMSO
Injectable anticholinergics
Muscle relaxants
Oral estrus control pills (Ovaban®)
Stimulants

not heal at all. Antibiotics are among the most valuable drugs available, but only if they are used properly.

Hematinics

Hematinics include iron, copper, cobalt, vitamin B-12, and liver extracts. These substances can improve the red-blood-cell count and hemoglobin content, increasing the oxygen-carrying capacity of blood. They are basically dietary supplements. Some are injected and others are given orally, such as vitamin-mineral supplements like Red Cell®. While hematinics benefit dogs with deficiencies, noticeable improvement is less likely in dogs fed a good, well-balanced diet. Nutritional imbalances can result from their use, and excesses of some cause poisoning.

Aspirin

Aspirin is often used for treating arthritis and other causes of inflammation and pain, including initial treatment of strains. Unfortunately, it can cause bleeding stomach ulcers and even death in dogs. Administering it with food decreases this possibility, but do not use it for an extended period of time. Aspirin is restricted or banned in many races; Yukon Quest veterinarians recently banned it because of the possible danger to dogs.

The anti-inflammatory and analgesic effects of aspirin can mask pain so that the dog — and the musher — underestimate the injury, and this can result in overuse of the injured limb. Consult your veterinarian for dosage; veterinarians have recommended that we use dosages ranging from one five-grain tablet per thirty pounds, to one five-grain tablet per dog (including one that weighed 110 pounds). Do not administer aspirin more often than every six hours, and if in doubt, use smaller amounts less frequently or not at all — aspirin use in dogs can be *dangerous.*

Phenylbutazone ("Bute")

"Bute," another oral anti-inflammatory drug, can also mask symptoms without effecting a cure. Although fairly safe when used as directed for short periods of time, prolonged use can cause a number of serious side effects ranging from bone marrow depression to kidney, liver, and intestinal damage.

Dimethylsulfoxide (DMSO)

DMSO is a topical drug used widely to reduce pain and swelling. It is most effective when used within twelve hours of the time of injury. It penetrates the skin rapidly but has little effect on deep pain and is ineffective when applied through thick fur. DMSO carries some drugs, including antibiotics and steroids, through the skin to under-lying tissue. (It also carries these drugs into *your* body if you do not wear protective gloves when applying it.) Some races ban it or limit its use to topical foot preparations. DMSO can introduce illegal sub-stances into the bloodstream, which subsequently show up in drug tests.

DMSO slows healing and increases the likelihood of infection occur-ring. It therefore should *not* be used if an infection is present. Some veterinarians use it generously, others only with caution. As with any anti-inflammatory drug, remember that just because the swelling and pain go down dramatically when you splash it on, healing has *not* taken place.

Steroids

Corticosteroids. These drugs reduce inflammation, swelling, and pain. They also increase red blood cells and reduce scarring. They are used topically (often in foot ointments, which are discussed in Chapter 7), or are given orally or through injection to relieve muscle and joint injuries.

Several forms are used. Cortisone must be changed to hydrocor-tisone by the liver and therefore is ineffective topically. Hydrocortisone is a natural substance; dexamethasone (Azium®) is a more potent analogue (similar compound) of hydrocortisone. It is commonly used in topical skin preparations, often in combination with DMSO.

Corticosteroids, especially taken internally, can cause problems. They slow healing, depress the body's natural immune response, cause muscular weakness and exercise intolerance, weaken the skeletal system, and reduce peripheral circulation; therefore, they should be used sparingly. Internal use should be on the advice of a veterinarian only. Taken correctly, these drugs reduce the suffering of an injured animal, especially if rest is enforced. Additional injury can occur if the dog is worked, because pain is not present to warn him of damage.

Corticosteroids are banned from some races, except for topical use.

Anabolic Steroids. These male hormones and synthetic analogues are used to increase muscle mass, and some feel that they can improve the physical abilities of a healthy dog. Under veterinary guidance, they can reverse anemia due to parasites or infection, strengthen emaciated animals, and rebuild weakened muscles. They can increase appetite, red blood cells, and hemoglobin and make the dog feel better.

In most dogs, anabolic steroids will build muscle mass if the dog is trained strenuously and is well-nourished. However, most studies show that anabolic steroids do not improve endurance. The increased muscle mass is unlikely to benefit race dogs if they become over-muscled or muscle-bound. Human sprint racers, marathon runners, and ballet dancers could not perform with the muscle mass of weight lifters and wrestlers. Most mushers and veterinarians frown on the use of steroids to increase a dog's physical ability. While harmful effects in dogs are as yet undocumented, steroid use in humans causes a decrease in the natural production of testosterone (a male hormone) and an increase in tendon injuries, birth defects, and heart problems in males. Anabolic steroids are banned from most races.

Stimulants

Amphetamines and similar drugs affect the nervous and cardiovascular systems. While they stimulate a dog for a short period of time, the depression that follows is often more pronounced than the "high." They are banned from races, and the use of these drugs for increasing performance is harmful to dogs and to the sport of dog mushing.

Alcohol, incidentally, is *not* a stimulant; it is a depressant. The practice of giving it to cold or hypothermic dogs (or humans) is actually counterproductive.

Euthanasia

Unfortunately, serious life-threatening injuries occasionally occur on the trail. If a dog is hopelessly injured and suffering, it is far more humane to put him down immediately than to carry him all the way to a clinic so that someone else can do it. Additionally, if a dog is very old or disabled, euthanasia is necessary. A musher may opt to do this himself.

A bullet fired properly into the head delivers instant, permanent relief to the dog (leaving the human to suffer alone). This is as effective as an injection by a veterinarian. Do it at close range, using necessary firearm precautions. Aim at the center of the forehead about one inch above the eyes, and direct the bullet toward the base of the skull. A large-caliber firearm offers more assurance of an instant death. Be sure, of course, that the dog's injuries warrant this. A broken back is generally incurable, but a partial evisceration or a compound fracture can heal *if* professional help is obtained promptly.

Do not resort to evasive tactics such as overdosing with sleeping pills or aspirin. The dog may go to sleep only to wake up hours later, or may suffer from poisoning without dying.

Musher Maladies

Dog drivers have been bitten in fights, run over by sleds, and tripped up by traces. Broken teeth, scarred faces, concussions, and broken bones are potential side effects for dog-team devotees. Mushers have been slammed into trees, fallen through river ice, floated off on ice floes, suffered from frostbite and freezing of body parts, and been abandoned by Fido the Faithful and crew at inopportune times. A sound knowledge of first-aid techniques and wilderness and cold-weather survival might save your life. This information is available in other books. A few conditions peculiar to dog mushers are worthy of note.

"Musher's knee" is a seemingly perpetual knee sprain caused by pedaling too much. An elastic supportive bandage helps if you cannot rest (and who can rest during the mushing season?).

Carpal tunnel syndrome sometimes results from gripping the handlebow for long periods of time. This is a pinched nerve in the wrist that creates pain or numbness. The pain spreads from the hand up the arm and even into the shoulder. It usually strikes while sleeping. It can be diagnosed by a physician, who may recommend wrist braces, cortisone, surgery, or other treatments. B-vitamins sometimes alleviate the symptoms.

Hydatid disease is a serious, bizarre, and little-known problem that strikes mushers more often than the general public. It is caused by *Echinococcus*, a tiny tapeworm that infects dogs when they eat infested beef, sheep, or raw game (inspected meats are generally safe). The meat is infected with the encysted larval worm (hydatid form). In the dog, it grows to the rather innocuous adult stage in the gut.

However, the microscopic eggs that are passed in the stool can be inadvertently ingested by humans, leading to hydatid disease. The larvae move to the human liver, lungs, brain, or other organs, where they grow into large cysts containing up to fifteen quarts of foreign material. Death occurs when the affected organ can no longer function, or if the cyst ruptures, releasing the contents into the body and pro-

Gripping the handlebow of a sled, especially on rough trails at high speeds or for long periods of time, can cause carpal tunnel syndrome, in which a pinched nerve causes a deadening sensation or pain in the hand, wrist, elbow, or even the shoulder, typically during rest. Mushers whose hands become numb from this or other problems can also suffer from frostbite, due to poor circulation or lack of warning pain.

ducing a severe reaction. Surgery may or may not be possible to remove the cyst. Dog handlers are known to be at risk for this disease, because they work in such close proximity with canines, and mushers have a tendency to feed their dogs raw meat.

Because of this, dogs should never be fed raw game, including moose and caribou. (You yourself cannot get this disease directly from infested meat.) The microscopic eggs can be missed in routine fecal exams, and only a few wormers (notably Droncit®) are effective against the adult stage living in dogs. The disease is more prevalent in coastal areas of the North, where it is also harbored by fox; in this case, the larval stage is found in microtine rodents such as voles and lemmings.

The main disease suffered by nearly all mushers is sled-dog addiction. One Iditarod musher told us that he was going to hang up X-rays of the injuries that he had sustained in his recent race as a warning not to run again. His plan failed, because he mushed to Nome again the following year.

To the best of our knowledge, there is no cure for the hopeless disease of sled-dog addiction.

CHAPTER 7

NO FOOT, NO DOG

Sore or injured feet are common problems, but the symptoms of bad feet vary and can be deceiving. Over the years, we have seen foot injuries cause an array of other problems.

Comet was limping. I stopped and checked his feet and found a reddish, worn area between the pads caused by abrasive snow. Ivanhoe was not pulling; he seemed happy and willing, but his line was never tight. He had tender feet. Trapper suddenly developed a severe limp. Balls of ice had collected on the long hair between his toes, and when I melted off the ice, his lameness disappeared. Streak was not hungry; examining him, I saw the swollen, inflamed feet of a dog that had been pounding down a trail for too long, with cracks and a systemic infection setting in. But he had not been limping. Legs seemed fine after a long run, but later he started hopping around holding a back leg high off the ground. He had a badly lacerated foot.

If something is wrong and you do not know what it is, check the feet. If a dog has pus draining from his eyes, he might have a systemic infection, possibly originating from infected feet. Symptoms can seem totally unrelated. Maybe they *are* unrelated. Check the feet anyway. You might be surprised at what you find.

Damaged feet sometimes cause lameness. They can also cause fever, depression, and appetite loss, and the dog may be reluctant to drink, to pull, or to run. He might avoid walking on straw, spruce boughs, broken ice, gravel, or other coarse surfaces. He may be reluctant even to stand up. Dogs have died when infected feet caused a systemic infection. All of this can occur *even without signs of lameness*.

A sled dog is only as good as his feet, so it is critical to avoid foot problems. Unfortunately, the feet take a great deal of abuse, especially when they are needed the most — on long races. But many foot injuries can heal even as the dog continues traveling seventy or even

Iditarod Trail Race leader Eep Anderson of Takotna, Alaska, tapes colorful booties to his racing dogs' feet. The Iditarod Trail Race, from Anchorage to Nome, covers more than 1,000 miles of the Alaskan wilderness. The booties protect the dog's feet. *Photo by Eric Muehling; courtesy* Fairbanks Daily News-Miner.

a hundred miles a day *if* the musher is dedicated enough to care for them properly and in a timely fashion. If the musher is not prepared to do so, he or she should drop the dog to avoid permanent damage. Crippling injuries can be headed off by using foresight in judging trail conditions (using booties when needed for prevention of injury) and by spotting and treating a problem quickly while it can still be reversed.

Dogs with exceptionally tough, care-free feet are especially important to the long-distance racer. Booting up sixty-four feet at 3:00 a.m. on a forty-below morning takes a lot of dedication, particularly when your competitor is beating you, not with better dogs but with better feet. He leaves half an hour before you do because he knows that his dogs' feet are tough enough to withstand the conditions without booties.

On a long race, your dogs' feet are tested to the limit. In many dogs, the feet are the first parts to wear out. Sore feet can lead to the breakdown of the mind from pain and depression. The rest of the body can be affected by infection and even by sprains caused by the overworking of an opposite leg in order to favor a foot injury.

All About Feet

A dog's foot has thick, tough skin over pads of dense fat that act as cushions, absorbing the first impact every time the foot strikes the ground. The skin of the pad should feel tough but pliable, be resistant to abrasions and lacerations, and be free from cracks, dryness, or scarring. Some mushers believe that black pads are tougher than pink ones; other discredit this theory.

If the hairs underneath the feet are stained reddish, the dog probably has been licking his feet excessively. (You can see the same reddish discoloration on the sparse udder fur of a nursing bitch, caused by the pups' licking.) This dog may have sore feet, or he may have developed the habit of licking his feet when he *did* have sore feet. Some dogs seem to lick from boredom. It appears that this reddish hair is more likely to collect snow, because the natural oils have been licked away.

A smallish, tight foot with a high arch is more resistant to injuries. Big, splayed feet (often seen in some hound breeds) expose more of the thin-skinned webbing to the abrasive snow. (Large feet do offer a snowshoe-like quality.)

A dog's conformation affects the feet. Dogs that tend to pound on their front feet are more susceptible to foot soreness. A heavy head and shoulders can stress the front feet. Our tender-footed Ivanhoe had straight, vertical shoulders and a short stride that probably contributed to his foot problems.

A light, well-angulated, long-legged dog has a light, long stride and takes fewer steps to cover the same ground, thus abusing his feet less. His feet might not actually be tougher, but because his stride

Avoid flat feet. This foot has nicely arched toes and is fairly compact, which are good points.

stresses them less, they hold up better. The front feet carry over half of the dog's weight and absorb the forward momentum of every stride; therefore, they are more susceptible to injury. However, sometimes the hind feet are affected instead — so always check all four feet.

Genetics plays a strong role in foot quality, with some lines of dogs reliably having good feet and other lines lacking this quality. (Some dog owners can truthfully report that their dogs never have foot problems — but only because the dogs' feet never have been stressed.) Pay close attention to this if you are breeding distance dogs. A dog with weak feet should not be bred at all. Feet are somewhat less critical in sprint dogs. Most dogs whose feet would not hold up to the shorter distances have already been culled from competitive strains of sled dogs.

If you plan to race mid-distance or longer races, you must know which of your dogs require booting to prevent snowballing under what trail conditions. Which dogs' feet are prone to abrasion? Which ones to swelling and cracks? (These are discussed under foot injuries.) Discover as much as you can during training and during races. Remember — prevention is the key!

This is a big, loose, hairy foot. The splayed toes expose the webbing to abrasion and are considered a weakness. The hair, although it protects the webbing between the toes, also tends to collect snow. This dog, despite his poor foot construction, has few foot problems — a tribute to good breeding.

Preventative Foot Care

If the elusive miracle foot toughener has been found, it is still somebody's secret. Most of the "tougheners" on the market have a high alcohol content that dries the skin, leaving it more prone to chapping and cracking. Alcohol also dissolves away the natural oils in the hair. Chrome Tan®, Kopertox®, and Preparation H® do not help much either. The three best methods of toughening the feet are careful breeding, judicious training, and good health care.

When a dog is run, the hide on his feet toughens in a natural response to the stress. If he is run too much, the skin wears away faster than it forms. Housing dogs on gravel keeps the feet tough during the summer, just as walking barefoot on gravel toughens human feet faster than walking on dirt.

Dryness and cleanliness cut down on parasitic, bacterial, and fungal infections. Parasitic infections weaken the dog, and hookworm larvae damage the skin itself by boring right through it. (This is generally not a problem during winter months, because the larvae require warmth to develop.)

Many health problems show up first in the skin — including the feet. Some are cleverly disguised as a simple but persistent foot problem. A lack of fat or zinc in the diet, or an absorption problem, can weaken the feet. A biotin supplement (which helps in fat absorption) may help. Liver disease, hormonal changes, and other conditions also affect the feet.

One of our lead dogs, Legs, finished the 1,000-mile Yukon Quest Race without ever having a sore foot, so when he suddenly developed a string of foot problems ranging from weakened pads to abscesses, we suspected an underlying medical problem. A veterinarian diagnosed kidney infection and a borderline low-thyroid condition. Antibiotics cleared up the kidney disease, but the foot problems persisted until we started him on thyroid hormone.

Some people do not clip the claws, thinking that they help to grip ice. If the claws are long enough to force the toes upward when the dog is standing on a hard, level surface, clip them! Long claws are prone to cracking, breaking, and tearing. Running on a hard surface can cause bruising up inside the nail, and, according to one veterinarian, it can stress the carpals and tarsals, leading to arthritis. Nails do dig in under certain conditions of hard-packed snow and rough ice. But on glassy ice, an experienced dog runs on his pads without digging in his claws, because nails skid like ice-skate blades, while the soft pads offer greater contact and better grip. (The same is true on slippery tile floors!) Clipping nails also lessens the likelihood of the dog wearing holes in his booties. (Nail injuries are discussed under foot injuries.)

Booties

Booties can keep a dog in your team and your team on the trail. Improperly used, they can cause dropped dogs or scratched teams. Use booties **only** when you must but **always** when you must. Use them if snow is abrasive or if the trail is icy. Use them on roads to protect the feet from salt and chemicals. If you do not put them on *before* running your dogs over a bad trail, the feet will get sore, and you will be forced to use the booties even on better sections.

Although they protect the feet, booties can interfere with circulation if they are fastened too tightly, causing swelling, cracks, infection, and possibly even frostbite. Even when applied correctly, the fastener can get too tight if the foot swells for any reason, or if the bootie is left on for too long. Always remove them when stopped.

Bruce Johnson boots up his dogs when he has to — and goes on to win the 1986 Yukon Quest.
Photo by Ron Lambert.

If a dog wearing a bootie starts to limp, inspect his feet immediately. When booties wear through, ice and snow collect inside, abrading the feet worse than the trail. Check and change booties religiously! When dogs run through overflow and then on soft snow, balls of ice form around the rim of the booties, causing sores and discomfort. Unless the weather is warm and the trail is hard-packed, change booties immediately after running the dogs through water.

When sizing booties, have the dog place his weight on the booted foot. If the boot is too small, it will interfere with the expansion of the foot and will pinch the toes. This can cause sores between the toes, often on the upper side of the webbing. A bootie that is too big flops, hindering the dog's movements, and is thrown off easily.

Ideally, your team will be matched closely, and all will wear the same size booties. However, because the front feet are larger than the hind feet, you may need two sizes for one dog. If your booties are sized by color, your weary, befogged brain can tell different sizes at a blurred glance during a distance race.

Booties help to keep medication in place when the dog must be run, and a bootie fastened on lightly will keep him from licking off medication when he is resting. You can pad an injured foot with a thick bootie or place one over a dressing.

Sprint racers use booties to protect injuries on their dogs during training or to hold on medication. If a dog's foot is so bad that he needs a bootie, he probably will not help you much in a fast race. A bootie can throw a dog off stride and slow him down, disrupting the rhythm of the team. Most dogs hop around and flip their feet trying to get rid of booties, and this is not something that you want to tolerate at the ALPO International Sled Dog Race at Saranac Lake.

Booties play an important role in long-distance races where protection from injury is as important as protecting an existing injury. Trail conditions vary greatly from year to year, and mushers must be prepared for the worst. Race rules require two sets of booties per dog, or 128 for a sixteen-dog team. Five hundred to 1,000 booties are commonly sent out for a 1,000-mile race.

Materials

Booties must be made of very durable material. The thickness of bunting offers extra protection on crusty, icy trails, during cold weather, or for injuries, but it soaks up water. Nine- or ten-ounce polypropylene is lightweight, stretchable, compact, and more durable than bunting. Cordura offers excellent durability but is abrasive on the foot. Ivanhoe, our tender-footed dog, traveled 400 miles in ten days

Bootie Styles
Top, left: Cordura booties. *Top, right:* Lined cordura (the Velcro strip is too narrow here). *Bottom, left:* Polar fleece booties. *Bottom, right:* Cordura foot pad sewn over polar fleece.

Figure 7-1
Booties

Many types of booties are available, but this is a basic type. The flare at the top does not help much on softer materials. Hem the bootie top if the material might fray. Unless you use an industrial-strength thread, double-stitch the entire bootie.

Steps:
1. Sew velcro tabs/elastic together.
2. Sew velcro to bootie.
3. Hem if necessary.
4. Place velcro to inside and sew up bootie.
5. Turn right-side out and make *sure* that it fits the dogs *before* you cut and sew 500 more!

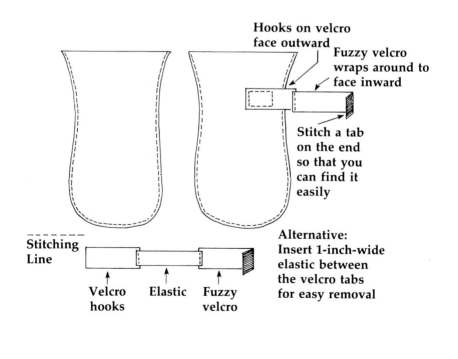

Hooks on velcro face outward

Fuzzy velcro wraps around to face inward

Stitch a tab on the end so that you can find it easily

Stitching Line

Velcro hooks   Elastic   Fuzzy velcro

Alternative: Insert 1-inch-wide elastic between the velcro tabs for easy removal in the same pair of cordura booties (removed at night and during breaks). The same material wore out on two miles of pavement.

Thick, soft leather (elk, moose, cow) is durable, soft, and protective and offers a better grip on ice. But it is also very expensive and harder to sew and tends to stiffen after drying. Gortex® and canvas also have been used.

Cheap fabrics wear out in just a couple of miles, resulting in further injury when holes develop. You end up using many more booties — or no booties at all — instead of saving money. Even blue-jean denim will not hold up more than five or ten miles.

Velcro is the most popular fastener. It is quick to use and unlikely to cause constriction if the strips are ¾ inch wide or wider. Inserting a short elastic strip between the bootie and the velcro allows the booties to be pulled off simply, saving valuable time (and the stress of not being able to find the end of the velcro!). However, elastic can cause constriction if it is too tight or twisted, if it folds up, or if the foot swells. You can use black electrician's tape or first-aid tape if you do not apply it too tightly. It is easy to get tape too tight. Again, a wider tape is less likely to bind and constrict.

When applying booties, be sure that the dog's feet are free of snow and ice and that they are relatively dry. Fasten booties tightly enough to keep them on without constricting. If the booties fly right off, you did not fasten them tightly enough. If the foot is swollen, or if you see a puffy area above and below the fastener, you either fastened the bootie too tightly, or swelling occurred for some other reason.

Foot Injuries

Always be alert for signs of foot injury — a spot of blood in the snow, lameness, or a dog licking his feet frequently. Check the feet often during a long-distance race — once or twice a day, or after running on a bad trail. Always spread the toes and inspect the deepest recesses underneath the foot, where cracks are usually found.

In normal training, a dog developing bad feet should be rested until the feet heal. Some people feel that, in general, *moist* conditions (like weeping abrasions or moist dermatitis) are best treated with a drying agent (such as Betadine®) and that *dry* conditions (including cracks and dry, abraded skin) do better when a moisturizing agent (such as Furacin® ointment) is applied. Sometimes the best course is to treat first with the Betadine® ointment until the injury dries out, then

A dog holding his foot up may have cold feet, sore feet, or nothing wrong at all. The worn, discolored hairs (more evident on the back feet) can be caused by excessive licking. This also can be caused by running on soft or windblown trails where the dog repeatedly punches through.

switch to a nondrying agent. Keeping the feet clean, warm, and dry greatly speeds healing. That sometimes means keeping the dog inside.

Ice Balls or Snow Balls

When grains or marbles of ice build up on the fur between the toes, they abrade the skin. Some dogs, especially those with long, fine, soft fur, pick these up faster than others, and ice balls or clumps of snow can even form up the backs of their legs. Ice balls range from the size of crumbs to over an inch in diameter. On one run, when a warm spell broke and the temperature dropped to -20° F., Miki ran into damp snow and overflow underneath cold snow. The odd combination caused ice balls three inches in diameter to form on the *toenails* of her dogs.

Dogs with ice balls may (or may not) limp, shake the foot, look back at you, or bite at the foot while running. Remove ice balls

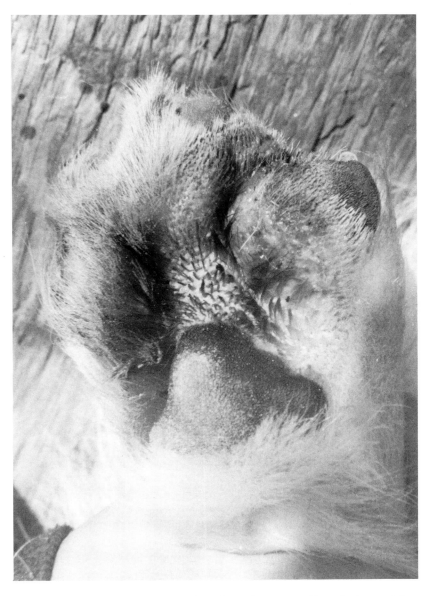

A mysterious foot infection caused Amber's foot to swell up during a night-long run. Antibiotics and twice-daily cleaning cleared it up. The hair was also clipped away. A moist infection like this can be treated with Betadine®, which is a drying agent.

On long-distance races, the endurance of a dog's feet is no laughing matter. Dogs licking their feet may be helping, by cleaning away snow and ice; or they actually may be harming their feet by habitual licking. Licking removes the oils in the fur and can even wear down hair and skin. *Courtesy* Fairbanks Daily News-Miner.

promptly to prevent abrasion; this will provide instant and complete relief if no damage has been done. Melt them off with your hands, or crush them with pliers or your teeth. A relaxed team, given the opportunity, will lick them off, but most dogs tend to rip them out hurriedly, hair and all, trying to finish before you start the team again. This leaves bare, sore skin.

Clipping excess fur reduces the problem but also eliminates an important protective shield from the underside of the foot. Vaseline®, greasy ointments, and Pam® no-stick cooking spray all retard ice balls when smeared on the hairs, but they wear off in a few miles.

Booties offer the best protection and should be used when your dogs start icing up. Ice balls are especially likely to be caused by moist snow, but they can form on certain dogs under many other snow conditions.

Lacerations

Jagged ice and dog bites are two common sources of lacerations. A small nick usually heals without care. If severe bleeding occurs, apply a compression bandage over a thick surgical pad. Vetrap® works well and stays in place better than a conventional bandage. Put cotton balls between the toes to prevent sores from developing, especially if the bandage is going to be in place for very long.

Washing a cut (we use diluted Betadine® scrub) and applying an antibacterial powder or ointment helps to prevent infections. A veterinarian may prescribe oral antibiotics.

Some veterinarians feel that suturing does not help a cut pad, because the skin is so inelastic that the stitches tend to saw through it at every step. Others recommend suturing if the fat pad underneath the skin is visible. As an alternative, butterfly bandages held in place with Super Glue® or Skin Bond®, can be used to hold the edges together. (Skin Bond® is less likely to cause cracking, because it has some give to it after drying.) Because the dog traumatizes any foot injury when he walks, healing is slow. If the dog must work, a thickly padded bootie, or a bootie over a dressing and bandage, offers some protection.

Abrasions

Very cold or wind-blown snow has tiny ice crystals that sandpaper away the fur and abrade the skin. Ice balls also abrade the skin. *Prevention is the best cure!* Boot your dogs if conditions warrant it. Often the first sign is hair loss between the pads, followed by inflamed ("raspberry") skin. Swelling, bleeding, and infection can result. Damage frequently occurs on the webbing between the pads, where it can be overlooked unless the toes are spread apart. Pads can also be worn thin, especially when the dog is run on gravel. Booting protects the injured area, which you can treat with an antibiotic ointment. Some people affix a cloth or surgical tape over the affected area with Super Glue® for further protection.

Swelling and Cracks

Feet swell in response to constant pounding on the trail, from booties being applied too tightly, or from infection or injury. Swelling can spread upward into the leg and shoulder. It can also cause cracks, which appear as dark spots or cuts, usually deep in the webbing. Infected cracks can cause a systemic infection with an elevated body temperature, and, in extreme cases, death. Cracks commonly occur on long races. Small cracks, unless they become infected, do not seem to bother the dogs much.

Treat swelling with rest if possible. A veterinarian may prescribe DMSO or a topical corticosteroid to reduce swelling, inflammation, and pain. Cracks benefit from antibiotic ointments, rest, and a warm, dry, clean environment. You can protect feet with booties if additional swelling is not a problem (remember — booties might have caused the problem initially).

Abscesses

When an infection develops in an isolated spot underneath the skin, the body may wall it off, creating an abscess. In the foot, an abscess usually appears as a red swelling on the side of the toe or in the webbing. (A broken toe with bone fragments can also look like this.) Keep the area clean, and use antibiotics (if recommended by a veterinarian) to keep the infection from spreading. Boot the foot if the dog continues in harness. An abscess sometimes breaks open and drains, or it might just shrink with healing. It can be lanced when it softens and be allowed to drain.

Toenail Injuries

When a dog's toenails are too long, or when he is run on a hard or rough surface, the nails can tear or split to the quick, causing lameness. Remove the broken part with nail clippers. If no infection is present, paint over the break with Super Glue® to protect it and nerve endings, or fix a temporary dental cap to it.

Nail beds can become inflamed, especially if the dog is punching through crusty snow. Clean them, apply antibiotic ointment, and use booties for protection and prevention. Keeping the nails clipped helps to prevent many nail injuries.

Dewclaw Injuries. Dewclaws can be torn when the dogs punch through hard, crusty snow, or when the dewclaw is caught on brush. Again, clean and apply ointment. An injury can be protected with a bandage or with Vetrap®. Place a piece of cotton between the dewclaw and the leg before applying the bandage to prevent the claw from irritating the leg.

Because bootie fasteners lie directly over the dewclaw, the nail is pressed into the flesh of the leg, often resulting in a serious sore. If the dog must continue in booties, wash the sore carefully, apply antibiotic ointment, and place a cotton ball between the dewclaw and the leg. Lubricate the sore well with ointment so that the cotton does not stick to it. Wrap first-aid tape around the leg over the dewclaw to hold the cotton in place, then replace the bootie.

All dewclaw problems can be eliminated by clipping off the dewclaws when a puppy is a few days old (see Chapter 8).

Topical Foot Ointments

Veterinary foot ointments have improved greatly in recent years and are available with a bewildering array of ingredients that can help prevent infection, decrease harmful, painful swelling, and speed healing. Medications containing DMSO, steroids, or other anti-inflammatories can keep a dog in harness. However, they also slow healing, mask symptoms, and leave a dog more susceptible to infection by suppressing the immune system.

Most ointments contain antibiotics (usually nitrofurazone 0.2 percent, found in Furacin® ointment) or an antiseptic (such as povidone-iodine, found in Betadine® ointment). Antibiotics do not dry the skin like iodine can, but bacteria can become resistant to them. In some cases, such as in moist dermatitis, drying the skin is necessary.

Many ointments also contain a compound to decrease inflammation (swelling, heat, pain, redness). DMSO (dimethylsulfoxide) or a corticosteroid can do this, but both also have drawbacks (see the drug section in Chapter 6). Some people claim that DMSO toughens the feet; others avoid it, believing that it softens the pads.

The use of anti-inflammatory agents is controversial, and some races prohibit their use. Some people feel that anti-inflammatories are invaluable in reducing swelling, which is a primary source of soreness and cracking, and that they quickly relieve pain. Others feel that they should not be used because of their adverse effects (slowing down healing, increasing infection, and masking symptoms). Some veterinarians recommend oral antibiotics to prevent infection and speed healing whenever DMSO or steroids are needed. Others feel that this practice leads to bacterial resistance and other problems.

Many mushers use these compounds only if the dog must stay in the team during a race (assuming that race rules allow their use) and do not use them if the dog can be rested. Other mushers use them on a daily basis when the dogs are run hard, to prevent swelling.

Of course, you can prevent and treat many problems by using booties. If in doubt, avoid the fancy drugs. Even highly experienced trail veterinarians disagree on when anti-inflammatories are beneficial or harmful, and mushers must often decide for themselves what will

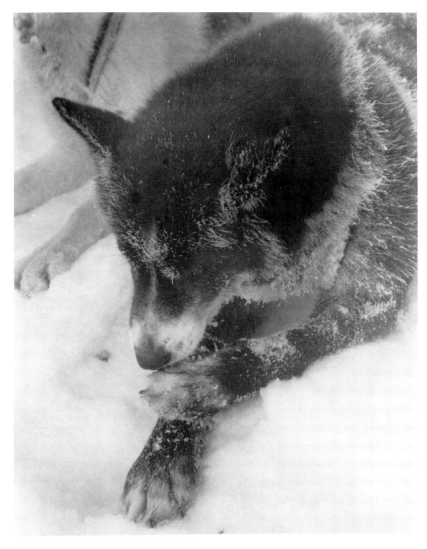

A foot ointment doesn't do much good if the dog licks it all off. To prevent this, booties should be applied lightly even if the dog is resting.

work best for their dogs on the given trail conditions. The jury is still out on this one!

One drawback of medicated ointments is their high cost. The late Dr. Del Carter, DVM, who was deeply involved in long-distance racing, suggested that mushers mix their own and recommended the following recipe:

> 3 pounds Vaseline®, 50 to 70 cc Betadine®, 1 pound lanolin, and ½ pound glycerine (to prevent freezing). To this basic formula, 40 cc of 90 percent medical grade DMSO (or 40 cc of 4mg/ml dexamethasone, available by presecription) can be added if desired. Vitamins A and E may also be beneficial. Melt slowly, stirring constantly, and pour into containers.

We sometimes use nitrofurazone ointment, available in one-pound containers at a reasonable price from some mail-order veterinary supply companies.

Warming or preferably melting the ointment before application greatly increases the penetration and ease of use, and a smaller amount goes a lot farther than a cold, stiff glob. You can heat metal containers by a fire or camp stove; plastic tubes can be kept warm in an inner pocket. To prevent greasy fingers, apply the ointment with a small paintbrush or squeeze bottle, or wear surgical gloves.

With the inventiveness and drive of competitive mushers, advancing medical knowledge, and ever-increasing trail experience of mushers and veterinarians, ideas on foot care and treatments are expanding and evolving constantly. You can keep updated by talking to different people involved in distance racing, especially the experienced trail veterinarians — whether you plan to race, or whether you just want to provide the very best care for your dogs.

Take care of a dog's feet, and the dog will take care of you — and will get you where you want to go.

CHAPTER 8

THE NEXT GENERATION: BREEDING, RAISING, AND TRAINING PUPS

If you are a small-time musher, it is to your advantage *not* to breed. Buying good adults is cheaper and less risky than raising pups, especially if your breeding dogs are not top quality. The small income from selling extra puppies will not offset the cost and time invested in raising them. Enough mediocre dogs already exist without having inexperienced breeders adding to the numbers.

However, most top mushers must breed their own dogs to maintain a strong continuity in their teams. Many a musher has reached the top of his or her field only to drop from sight after a few years. Others, like George Attla and Harris Dunlap, stay on top for years — even decades. Mushers who only briefly touch the top ranks typically have a crackerjack team or even just one outstanding leader, but as those dogs age, the team slips. To stay on top, you must constantly replace aging dogs with young ones of an equal caliber. This means expending considerable time and money in an aggressive breeding program. It also means planning in advance, because replacements should be born at least two years before older dogs retire.

It is important to develop a team of dogs with consistent sizes and gaits, and this is more likely to occur among related dogs. Unrelated dogs might be individually good, but they just will not "fit in." It is difficult to maintain this consistency if a line does not replace itself fast enough, and this will cause you to lose the winning edge. Once lost, it will be very hard to regain.

If you own an unusual type of dog, you also might need to raise your own pups. We run eighty-pound old-time huskies on our trap-

167

Toulouse, the brown leader, matches his stride with that of his father, Legs, beside him. The three dogs in back are mother and offspring. Even though all five dogs are in the same size range and travel at the same speed, they have different builds and different attitudes.

line, and these big, long-legged working dogs are hard to find in this era of race dogs; therefore, we need to raise our own replacements. Chinooks and other rare strains and breeds are also difficult to replace unless you breed your own.

Breeding Stock

Do not breed two dogs just because they are your best dogs. Aim for better dogs, not just replacement stock. A poorly built dog might excel from pure heart and drive; that might be enough for your team but not for breeding. Instead of breeding for a single trait such as speed, consider the dog as a whole, looking at conformation, stamina, attitude, intelligence, and general health. Do not just better your dog yard — better the species.

If you choose your breeding stock carefully, you will avoid years — even generations — of experimentation to perfect your stock. Serious mushers breed for performance, not for the little dots over a husky's eyes. They give coat color and markings a low priority, finding it hard enough to breed for all the other required traits. (With purebred dogs destined for the show ring as well as for the trail, color and other "show" traits must be dealt with according to the breed standard.)

Choose proven bloodlines for your breeding stock, in which weaker traits have been culled for generations. If you invest in a proven bitch from an established bloodline and breed her to the best stud available that complements her type, the offspring might pay off your investment by commanding high sales prices, more race winnings, and a better reputation. You can often buy a good bitch that is retired from racing but still able to produce top-notch pups. If you cannot buy or lease a tried and true bitch, it is still better to obtain one of her pups for breeding than it is to breed a lesser bitch.

Beware of breeding "the best to the best." While this is certainly better than breeding indiscriminately, the best of one team may not match up with the best of another. Aim for consistency. Ideally, the parents will have matched gaits, conformation, and sizes to ensure uniform, efficient teammates in the offspring. Consider the suitability of one dog for the other, and of both for your team. Avoid breeding two dogs with the same fault. Decide which traits you require and which are unacceptable, and go from there.

Careful, planned breeding does not guarantee outstanding pups, but it does improve your chances. Remember — some outstanding dogs fail to pass on their traits, while a few mediocre dogs produce outstanding pups.

Bloodlines

A dog's pedigree can reveal the potential of its offspring. For the pedigree to be meaningful, the breeder must be familiar with most of the dogs listed on it. The ancestors' traits will appear in the off-spring, and the traits of a dog listed two or more times are most likely to make a strong showing. Bloodlines are even more important than the parent when breeding.

Look at previous litters of both potential parents, as well as at any other relatives you can find. Examine photographs, especially action photographs showing gaits, and peruse track records. The more investigating you do, the less surprised you will be with the outcome. We once bred two 80-pound dogs, and the resulting pups each grew to 115 pounds. If we had known then that the mother's Malamute ancestors were in that size range, we would not have been so astonished.

The Brood Bitch

In addition to the hereditary power that she shares with the father, the mother influences her pups psychologically at a young age. Thus, the temperament of the female is more important than that of the male. Timidity or wildness is learned as well as inherited, and the pups will mimic a spooky dam. (Removing the pups at an early age sometimes prevents them from adopting her faults.) Good nutrition, parasite control, and current vaccinations are also more important in the dam than in the sire.

Heredity

Physical traits and intelligence are genetically controlled, and heredity affects many less obvious traits as well, including tendencies toward disease resistance, overheating, shyness, and recovery time after running. Just how much genetics affects the end product is still being explored.

Heredity determines the outer limits of a dog's potential — how fast he might run or how tall he might grow. Environment takes over, even before birth, to influence how much of that potential will be realized. If a dog lacks the genetic makeup for speed, no amount of training, vitamins, or gimmicks will make him fast. But even the best genetic background cannot overcome the physically stunting effects of malnutrition or the psychological stunting that results from improper socialization. Nutrition, health, socialization, conditioning, and a host of other factors influence the ultimate result.

Pups show traits of ancestors as well as of parents. However, due to a shuffling, splitting, and recombining of genetic material, they might not closely resemble any one relative. Many traits will be either present or absent, rather than blended. For example, pups out of a blue-eyed mother by a brown-eyed father usually will have either blue eyes or brown eyes, and only rarely will they have one of each color. This is true of many traits. Even size differences generally represent either the mother or the father rather than an average of the two. Breeding divergent strains, such as a sprint dog with a heavy freighting dog, can result in an unbalanced combination, such as a dog with a heavy front and a light rear.

Each inherited trait is controlled by one or more genes. Recessive genes may not be expressed or apparent in a dog, but he still can pass them on to his offspring. These traits can remain hidden for generations, only to crop up unexpectedly when haphazardly matched with a similar gene from the other parent. Dominant genes are always expressed, although their appearance might be altered by other genes.

The key to obtaining good, consistent, uniform litters is to use breeding stock known to consistently pass on good traits. Some dogs are famous for their ability to pass on their good qualities. These propotent dogs, male or female, possess concentrated genetic material and are often the result of inbreeding or line breeding.

Inbreeding and Line Breeding

Inbreeding usually, but not always, refers to the breeding of closely related dogs, such as between a father and a daughter. This concentrates the genetic material and allows hidden genes, both desirable and undesirable, to be brought out. Inbreeding also results from repeatedly introducing the same dog back into a line of dogs (also called line breeding). Most top dogs have some inbreeding in their background; the names of one or more dogs appear several times in their pedigrees.

Inbreeding exaggerates both the good and the bad qualities of the parents, and the offspring will pass those traits to future generations more reliably. By selecting the best pups and culling the worst, an improvement in both type and genetic consistency is possible. Only dogs with excellent traits and no serious faults should be inbred closely. Ruthless culling may be required, which is why most mushers do not inbreed their dogs closely.

Close inbreeding is indeed a risky business. Some genes harbor bad traits that have not been expressed in (and consequently have not been culled from) previous generations. Inbreeding causes these traits to appear again. Inbreeding over a few generations also reduces the size and vitality of the dogs. Because of their prepotency, bad traits are difficult to eradicate from future litters. Hereditary diseases, including PRA and insufficient digestive enzyme production (see Chapter 6), may also occur more frequently with inbreeding. Some problems do not appear until middle age, by which time the dog already may have been bred and passed on the problem.

To avoid these problems, line breeding is a better option than close inbreeding. Because the genes are less concentrated in a grandfather-granddaughter mating, line breeding can stabilize a strain without the risks of close inbreeding; however, if taken through enough generations, the end results (both good and bad) will be the same.

If two totally unrelated strains or breeds are mated, the offspring often have "hybrid vigor" — exceptional strength, size, stamina, and resistance to disease. This is especially likely to occur if each of the unrelated parents is also inbred. However, uniformity will be sacrificed, and hybrid vigor will rarely be passed on to future generations. This is why some outcrosses, such as husky x Irish Setter, will produce outstanding dogs that are relatively worthless as breeding stock. Crossing two dogs of the same strain will rarely produce hybrid vigor even if the dogs have no common ancestors.

If you intend to breed seriously, and especially if you intend to do any line breeding or inbreeding, you need a sound knowledge of genetics and of your strain of dogs, including pedigrees, genetic weaknesses, and hereditary diseases. Know your goal before you begin. Many good books on dog breeding and genetics are available; a couple are listed in the bibliography.

Raising Pups

Raising puppies is covered in many reference books. You should be informed on breeding, nutrition, parasite control, health and disease, and puppy psychology. Here we will only cover subjects specific to raising sled dogs.

Nutrition is critical before, during, and after pregnancy. Start the puppies on soaked food when they begin toddling and coming out of the dog house. Nutrition during the first year will affect pups for the rest of their lives. If you shortchange them with a cheap or unba-

These winter puppies stay comfortably warm in a dog house big enough to share with their mother. A burlap sack insulates the door, and snow packed around and over the house provides extra insulation and protection from winter. (Don't use snow insulation unless temperatures average below zero.)

lanced diet, they will never reach their full potential.

Huskies are extremely hardy, and pups usually can survive birth in an unheated dog house in subzero temperatures, but in winter conditions it is best to provide a heat source.

Dewclaws

Dewclaws cause problems in distance-racing or cross-country dogs. Booties press the claw into the leg to cause sores, or the claw catches and is torn when a dog goes through crusted snow. Pups destined for this kind of work should have their dewclaws clipped off.

Clip off the claws when the pups are three days old. We use sterilized nail cutters. Be *sure* that you cut off the entire toe, going through the bone as close to the leg as possible, or the nail will grow back deformed. A dab of styptic will stem any bleeding but often is unnecessary.

Removing dewclaws is usually unnecessary in sprint dogs and most recreational dogs. Dewclaw sores are covered in Chapter 7.

Culling Puppies

Culling pups does not have to mean killing them. It is irresponsible to breed many dogs with the intention of killing all but the very best. Instead, more care should be taken to breed better dogs, and more work should go into helping problem pups mature into good dogs. When you do decide to cull a pup (or an adult) that is not equal to your team, try to find a good home for him as a pet or in a recreational team. When you give away low-quality dogs, encourage the new owner to spay or neuter them to avoid perpetuating that type.

Cull obvious abnormalities at birth if nature does not beat you to it. A young or underweight bitch might not be able to handle a large litter, and you might need to cull some pups if you cannot hand-raise them. Pups culled at birth are picked according to size and vitality. Experts can judge angulation in the very young by feeling leg and shoulder bones. You can also compare bone structure and leg and neck length and cull on the basis of whether you want heavier or lighter dogs.

Some bad traits, such as serious conformational faults, extreme wildness, and inappropriate sizes or builds, show up by weaning time. These dogs can be culled if necessary. (Remember, though, that the puppies will change as they grow, and even some conformational faults may straighten themselves out.)

As the pups begin running around, watch for bad movement such as jerky gaits and legs that do not fly straight. Also watch for attitude problems such as violent aggression or wildness. Some pups act too lethargic or too crazy; they might still develop into fine dogs, but if you need to cut back, start with them. (One of our lie-around pups became our main leader.)

Pups may be brought on walks or may run loose behind a slow team as they approach four months of age. The slowest ones can be culled. Later, as they are put in harness, you may again look for smooth gaits, good attitudes, and, of course, that burning desire to pull. Some mushers give males longer to prove themselves because they are slower to mature. Many pups make it to this point only to be culled during the breaking process.

Psychological Growth
A single puppy with a loving family will have his psychological needs met almost automatically, but the sled-dog breeder who is not aware of the critical periods in the mental growth of puppies might not realize the importance of spending time with them.

When puppies are four weeks old, they are bombarded with a dazzling array of new subjects with which to cope. A stable home environment gives them the security to accept these experiences with curiosity. From now until the twelfth week, they are especially responsive to human handling. Handling puppies is particularly critical during the fifth, sixth, and seventh weeks. If puppies are not handled *as individuals* during this time, they might grow up shy, nervous, or standoffish. You do not need to spend much time with each pup — just a couple of minutes a day — but if you neglect this socialization now, it will affect them for a lifetime.

During this early period, the puppies investigate everything virtually fearlessly, and sudden scares have no lasting effect. However, during weeks eight and nine, they go through a "fear period." They are frightened easily, and bad scares might affect them for a lifetime. Again, consistent support and a stable environment help to avoid lasting effects.

From nine to twelve weeks of age, puppies learn to control their behavior, and you can teach them simple lessons. Use positive reinforcement (praise), and limit punishment to moving a puppy away when he is bad. As the puppies grow, expose them to many new objects so that they learn not to fear strange objects or situations. (This begins the obstacle training discussed in Chapter 11.) Put them on different surfaces — cement, dirt, gravel, carpets, and linoleum. Give them ramps and stairs to climb. Have other people handle them. Accustom the puppies to having their feet and mouths handled. If the puppies are afraid, especially during the eighth week, avoid introducing too many new objects.

At four months of age, the pups might go through another period of anxiety, marked by an avoidance of new objects and places. Encourage their self-confidence, and do not force new experiences on them. At six or seven months of age, and again around one year, the pups might question your authority and resist training. Try to avoid frustrating battles during this time, but do not lose your dominance.

Healthy, happy puppies.

Teach your pups a few simple commands as early as two months of age. This is not to teach them the commands so much as it is to teach them how to learn. Make them aware that you can communicate your desires and that they must respond to them. Ideally, teach them courtesy commands such as "Sit," "Down," and "Stay."

By following these suggestions, you will help your puppies to mature into well-adjusted sled dogs that can handle crowds and new experiences without anxiety. If you do not at least socialize with your pups, they might never respond to you, or they might be fearful or aggressive toward other humans. Potential leaders in particular will benefit from individual handling as pups.

Disease Prevention

A little labor can save a lot of grief when it comes to preventing disease in puppies. Sick pups can be very hard to save. Provide your puppies with a warm, clean, dry home, clean water, and good food. Pick up droppings twice a day. Keep the puppies in a suitable roofed pen.

Pups are more susceptible to parasites, especially roundworms. Worm the pups frequently, as recommended by your veterinarian, with a mild wormer. Also consult your veterinarian about a vaccination schedule, because many different schedules have been suggested. Dr. Robert Stear of Norden Laboratories advised vaccinating pups with distemper and measles vaccine at six or eight weeks of age; against parvovirus every three weeks from nine to eighteen weeks of age; and with the seven-way shot at sixteen weeks. Do not give shots more often than every other week, or you might damage the pup's immune system.

Pups are most vulnerable to disease between ten and eleven weeks of age, when their maternal antibodies are dwindling. These antibodies come from colostrum, or the first milk produced by the bitch. Just as the pups lose their resistance, they also are exposed to stresses such as weaning, parasites, wormers, new environments, and infectious agents as their world expands.

Parvo has been a nightmare for some mushers, because regular vaccinations sometimes fail. Maternal antibodies offer pups temporary immunity (if the bitch has been vaccinated), but they also render puppy vaccinations ineffective. As the antibodies fade, the pups become susceptible to disease, but this period varies greatly among different pups and different litters. It is hard to predict that variable fraction of time when the pups become responsive to the vaccine, but before they contract the disease. Even a religious vaccination schedule might miss that window of susceptibility.

Do not assume that the vaccinations will work. Keep your puppy area scrupulously clean. Joe Runyan, 1989 Iditarod champion, lost up to half his litters to parvo until he isolated his pups in pens that were elevated so that the droppings fell through the wire mesh to the ground. By coupling this with strict sanitation, Joe almost eliminated his parvo problem.

Veteran musher Joe May, another Iditarod champion, gave us his own excellent opinion: "I consider vaccine to be one-third of the parvo

Confinement keeps pups safe and reduces their chances of coming in contact with infectious diseases. *Courtesy* Fairbanks Daily News-Miner.

prevention program for pups. One-third is a clean pen or living area — pen *must* be cleaned once and preferably twice daily. One third is dry ground and shelter — mud, cold, and wet environment are deadly to young pups with no reserves to draw from — with this combination I raised hundreds of pups without *a single* mortality [to parvo] following the advent of parvo vaccines. A roofed puppy pen is very very cheap medicine."

Training Pups

Training pups can be infinitely rewarding or endlessly frustrating. Some young dogs go at the word "Hike," and others do anything but go. Throughout the process, *patience* is the first rule. Pups are harness-broken much like green adults are (see Chapter 11), but we will include a few differences and additional information here.

Teach the pups to respond to "No!" by three months of age, and instill good manners early. Discourage them from chewing on rope. Do not let them jump on you if this is not accepted in your adults.

Discourage fighting. Handle each pup's feet and mouth frequently so that he will accept medications and booties. Introduce the pups to chaining at four to six months, gradually increasing their periods of confinement until they accept it. They will learn restraint and patience as well as the rudiments of untangling themselves, which will carry over to harness work.

If possible, run your pups loose behind the sled starting at four or five months of age, when they can keep up with a slow team. Even if they are old enough to harness-break, they will benefit from the conditioning and training. Our pups run behind (and beside or ahead of) our team from four months up to six or eight months of age. They know "Hike" and "Whoa" before they get in harness. They also learn that adults will not tolerate playing and become familiar with the

Joe Runyan has almost eliminated parvovirus from his kennel by raising pups in elevated wire pens. The pups are kept in the pens almost until they are put in harness, yet the confinement doesn't seem to affect their performance.

Running young dogs loose behind a sled before harness-breaking not only builds their physical abilities, but also teaches them basic commands.

towline. In areas where dogs cannot be run loose safely, you can individually handle each pup in harness to give him a head start.

Some mushers start to harness-break a pup before he can walk in a straight line, and others wait until the pup is a yearling. If you work with a pup under five months old, do not do more than just tie a light weight to his little harness. A pup can be run in a small team at five or six months, but it is better to wait another month or two rather than risk overstressing him. A five- to eight-month-old pup should be run only a mile or two, and certainly not over five miles, even though he can run farther when he is loose behind the team. Do not expect a younger pup to have a sense of responsibility, either.

Before hooking a pup in the team for the first time, confine him for several days so that he is crazy to go. Running him in harness should increase his freedom, not restrict it.

The first run is critical. Make sure that it will go smoothly and that his harness fits well. If a pup is not eager when you hook him up, consider letting him mature a few more weeks. Hook the pup up last so that he will have less time to mess up or chew his harness. In our experience, if a pup never has a chance to chew, he will rarely start

This young dog has proven himself to be a steady, fast worker, but at eighteen months of age, he is still impressionable, and his body has not reached its full potential. Working him too hard or too fast, or putting on too much pressure, can still ruin him.

after maturing. Preventing the habit from starting is *much* easier than breaking it.

Start the pup in a slow, reliable team, preferably beside a dependable dog that will neither intimidate the pup nor tolerate playing. The novice will quickly pick up his teammate's good habits, but he will also notice the antics and bad habits of irresponsible dogs. We like to run just one or two pups in a five-dog team, but when breaking a lot of youngsters, it is necessary to run several in one team with a couple of steady dogs up front to keep control. Avoid using your prized leader for this, if possible, because it can affect his intensity, speed, and quick responses.

When you first hike up the team, do not let the dogs start too fast or the pup might never get his stride. Do not go very far — just half a mile to two miles — to keep him wanting more. Do not go more than four miles even if he can take it physically. At this point, his psychological well-being is far more important. Stop frequently to walk up to praise the pup (anchor your team well). Even if he is doing badly, do not punish him. Just untangle the lines and pull him forward to tighten the tug.

A bad first run can ruin a pup. If the team is uncontrollable and runs too fast, especially on a downhill, that pup might be injured or scared so badly that he will never run flat out, or he may balk on steep downhills. Do not expect perfection. In fact, do not expect anything until the second, third, or fourth run. First your pup must learn to enjoy it. *Then* he learns what to do. Finally, he learns that sledding is serious work and not all play.

As always, judge each situation separately. We rarely run two pups side by side; however, once, when we broke two littermates, Streak was a natural and Comet panicked. Before the situation grew frightening, we put Streak beside Comet. Comet saw his brother's eager performance and instantly caught on. Streak unraveled the mystery for him better than any adult dog could have done. Both dogs went on to log thousands of miles of trapline and cross-country sledding.

Once a pup's training begins, run him three or four times a week — not every day, and not just once a week. If you run him too much — too far, too fast, too often — he will learn to slack up to protect himself. He will get bored or stressed, his attitude will dry up and blow away, and you might overstress his young body. On the other hand, if he is not run enough, he will lose condition and forget his lessons. The way in which you handle this dog will affect him for the rest of his career. Aim for the optimum number of runs, not the

With the proper care and training, there's no telling how far well-bred pups might go.

maximum or the minimum. This optimum will vary from pup to pup and will depend upon trail conditions.

After a few good runs, move the pup to different positions in the team. Give your poor old dog a break and run the squirt by some other old-timer. Try him on both sides of the towline, in wheel, and in swing. (Be *very* careful not to scare him with the sled; move him forward if there is any trouble, and let him mature and gain experience before putting him in the wheel position again.) Try him in the lead if he shows potential, but do not run him there very long or very often even if he does well. You will not ruin him by waiting — he will only improve with maturity and confidence.

A pup that drags against his neckline is not hopeless, but he needs training. Maybe he lacks maturity, or maybe he is afraid. Run him in a slow, small team or alone pulling a weight. Once these puppies realize that pulling forward is more fun than pulling backward, they may become as dedicated as they once were obstinate. One of our pups necklined for three months. When she finally started pulling, she was the toughest of our eleven dogs — at one year of age!

The pup that runs without pulling is actually less promising than the one that necklines. This pup might be too slow or may have physical problems. If he *can* work, but simply won't, you may try to retrain him. However, you will need to decide if this dog is worth the effort. Suggestions for retraining are discussed in the section "Dogs That Do Not Pull," in Chapter 11. If nothing works, this pup might be incompatible with your team or with harness work. Do not wreck your entire team trying to cure a problem pup that will never make it.

Dogs that constantly look backward are covered in Chapter 2.

If you ask too much of young dogs, they might never become hard workers, because they will learn to slack up to avoid fatigue. Yearlings and eighteen-month-old dogs have finished the Iditarod, but some have been ruined in the attempt. Physical conditioning is important in a young dog, but good training is even more important. Do not ask for his greatest effort until his second or third year in harness.

Genetics determines a pup's potential, handling molds his character, and training conditions and hones his skills. It is up to you to develop his potential to the fullest extent. No matter how pleasing it is to run an outstanding dog bought from another musher, it is infinitely more rewarding to run an outstanding dog that you have bred, raised, and trained yourself.

CHAPTER 9

TRAILS AND TRAIL CONDITIONS

"Oh, NO!"

We had just broken trail out to a winter cabin, only to find the creek right before it running wide open. The dogs faltered at the sight of that black, hip-deep water. On the far side stood our little cabin, but the thirty feet of swift water looked too dangerous to attempt wading.

A hundred yards upstream we found an island of ice, separated from each bank by only twelve feet of water. Undaunted by the treacherous appearance of the ice, we eased a couple of driftwood logs over the gap, and I edged across as rushing water painted the makeshift bridge with glassy ice. Miki sent the unhooked dogs across one by one and finally tiptoed over herself. Hauling the logs across the island, we threw them down again to make the final crossing. By the time the dogs, sled, and mushers were all safely ashore, the ice island had begun to disintegrate, but we were soon toasty warm in our cabin, surrounded by a pack of relieved canines.

You may never have to resort to such tactics in your mushing career, but whether you train and travel on back-country trails or through city streets, plenty of different conditions and challenges await you.

Where To Run

Almost every populated area in Alaska and Canada has trails in or around it. Some may be hundreds of miles long; others just go to the city dump. Most are open to public use, but some trails lead across private property or native corporation land, or are maintained by trappers who object to trespassers. Other dog mushers can tell you which ones you may use.

Trapline trails, when open to the public, offer miles of untouched wilderness, but are not always in the best of condition. Running the first two or three dogs in single file helps on soft, narrow trails like this one near the Alaska Range.

In more densely populated areas of Canada, the United States, and Europe, where snow machines are not used for serious travel and where more land is restricted, trails may be harder to come by and may be more regulated. Many parks and national forests maintain trails for public use. Logging roads can make fine trails for winter sledding or snowless carting. Abandoned railways, frozen rivers, and summer horseback trails are possibilities. In farm and ranch country, many routes are suitable for either summer or winter use, but any time you cross private property, you need permission.

Seldom-used roads, whether they are in remote ranching areas or quiet suburbs, are usually suitable. Sandy seashores or barren deserts provide miles of carting (be sure that dogs are allowed in the area).

Many trails follow frozen rivers, which usually offer relatively flat, smooth traveling and good visibility of obstacles ahead. But they can be windblown, over-flowed, or have other hazards, such as those found on the Porcupine River Trail in north-eastern Alaska.

You can even run a wheeled rig on paved roads, but watch your dogs' feet closely — pavement is extremely abrasive and gets burning hot on sunny days. For specific ideas on where to mush, see Table 9-1.

Talking to other mushers is the best way to learn about trails. Many well-used trails are mapped by local organizations or borough planners. Other recreationalists — skiers, snow machinists, bikers, ATV users, and horseback riders — can give you ideas on where to run. Just remember that they will all be out there, too! (Do not run a dog team on established ski trails, because the wide sled tracks will completely spoil the easy glide of a skier.)

In some areas, dogs must be trucked long distances to good trails or to snow. This is even true in parts of Alaska. Where snow is absent,

Table 9-1
Popular Mushing Areas

Many of these places also hold races. You may need permits to bring dogs into some places (especially national parks), and some areas require permits for overnighting. These are only suggestions; there are many other places.

ALASKA
- Anchorage area, including Knik, Wasilla, and Trapper Creek
- Bettles/Coldfoot area
- Fairbanks area, including North Pole, Two Rivers, and Nenana
- Iditarod Trail, 1,100 miles from Anchorage to Nome (some parts are not broken out until early March)
- Tok
- Yukon Quest Trail, 1,000 miles from Fairbanks to Whitehorse (Yukon Territories) (some parts are not broken out until late February)
- Most populated areas in the interior and western sections have trails suitable for dog mushing.

FORTY-EIGHT STATES
- Adirondacks, New York
- Allegheny National Forest, Pennsylvania
- Beargrease, 250-mile race trail, Duluth, Minnesota, to Grand Portage (500-mile round trip)
- Ely, Minnesota
- Jackson Hole, Wyoming
- Michigan: In 1985, a race was run from Empire on Lake Michigan to Tawas City on Lake Huron, 325 miles
- Montana 500 Race Trail
- Oregon Dunes National Recreational Area, Oregon (suitable for wheeled rigs)
- Saranac Lake, New York

Table 9-1 (Continued)
Popular Mushing Areas

- Superior National Forest and Boundary Waters, Voyageurs National Park, Minnesota, and adjacent areas, including Canada's Quetico Provincial Park (Ontario)
- Red Feather Lakes, Colorado
- Yellowstone National Park, Wyoming

- Many other national parks and national forests have trails suitable for mushing.

CANADA
- Northern British Columbia, especially the Fort Nelson area
- Northern Ontario
- Quetico Provincial Park, Ontario (and adjacent areas in the United States)
- Whitehorse and Dawson City, Yukon Territories
- Yellowknife, Northwest Territories

- Canada has many other parks suitable for mushing.

EUROPE
- The Alps and other mountainous areas
- Britain: On private land, forest commission land, or country council land, by permission or permit; Sled Dog Centre at Hafod Llan near Llyn Alwen in Northern Wales. Illegal to run on public roads. Usually limited mileage of trails.
- France: Train with carts instead of sleds, or in mountainous areas

wheeled rigs are an option (see Chapters 3 and 11).

Anytime you run your dogs, have a good idea of where you are going, how long you will be gone, and what kind of weather or trail situations might present themselves. By planning ahead, you can forestall potential problems, protect yourself from frostbite, keep your dogs from suffering heat stroke, or prevent your sled from getting wrecked because you brought more dogs than were safe on a rough trail.

Training Trails

Many people make their own trails either with a good gee-haw leader, with snowshoes, or with a snow machine. This usually is done with some specific training purpose in mind, such as a trail set up for leader training. A circular trail or one with a loop at the end eliminates the need to turn the team around (but then, the team will not get any practice at doubling back, either). One with several side trails that rejoin the trail allows you to turn around in different places or to drill your leaders.

A variety of trails is best, even if you must make them yourself. Running over the same route day after day bores both dogs and musher; morale suffers, and speed and enthusiasm wane. You might also go out with a snow machine or an ATV with an odometer and measure exact distances so that you can tell how fast your dogs are and develop a feel for judging and regulating the miles per hour that they travel.

Race Trails

Trails set aside for sled-dog races are generally open to public use anytime races are not being held. Do *not* use them on race days unless you are entered in the race!

Many race trails consist of two parallel tracks, one for outbound teams, the other for inbound ones. Connecting trails allow access from one to the other at given intervals: two miles out for a four-mile loop and eight miles out for a sixteen-mile loop (see Figure 9-1). To avoid tricky, sharp corners, the connecting trails should slant away at a forty-five-degree angle and arc back to join the incoming trail at the same angle. Each fork should be marked clearly and should have a warning sign well in advance indicating both the mileage ("turn

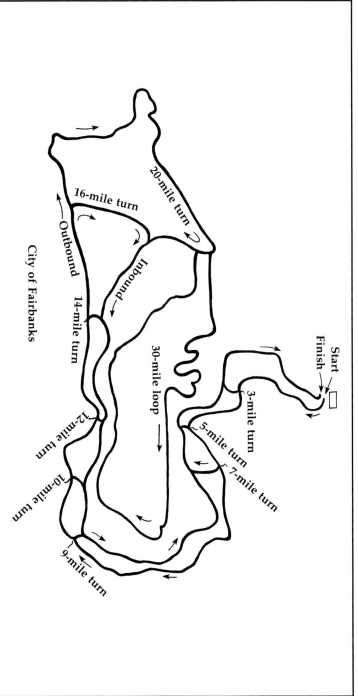

Figure 9-1
Race Course in Fairbanks, Alaska

Start
Finish

3-mile turn

5-mile turn

7-mile turn

9-mile turn

10-mile turn

12-mile turn

14-mile turn

16-mile turn

20-mile turn

30-mile loop

Outbound

Inbound

City of Fairbanks

The race course in Fairbanks, Alaska, maintained by the Alaska Dog Musher's Association, is simpler than it looks. Two roughly parallel trails are joined at intervals to make loops of various distances. Since the course is one way only, head-on passes happen only by accident. The North American Championship Open is raced partly on this course, and partly through downtown Fairbanks. Some training trails are set up similarly to this course.

here for eight-mile loop") and the direction (which is often color-coded). Most tracks use the ISDRA color coding: a red marker on the right side of the trail for a right turn; a red marker on the left side for a left turn; a blue marker for straight ahead; and an orange or yellow marker indicating a hazard. Curves may be marked as well. Your local musher's association can set you straight if you get confused by the layout or trail markers.

Night Travel

With dusk arriving early during midwinter months, many working people run their teams at night. In the summer, nighttime running decreases the possibility of overheating problems. Dogs are naturally dawn and dusk hunters, actually preferring very late and very early hours. Also, the colder temperatures lend the dogs an extra spark.

Always carry a headlamp, and in trafficked areas, keep it on to alert others of your presence. Reflective tape on the dogs' harnesses, on the sled, and on your outer clothing will alert motorists that your procession reaches thirty feet or more ahead of your light. (Remember — whether the dog team hits the car, or the car hits the dog team, it is going to be bad for the dog team.) Do not run more dogs than you feel comfortable with at night. Be especially careful to stay on the right trail, and remember that you may not be able to see hazards until you are right on top of them.

Trail Conditions

Whether you are mushing near your home or are on a thousand-mile trip, you may be exposed to difficult or potentially dangerous conditions. Knowing what lies ahead and being prepared for the possibilities decrease the chances of problems. Because information on survival, backwoods safety, and winter clothing and gear for humans is available from many other sources, we will not discuss it except as it relates directly to dog mushing. Be aware of peculiarities in your area and of the safety techniques that you need to know. At times, you may need to carry extra gear or clothing to handle the conditions. Additional information on what to bring on longer treks is found in Chapter 11.

An ideal trail is packed hard enough for the dogs to lope with little resistance from the sled, but not so hard that it has no give. Snow-machine trails can get so hard that dogs can injure their feet and

Traveling at night can be dangerous because of limited visibility, but the dogs are all for it. Loki leads out on an early morning run.

Some trails can be so hard-packed and unforgiving that they cause damage
to the feet and wrists.

wrists from pounding on the unforgiving surface. These trails are fast
and sometimes icy. A light snowfall actually improves them. Snow
machines also kick up snow, which builds into hard-packed, rolling
bumps that grow every time a machine passes over them. These
bumps, called moguls, create a roller-coaster effect that is hard on the
dogs and that stresses the front end of the sled. Pedaling as the sled
starts to break over the top of each bump reduces the jerk on the dogs.

Horses and other large animals punch deep holes in some trails.
A dog can trip and injure himself or even break a leg in these holes.
Slowing the pace minimizes this risk.

If there is a road crossing that you use frequently, consider putting
up a "Dog Team Crossing" sign to warn drivers. (These signs are
available from some mushing-equipment outlets.) Remember — many

vehicle drivers cannot stop in time to prevent an accident. Remember, too, that dog teams do not always stop on command. Road crossings should have good visibility on both sides. Gravel and pavement on roads are destructive to runner plastic; if you run beside your sled, at least your weight will be eliminated, and damage will be minimized. However, do not do this if you risk losing control of your team.

Unfortunately, few trails are free of hazards. Conditions vary widely from area to area, so if you travel to an unfamiliar part of the country, try to be prepared.

Overflow

Overflow can be as innocuous as a half-inch of fresh water or as appalling as three feet of runoff rushing downriver over old ice. It can occur anytime during the winter and at any temperature, and it can occur on lakes, swamps, rivers, and creeks. Sometimes "glaciering" builds up layers of ice inches or yards thick from repeated overflows, either in smooth layers or in a waterfall shape. I once built a log bridge over a narrow creek with seven-foot banks; by March, the bridge was completely buried under layers of ice.

When you are breaking trail on a river, frozen overflow obliterates the deep snow and provides a solid, if slippery, surface on which to run. Fresh overflow under cold snow creates mammoth-size problems when it freezes to sled runners, boots, snowshoes, and dogs' paws. Sometimes you can travel on the river bank to get around it, but often your only recourse is to slog ahead or turn tail. If slush freezes to your sled, tip the sled over and bang the ice off with the back of your ax head or with your snow hook.

When you see water on the trail, be suspicious that it is also *beside* the trail, hidden beneath the snow. Your dogs may hop off the trail only to find themselves in soft slush without the benefit of a hard trail bottom. You are better off staying on the trail even though you cannot see any water elsewhere.

Sometimes creeks flood with yards or miles of water. The upper end freezes as the water moves downstream. When traveling upriver, you first encounter slush, then a deeper flood of water, then freezing water, and finally a river of frozen ice. Most sled dogs come equipped with an instinctive fear of water, but with consistent training and a strong front end to your team, they can overcome it.

If you anticipate overflow, wear waterproof boots and carry a change of foot gear. Bring matches and tinder, because they can save you from becoming a double amputee from frozen feet. Carry extra dog booties, because they must be changed when soaked.

A small amount of overflow like this is not dangerous as long as the weather is not too cold and the ice underneath is safe. Dogs learn to go through it without balking. The best teacher is a dog that is unafraid.

Dangerous Ice

One inch of good ice usually will support a dog team, but not with much margin for error. Anytime the ice is questionable, carry an ax to test the thickness. If a single blow with the ax reaches water, you are safer to stay off of the ice. Newly frozen ice is strong and flexible, but it grows brittle with age. A thaw can rot ice, making it much less safe, and spring ice rots until a foot of it will not support a man. Ice is weakened when bubbles, plants, and other foreign objects are frozen into it. Clear black ice can be thin or several feet thick; thickness often can be estimated by the depth of cracks or bubbles leading down through the ice. White, yellow, or gray ice is more likely to be safe unless the color is caused by incompletely frozen slush or overflow. If you hear running water, or if your footsteps sound hollow, you are walking on a thin shell of ice hanging above the water. Back off — this is very dangerous! The water might be a foot below the level of the hollow ice, and you would have a heck of a time getting out, assuming that the current did not catch you first. Even during cold weather, holes can open up on rivers, and some spots never freeze. These usually occur over swift water, although the water might be fairly shallow. Sink holes and frosty wrinkles in the snow also signal bad spots.

Watch for unsafe areas anytime that you travel over unfamiliar ice. Likely trouble spots include the mouth of a river; swift, shallow streams or riffles; river confluences; and marshy drainages weakened from below by the warmth produced from decaying vegetation.

Some river channels, especially fast, shallow, shifting ones, cause sections of ice to cave into the running water, leaving a hole several feet deep and yards long. Sometimes a long section will cave into the river; this is often spanned by an ice bridge over which you might be able to cross.

Sea Ice

Traveling on the frozen ocean has its own unique hazards. Leads (breaks) open up whenever the ice cracks and drifts apart. Ice can drift offshore, carrying unwary travelers with it. Because the ice has hundreds of square miles of surface area, all affected by the vagaries of wind and current, it has awesome power and unpredictable actions. One year as we mushed along the shore toward Nome, Alaska, we saw miles of solid ice stretching toward the south. On our return trip a few days later, all the ice had moved offshore, and cold blue waves, whipped by a sharp north wind, stretched as far as the eyes could see.

Occasionally, a storm combined with incoming tides causes rapid

Creeks can drop, allowing sections of ice to break away. These dogs are familiar with this condition and know that the water here is shallow. Unfortunately, they tend to start thinking that ALL holes are shallow and are not as careful as they should be when on unfamiliar rivers.

flooding of shore ice. Even in recent years, people have drowned or have died from hypothermia when caught by the rising waters. Take the advice of knowledgeable locals if they warn you off of the ice. Stay on marked trails when possible, and if you travel out onto sea ice, let someone know where you are going and when you will be back.

Rough Ice

During freeze-up, wind and currents on oceans, on big rivers, and on larger lakes force slabs of ice into piles or pressure ridges that vary in size from only inches to more than thirty feet high. Local trails usually follow the smoothest routes, but travel is still rough and many a sled has been torn apart. Long-distance travel on oceans can be difficult because of the hardship in getting heavy loads over these ridges. Plan to travel slowly, and run a smaller team if you anticipate trouble. When freighting, you may need to break down your load and carry half over at a time.

Dropping water levels cause ice to sink. This opens deep cracks paralleling the shore where the ice remains frozen to the bottom. These cracks can injure mushers, dogs, and sleds. A toboggan sled is much less susceptible than a stanchion sled. You may need to travel slower with fewer dogs to avoid injuries.

Sand, Gravel, and Mud

Sand and gravel are abrasive. You can use booties to protect the dogs' feet; however, sharp rocks can tear booties, and a rock trapped inside a bootie can make a dog lame.

When dogs are run extensively on muddy ground, the natural oils in their feet are washed away, sometimes resulting in chapped, dry skin. A moisturizing ointment (such as nitrofurazone ointment) is beneficial.

Rigs run over sand, mud, and other soft ground should have wider wheels to prevent them from bogging down. Also, remember that the dogs become more tired running through deep sand and mud, and your vehicle will drag harder.

Mountains

High terrain may be incredibly beautiful, but it comes with many hazards. Glaciered creeks are common and are often steep, slippery, and dangerous. In minutes, wind can whip snow into white-out conditions. Drifting snow may drop into sheltered places, creating ten- to twenty-foot-high drifts. Avalanches are possible in some areas. Weather can change rapidly in the high country, often without warning, and shelter is hard to find above treeline. Watch your map and along your back trail for sheltered spots that you could reach in an emergency. If firewood is unavailable, bring a stove and fuel.

Anytime you go into the mountains, be prepared for the worst. Do not dress too warmly on a warm day, but carry cold-weather gear with you, including windproof clothing and a good, warm sleeping bag, when you travel farther than shouting distance from help. If you are unfamiliar with the route, examine maps and talk to others about it. Be aware that you may have to turn back due to impassable terrain or adverse weather.

Steep slopes offer a challenge both in going up and coming down. If you have a heavy load, you can divide it in half, making two trips to get it up the steeper hills. When two teams are traveling together, both can be hooked to one sled at a time to get the loads up. Coming

Sand is quite abrasive on the dogs' feet. If you run over very much sand, check the webbing between the dogs' toes for abrasion or inflammation. *Photos by Pat Brawand; courtesy Oregon Dune Mushers.*

back down for the second load can be exciting. On steep descents, take off some of the dogs' tuglines so that the dogs will not pull as hard. On truly frightful hills, turn some dogs loose, especially your wheel dogs that are first in line to get run over. (Unfortunately, loose wheel dogs no longer provide your sled with "power steering.") You may want to turn *all* of the dogs loose, assuming that they will not disappear on you. In extreme cases, you can lower your sled or even the dogs with a rope or with your disconnected towline. Rough locks can help tame any slope (see Chapter 3).

Sidehilling

On a sidehill, when the trail is slanted, you might struggle constantly to keep the sled upright, on the trail, and tracking after the team. Sidehills also occur on some rivers and on the shore ice of large lakes when the water level drops, causing the ice to slope from the shore toward the center of the body of water. Riding the uphill runner helps, but dealing with sidehills for a long time is extremely tiresome when you have a loaded sled. If the bad section is extensive, you can adjust the way in which your sled tracks.

When you move the towline off-center, the sled will track differently. Move it toward the downhill side to make it pull more to the uphill side. The farther you move it, the greater the effect. This can be accomplished by shortening the downhill side of the sled harness (bridle). You can pull the line closer to the side of the sled and hold it in place with a double neckline or cord. Mary Shields, an Alaskan adventurer and racer, has even moved the towline to the outside of the runner to prevent the sled from slipping sideways to the downhill. These techniques are also helpful when the sled is tracking off to one side for any reason (such as warped runners or an unbalanced load).

A gee pole often makes it easier to keep the sled on the trail, especially if one person handles the gee pole and a driver stays on the runners. Gee poles are covered in Chapter 10.

Glacier Travel

Because of a team's length, with the towline dispersing its weight, a dog team can traverse glaciers more safely than a motorized vehicle. Novices should always go with companions experienced in glacier travel. Crevasses are the greatest danger. The dogs can sometimes see or sense the danger before you can. If some dogs *do* fall in, their teammates are most anxious *not* to and will gladly try to back away and drag out the unfortunates. If the sled falls through, quickly anchor it with the snow hook if possible before trying to pull it out. In especially hazardous areas, a person roped to the towline should walk ahead to find a safe passage. Because glaciers are so dynamic, a previously safe route may become impassable as cracks open up. Be sure to bring extra rope and a mountain ax, ice pick, or other implement for feeling out hidden crevasses.

Wind

Wind sucks away body heat, wears out teams, drifts in trails, creates whiteouts, and produces abrasive snow that increases runner drag and causes foot problems. Dressing appropriately is vital: fur, leather, and windproof synthetics all block wind. A fur ruff on a parka hood helps to protect your face. Bring extra booties to protect your dogs' feet.

If your team is not on a trail, it might drift downwind instead of holding a steady course; therefore, watch your landmarks or a compass. Strong wind on glare ice can knock down dogs and whip the sled sideways. An ice brake or stabilizing rudder on one runner helps to control the sled; ice creepers on one boot also help. Crouch to reduce wind drag; this also offers you some protection because the sled breaks the wind.

Wind obliterates a trail faster than snowfall. Good lead dogs learn to find the trail by feeling for a solid surface under softer snow, but sometimes you have to snowshoe or ski ahead to locate the trail. A stick pushed through a drift will stop if it hits a packed trail hidden underneath, and it will go on down through the drift if the trail is not there. Unfortunately, you or your leaders can sometimes mistake a hard snowdrift under fresh drifts for the trail.

Whiteouts and windy conditions are especially hazardous along Alaskan and northern Canadian coasts and in mountains. Although well-traveled routes often are marked with tripods or small spruce trees frozen in the ice, ground blizzards (windborne snow) can hide one marker from the next. If neither trail nor markers can be seen, you may need to hole up until visibility improves; therefore, be prepared with a windproof sled bag and a good sleeping bag. Huskies seem relatively impervious to camping out in cold and wind, but some with shorter coats or nonhusky breeds appreciate a dog coat (available from some mushing outlets). Occasionally, you can strike out in the right direction and catch sight of the next marker before the last one fades from view, but unless you really know what you are doing, never lose sight of a marker.

Cold

We have mushed at temperatures down to -60 degrees F. without

Mushers on distance races often must contend with severe weather conditions ranging from heavy snow, bitter cold, high winds, or melting temperatures. *Courtesy* Fairbanks Daily News-Miner.

injuring ourselves or our dogs, and we run routinely at -30 and -40 degrees F. When the temperature or windchill is colder than -30 degrees F., exercise extreme caution, and limit training runs. Long-distance race dogs should be exposed to these conditions so that they will be familiar with them, but you still should not run them extensively.

You will probably notice a much longer recovery time after running under such cold temperatures. We have never had an uninjured dog suffer from frostbite (except for males' scrotums and females' nipples, discussed in Chapter 6). Nor have they ever frosted their

Dogs can work in severe temperatures like this -45 degrees F. scene. Mushers should take care to avoid sweating and frostbite, however.

lungs, although cold air is irritating and causes a cough (seen more often in mushers than in their dogs). Cold snow is very abrasive to dogs' feet. Protect them with booties, but be careful not to fasten them too tightly or frostbite may result. Cold snow also causes sled runners to drag badly. Some types of runner plastics are better than others (see Chapter 3).

Clothing again is critical. Wear enough to keep warm but not sweaty, and carry extra clothes that you can put on if you are not warm enough. Nothing beats fur and leather for warmth; in addition to providing excellent insulation, they are breathable, allowing sweat to evaporate, and they cut wind and air movement from your forward movement.

You also can carry chemical hot packs for warming hands or your body. If you may need to start a fire, carry a small bottle of kerosene or diesel fuel, which lights quickly but is nonexplosive. Natural tinder and matches light reluctantly, and at -60 degrees F., even gasoline lights slowly.

Melting Conditions

When winter weather heats up, trails become soft and punchy. Slushy trails do not seem to hurt dogs' feet, but beware when that slush freezes into thousands of little pinnacles! Boot up!

Overheating will be a problem if your dogs are used to colder temperatures, and they can collapse from heat stroke even at 10 degrees F. or colder. Some trails, especially those that are not used heavily, will "bottom out," causing the dogs and the sled to collapse through the original packed snow a foot or more to the bottom of the trail. Running at night will prevent these problems if a good freeze sets in.

Overflow or actually flooding, unsafe ice, bare ground, and clothing wet from melting snow can all occur during melting conditions.

Punchy Snow

When a trail has been broken out only once or twice, or if it has drifted over, the surface becomes "punchy," and the dogs will break through the crust. This can cause cuts, abrasions, strained wrists, abraded toenail beds, toenail injuries, and other damage. Extra-deep punchy snow demoralizes the dogs as they drag each other out. It helps to move at a slower pace and to boot the dogs. Check their feet at the end of the run.

Deep Snow

By traveling off the beaten path, you can experience untouched, solitary country. Unfortunately, that often means snowshoeing out a trail, perhaps through three or four feet of powder. Miki and I once took more than three days to travel twelve miles on a particularly bad stretch. Be sure to plan accordingly.

When the dogs have a good base under the snow, they can break trail through eighteen inches of powder; however, they cannot haul much of a load. Tall dogs handle these conditions more easily. If snowshoeing is necessary, ideally one person snowshoes ahead while another drives the team. If you are alone, the dogs must follow unsupervised, or you will have to snowshoe back to mush them ahead periodically. A good sled tracks nicely behind the team without human guidance, and you should not have to backtrack too many times to get it back in line. Under these conditions, a toboggan sled floats much better than a stanchion sled, with greatly decreased drag. According to one musher, a flat-bottomed toboggan with no runners at all is less likely to tip over when cornering in deep snow.

If the dogs crowd forward and step on your snowshoes, use your ax handle or a green willow wand to slap their noses until they back off, or turn some loose so that, with fewer dogs to pull the load, the team follows more slowly. They will eventually learn not to rush forward or get tangled. Run the team in single file so that the dogs do not shoulder each other as they struggle to stay on the best footing. Dogs can be run on a standard towline with just one dog in each section. If you do not have enough towline, double the tugs back to shorten them, and snap alternate dogs onto the unused neckline. Although this crowds them, the dogs require only half as much towline, and in the slow going, they need very little spacing. Eight dogs run single file on a regular towline require enough line for sixteen paired dogs, which means that it is a long hike back to the sled. You might want to bring extra towline if you think that you will need to string out the dogs in single file.

Turning one dog loose to walk behind you takes some of the workload off of your leader. Pick a lazy dog and let him flounder along behind you, packing a trail for the team.

Just because it is cold does not mean that *you* have to be cold. When the going is tediously slow, you should not be discouraged if you know that it can be like this. If you look ahead, you will have those extra booties when the trails drift in. If you are prepared with proper gear and trail savvy, you can come through almost any extreme and arrive home safely with a good story to tell.

CHAPTER 10

ON THE TRAIL

Mail is flown to our remote village only once a week, so mail day is quite an event and we try not to miss it even if it means running down from a distant cabin at 5 a.m. For one predawn run, we decided to put twelve dogs in one team pulling two sleds for maximum efficiency. Five additional young dogs ran loose, and a pup worn out from the previous day rode in the basket.

Dogs love to run in the dark early-morning hours, and the huskies loped eagerly, intent on their work. Only their rapid panting, the quick patter of strong paws on the snow, and the swish and glide of sled runners sounded in the night. Those dogs were veterans, many with more than 5,000 miles in harness, and I switched on my headlamp only occasionally to check them.

Then Miki's loaded sled slammed into a stump. My sled was caught between the stationary sled and 800 pounds of dog moving at twelve miles per hour. My wooden craft burst apart with a small explosion, sending me flying over the crumpling handlebow as it collapsed lifeless to the ground. Examining the wreck with the light of the headlamp, I decided that it might hold together for the last six miles home. When I hiked up the dogs, the front half of the team shot forward into the night. The towline had snapped.

We grabbed a few loose dogs and threw them in harness, moving up a shaky but willing standby leader. A couple of miles later, the remains of our team careened into the original front half. One of the seven escapees had turned around and stopped the others. Whole once more, the dogs sped on home, distracted only one more time when our herd of loose pups galloped after a moose.

Dog mushing is thrilling! The dynamic willingness of the dogs, the unexpected twists in the action, and the sheer exhilaration of working with your team to fly down a trail or struggle through miles of snowed-

Roxy Wright-Champaine keeps her body low to maintain good balance. Staying in control at the race start is more important than anything else. These wheel dogs are running in perfect synchrony. *Courtesy* Fairbanks Daily News-Miner.

in trail make mushing burn itself into your addicted soul. Out on the trail, anything can happen, but learning the possibilities and knowing how to handle them go a long way toward ensuring a smooth, trouble-free run.

Riding The Sled

Many of your moves to stay on (and in control of) your sled come naturally with experience. Your actions often parallel those of a skier. Keep your knees and elbows bent and flexible to absorb bumps. Counter instability by lowering your center of gravity, bending over the handlebow or crouching on the runners. If you think that you might tip over on a sharp corner, crouch with your weight on the inside runner. (Unfortunately, this can catapult you far and wide if the sled snaps over anyway!)

You affect how hard your dogs must pull. Even subtly shifting your weight on a rough trail can decrease the drag. Pedaling decreases the weight that the dogs must pull. When you are traveling fast, each kick must be a smooth, hard action, with your foot swinging far backward and upward to prevent a jerk against the dogs. At slower speeds, just getting some weight smoothly off of the sled decreases drag. A steady rate helps more than an uneven, jerky pattern of kicks that can throw the dogs off balance. On a rough trail, however (such as one with snow-machine moguls), pedal just before the sled breaks over the top of a bump, when the drag is worst.

Lena Charley is preventing her sled from sliding sidewise off the trail by riding the uphill runner and keeping a lot of weight on that side of the sled. The increased drag at the end of that runner turns the sled slightly, counteracting the sidewise skid. *Photo by Ron Lambert.*

You can run up hills to lighten the load. Obviously, you must be in good condition to do this, and it is extremely wearing on a long-distance race. However, it does pay off *if* you do not get so tired that you cannot give your dogs top-notch care. Running up a short, steep bank can prevent a midway halt, which usually calls for shouting and pushing on your part, affecting the morale of all. Keep the sled tracking smoothly on sharp turns to lessen the strain on your team, especially on the wheel dogs who lever the load around the corner. Running around corners helps, too, if you can maintain control of the sled.

Braking

Braking is an art. A racer never brakes unnecessarily because it slows the dogs. However, neglecting to brake when necessary can lead to injuries or time-consuming tangles. Because standard sled brakes tear up trails, brake by dragging your feet, by digging in a heel, or by riding a dragging snow-machine track whenever possible. This is especially important on well-groomed trails that are used by many people.

A large, fast team needs some drag at the start or the hotshot dogs will run up on the slow-starting dogs, creating a tangle when the team is least controllable. Anytime slack lines might cause a tangle, slow down the sled. If a dog gets the towline wrapped around a leg, stop the team with a voice command if possible, and brake only with caution, because the increased tension in the line can injure the dog or at best give him a good scare.

Braking on a corner helps to swing the sled around, but it also slows the dogs, and when the sled swings too sharply, it jerks the wheel dog. Also, it is more difficult to steer your sled when you stand on the sled brake; however, the sled will track better.

Dogs lean into their harnesses for balance, and braking jerkily throws them off balance. However, you can bounce on the brake to get their attention. They also depend on the brake for security. On steep hills, dogs can go too fast and get out of control. Brake to prevent the dogs from gaining too much speed and to keep the sled from running over your wheelers on steep hills. (Dragging a snow-machine track is very effective — see Chapter 3.)

Miki was slow in getting on the brake on one particularly bad hill that had a rough ditch at the bottom. Even though she was not close to hitting her wheel dog, he tucked his tail, cringing as he rushed forward, for fear that the sled would run over him. He reacted in this way because he did not hear the brake when he knew that it was needed. The moment he heard it bite in, he relaxed, and his tail bounced back up even before the lines tightened enough to tell him that Miki had regained control.

Slow down *before* your dogs get out of control. It is easier to keep control of a slower team than to regain control of a runaway one.

If the brake will not bite into hard-pack, jump up and down on it, forcing it into the snow. If the sled is loaded, pull up on the handlebow while standing on the brake to lend more weight. This also allows a lighter person to brake more effectively. Jumping off of the runners, shoving the sled forward to slacken the lines, and then pulling it backward sharply will jerk the dogs and break up their stride — if you can do this hard enough. At least it gets their attention — and sometimes lack of attention is the main problem. Do not try this at a twenty-mile-per-hour lope! It can be effective on glare ice when the sled brake will not bite in. You can also create drag by sliding your feet on the ice.

Avoid braking to keep your dogs from running up on another team when you do not want to pass. Instead, stop and wait for the advance team to gain a lead, then let your dogs catch up. This spares your dogs, your brake, and the trail. You must do this sometimes when the lead team is breaking trail and traveling more slowly. Sometimes the back team is not really faster, but the dogs are excitedly trying to catch up. In a nonrace situation, two mushers traveling together may wish to adjust the sizes of their teams or move dogs from the back team to the front team to equalize their speeds. Remember, though, that the chasing team will be working much harder and will tire out faster. Many dogs will get accustomed to the situation when they are around other teams and will stop trying to catch up quite as much.

Passing

When overtaking another musher, you have the right to decide when and if you wish to pass. If your dogs have been chasing, resting them at a slower pace before pushing onward may be beneficial — or it may be a waste of time. Avoid passing on narrow or twisty stretches of trail.

When you are about fifty feet behind the other team, call "Trail!" and make certain that the other musher hears you. The lead team should slow or stop. The dogs will not spread out as much if the musher keeps them moving slowly, but on a narrow trail, they may need to be pulled off into the deep snow. Keep your dogs moving,

When a number of teams are traveling together, as they are here in the Oregon sand dunes, it's a real pleasure driving well-trained dogs. If your dogs are not well trained, they can ruin the fun for everyone. *Photo by David Waguespack; courtesy Oregon Dune Mushers.*

encouraging them strongly with your voice, but be ready to brake if a tangle occurs. Popping a whip, shouting, or stopping to hit your dogs will upset the other team, so keep as quiet as possible. Even if a tangle occurs, there is no need to get excited. Some well-trained teams pass with just a whistle, while some mushers feel the need to shout frantically.

If your dogs will not pass, do not make it a big deal. Walk up and quietly pull your leaders by. Do not make this a bad experience, or your dogs may be reluctant to pass next time, too; however, a well-timed cuff can be effective on a particularly balky dog.

To make a head-on pass, call "Gee!" just as the two teams meet. If the other musher does likewise, the lead dogs maintain their forward momentum, and the pass goes remarkably smoothly — theoretically. If a tangle does occur, be patient, and do not grab dogs on the other team. Let their driver handle them while you handle your own dogs.

After being passed by an overtaking team, maintain an interval of at least one team length, and do not repass that team if it has a problem. Even if the musher stops the team to fix a tangle, wait for them. You know that he or she has the faster team, and going by the team is not going to save time — you will just be caught, making a third pass necessary. In general, give the advance team two to four minutes to get its act together and pull ahead. Only then, if you feel that you can pass and hold a lead, should you do so. Race rules spell out specific policies on passing and repassing.

Most races have a "no-man's land" (free zone) at the end, where an overtaken team does not have to give trail, although it cannot interfere with the other team. The faster team must pass on the fly with no help from the leading team. This is one time when having good strong leaders really pays off.

Obstacles and Hazards

A well-trained team will, at your command, cross unfamiliar bridges, dart through underpasses, and ignore corraled horses, even if they have never been exposed to these situations. This is because you have trained them to follow your commands, and because they trust your judgment. A young, inexperienced dog may balk, but confident teammates usually give him the incentive to overcome his fear.

Once, while crossing a university campus, we came upon a flight of stairs. Our dogs had never seen stairs, but they loped right down them, with the sled clattering along behind as our nonmushing passenger shrieked with laughter. A strong front end, with reliable, confident leaders and swing dogs, can take a bunch of uninitiated hounds just about anywhere. Training techniques for accomplishing this are discussed in Chapter 11.

Other animals excite sled dogs. These include livestock, loose dogs and cats, and wildlife — from rabbits and ravens to moose and bison. Keep alert and spot distractions before your dogs do. Dogs have a feeling of power when running in a team; they know that strength lies in numbers. They tend to think like a pack and may chase animals that one dog would not tackle alone. Fortunately, they also realize the importance of not tangling the lines by leaping after something, and they rarely leave a well-packed trail to strike out through deep snow. Brake *before* your dogs try to chase. Let them know that you are in control before the idea even pops into their furry heads, and they are more likely to obey you.

If they do get out of control and you cannot brake effectively, tip the sled over into deep snow or run it into brush. The drag will slow

This is a situation that you should try to avoid. Do not approach the moose. If you have a firearm, shooting in the air might drive the moose away, or you may have to kill it. Otherwise, if you cannot safely pull or call off the dogs, there is little you can do. *Drawing by Diane Drashner; courtesy Pam Gilbertson.*

or stop a small charging team. (Try not to smash up your sled or lose the team.) This will *not* stop a high-powered team, so use this trick with discretion.

Should your dogs actually tangle with a large, dangerous animal and you are powerless to stop them, let them go and *stay out of the way* (funerals are expensive). You cannot drive away an angry moose unless you have a firearm, and even then you may have to kill it.

Consequently, many backwoods mushers carry firearms, especially in the Far North. One top contender in the 1985 Iditarod chose not to carry a weapon and paid the price when a moose attacked her team. Not only was she knocked out of the race, but two of her valuable and cherished dogs were killed and several others were injured. Moose and bear are the most likely problems; bison, wolves, rabid animals, bulls, and savage dogs are also possibilities. In some areas, such as the Pine Barrens of New Jersey, feral dogs have been known to maul humans. If you have dangerous animals in your area, find out if firearms are recommended for protection. (Firearm use is prohibited in most national parks; hand guns are banned in Canada.)

We carry a .44 Blackhawk pistol. A .357 pistol or .30-06 or heavier rifle are also effective against big animals. Try to scare away the animal with a couple of shots before actually killing it. If you must shoot an animal to defend life or property, follow game laws for your area. This usually means salvaging edible meat and promptly informing the proper authorities. However, if you are not competent with a firearm, you are safer leaving it at home.

Consistent training results in consistent behavior. These dogs are dependable and can be relied on to stay put until the sled is loaded with feed and they can head for home. The wheel dogs don't like each other — Trapper, on the right, might have his back turned, but his ears will tell him if Yukon makes a move.

Loose dogs present a special problem. An excited sled dog can easily kill a small pet. Bigger pets may fight when cornered. While pet owners should keep their dogs restrained, many do not, and they will be very angry (with good reason) if your brigade chases their precious one into their own garage. Use strict discipline if necessary, and run reliable dogs up front if you anticipate problems.

When overtaking a hiker, skier, or other pedestrian, call out before your team reaches them. Dogs are very quiet, and some people get quite a fright when they turn to see eight or twelve large dogs rushing at them.

Watch out for unexpected behavior from your team. For example, a leader might suddenly swing out across a busy road. One of our lead dogs once rushed into an open, parked van. He jumped into the lap of the astonished driver, towing along seven willing co-conspirators.

Occasionally, we read of terrified teams bolting. I cannot say that this never happens, but in sixteen years and more than 25,000 miles of mushing, it has not happened to us. When a dog team "bolts," the dogs usually are just excited, as when chasing a loose dog or charging into the crowd at the start of a race. The dogs may be running uncontrollably, but they are not bolting in a blind panic as a horse might. Dogs shy away when they are frightened suddenly, but they do not actually flee in an unseeing panic.

Handling Heavy Loads

During the gold rush days in the north country, when dog teams were used for transportation rather than for recreation or sport, large loads were the rule rather than the exception. In his book *A Dog-Puncher on the Yukon*, Arthur Walden describes freighting for Alaskan gold miners at the turn of the century with three full-size sleds cross-chained together, loaded with 1,200 pounds of freight and pulled by six dogs. The dog drivers learned the best ways to handle such payloads, and many of their methods still apply today.

Sleds with eight- or ten-foot baskets look intimidating, but they actually are easier to handle than an overloaded six-foot sled. We used a nine-foot basket sled for our longest cross-country trip of 1,900 miles, and I am sure that the length contributed greatly to the sled's durability. No one part took too much stress. With the load distributed properly, the sled handled like a charm even with a 300-pound load.

Keeping the center of gravity low prevents the sled from tipping

A large sled can handle a big load much more easily than a small one because the weight is distributed properly, without being stacked too high or too far forward. On a nice trail like this, dogs can handle fifty or even a hundred pounds each without any trouble.

over. Most sleds handle best if the heavy weight is placed in the back, allowing the nose to swivel after the team. A very long sled (usually with an eight- or nine-foot basket or larger) might steer better if the center of gravity is farther forward, causing the sled to swivel in the middle rather than at the end. Knowing your own sled is a great asset.

If a load is only slightly outsized for our sled, we put fifty pounds into a red plastic child's sled and tow it behind. Very large loads can be broken down into two sleds. The driver has a difficult time if any hills or corners are involved unless a second driver is on the second sled. We have found that one team of twelve dogs can pull two coupled sleds (each with a driver) more easily than two six-dog teams each pulling a sled.

Gee Poles

The most valuable tool for controlling an overloaded or unmanageable sled is a gee pole. Some freighting sleds come equipped with a gee pole. It is usually on a hinge so that it can be folded back against the sled when not in use. You can jury-rig a highly effective gee pole quickly by lashing a long thin pole (usually cut from a small, dry spruce tree) to the front two stanchions on the right side of the sled. It should angle upward and project about six feet out in front of the sled. The front end of the pole, held by the driver, should be waist high. By levering it right or left, you can turn the heaviest sled with astonishing ease. You have to move the wheel dogs one position forward so that you can straddle the towline between the team and the sled.

Most gee-pole riders today use a pair of short, broad skis, but in years past, when heavy loads slowed the team's pace to three miles per hour and payloads were at a premium, the musher often walked or snowshoed while holding the gee pole. Some balanced on an infamous contraption known as a ouija board, which was a short toboggan tied into the towline.

You can fasten the skis into the towline by attaching short ropes to each ski tip, so that you are towed by the feet. I prefer to leave the skis free, and I lean on the gee pole for forward momentum. Although this requires more physical effort, it frees my feet so that I can balance and maneuver better and can ski along to lighten the load. I also can step more easily from one side of the towline to the other as needed. (Try this and you will appreciate the skill and dexterity, not to mention the courage, that your dogs need when untangling themselves while running.) I am also more free in case of a crash.

Gee poles are dangerous. Broken gee poles have run through dog drivers, killing them. Except for skidding the sled into deep snow, you have only vocal control over the team. On some corners, the sled takes control of the skier instead of the other way around. Miki has been lifted clear off of the ground and hurtled into the bushes by a gee pole. When dropping down banks, the sled can shoot forward and crash down on you. For these reasons, we rarely use a gee pole without a second person on the runners who is ready to brake or to offer assistance. When my dogs are traveling slowly on a familiar trail with no steep hills, I use a gee pole alone without undue terror. You do need to be adept on skis, however.

In addition to steering a sled, a gee pole helps you to keep the sled from tipping over. You can swing wide or turn on a dime and can break runners loose when the sled has been sitting for awhile. Two

Mark Worcester handles the gee pole behind Roger Burggraf's team of registered Alaskan Malamutes as they climb Sable Pass in Denali National Park.
The gee pole is attached to the right side of the sled, with a brace going to
the left side to equalize the force. A hinge allows it to fold up. Mark is on
the right side of the gee pole for better control on this sidehill; normally, the
musher straddles the towline, holding the gee pole in the right hand. *Photo
by Roger Burggraf; courtesy Sue Renkert.*

A jury-rigged gee pole lashed to the first and second stanchions of the 8½-foot freight sled helps Miki to steer the 300-pound load. The leverage turns the most obstinate sled with ease.

people can travel with one team without weighing down the sled. We also have used the gee pole to keep the sled tracking properly on a sidehill or on trails slanted by shelf ice, drifts, or spring melt.

We were traveling on the Yukon River one March, and Miki was riding the gee pole of our nine-foot basket sled with its 280-pound load, when we came upon a gaping section of open water. The trail was set high on the steeply sloping bank above the water to avoid the dangerous ice, and, with swirling black water just two feet below, it wiggled up and down and back and forth. Without a gee pole, our heavy sled might have skidded or rolled right into the water, but with Miki levering the front and me riding the uphill runner in back, we passed safely — thanks to using a dependable method dating to the gold rush days.

Traveling with Two People and One Team

Because we usually keep about twelve dogs, and because one team is more efficient than two, Miki and I frequently travel together with one sled. The obvious solution is for one person to ride in the basket, but when the sled is loaded, this is not always possible.

The most efficient way (efficient for the dogs, not for the mushers) is for one person to ski on a gee pole or on a tow rope behind the sled. The person can ski along to help ease the load, and skiing permits you to let go and walk up steep banks, greatly reducing the workload on the dogs. The musher has control of the dogs, so the skier only has to stay upright and sightsee. When you are skiing behind, be very careful not to let the rope tangle in your skis and drag you, because you will have a *lot* of power pulling you in a most awkward and painful position. (Skijoring techniques are discussed in Chapter 15.)

If you are traveling with three people, one can ride on the gee pole and another can ski on a tow rope behind. If you have more people than that, consider getting another team!

Another method is to tow a second sled, preferably a light one. An extra payload can be carried this way. Once again, the musher on the front sled controls the dogs, but the back musher can add greatly to the braking power by dragging his or her feet or by using the second sled's brake. This method also allows one musher to hold the team while the other handles dogs.

Be careful that the back sled does not run up and hit the front musher when going down hills and banks. Also, the front musher must contend with the tow rope leading back to the other sled, which may interfere with braking and footwork.

The sleds can be coupled by a tow rope leading under the first sled directly to the main towline of the team. A simpler method, which also controls the second sled better, is to wrap the tow rope around the back stanchions of the lead sled. However, if the back sled is snagged and slams to a halt, you run the risk of having the front sled "burst apart and collapse lifeless to the ground," as happened to us. At least if one sled disintegrates beyond repair, you will have an extra one with which to get home!

Sled First Aid

We are not going to discuss in-depth sled building and repair, but you should know how to patch up a broken sled on the trail so that you can proceed. If your sled cracks up en route, do not despair. If a sled has a part, Miki and I have broken it — and fixed it. We are living, breathing experts at putting sleds back together out in the boonies after a crash (or series of crashes), and we have two secrets to pass along.

The first is the most important — attitude. Saltwater tears do not put sleds back together; determination and improvision do. The second secret is having a good repair kit, including a trail ax (which doubles as a hammer), appropriate nuts and bolts, nails, string, cord, wire, duct tape (cloth-backed), screws and a screwdriver, and pliers. Remember — you create your own insurance, and carrying one or two pounds of extra weight is a small price. We carry a repair kit anytime we are traveling more than a day from home, but on shorter runs we just hope for the best. Even when a sled does break down, it usually can limp a few miles home, where you can repair it with proper tools or send it to a sled shop. (Some sled builders are listed in the appendix, and local mushers can tell you of sled builders in your area.)

Many broken sled parts can be ignored. If you have five crosspieces, who cares if one gets bashed? You still have four. A broken stanchion or two will not cripple a sled. However, every piece is there for a reason, and one broken part weakens the integrity of the whole sled, leading to snowballing breakdowns.

Boards that crack and splinter at an angle often can be bound tightly with string to hold them together. If the board shears off straight, reinforce it with a matching board — one can be chopped from a small tree. Shape it while the tree is still standing (so that it will hold still for you); hack down the sides, square it, then chop or saw it to the correct length. Lash it as tightly as possible to the full length of the broken board.

A broken railing can be splinted or replaced with a sapling one-half to one and one-half inches in diameter. We have found that green birch saplings invariably outlast the original railing. Cracked or broken false runners usually can be nailed back in place.

Nothing incapacitates a sled faster than a broken runner. On cross-country trips, we use one-half-inch plastic that can serve as a runner itself. Most runners break directly in front of the first stanchion, at the base of the curve — the worst possible place. If you must splint

When your sled needs work, you may need to do it on the trail. Mary Shields changing plastic at Carmacks during the 1986 Yukon Quest. *Photo by Ron Lambert.*

it, find a tree with a natural curve. A young birch tree curving up from a bank or from the trunk of a parent tree works well. Chop it into an appropriate board, preserving or exaggerating the curve. Nail the board to the underside of the runner, extending it well beyond the break. It will drag, but it should allow you to limp on to a place where in-depth repairs can be made.

Toboggans, having fewer parts, are less prone to breakage than wooden stanchion sleds. The tall, straight handlebows, however, are especially vulnerable, and some people carry a predrilled board that can be bolted quickly onto a broken handlebow to make a secure

A rough trail with little snow can lead to broken sleds, especially if you run very many dogs or have a loaded sled.

splint. Bolts in toboggans can shear or jiggle loose, so be sure to carry more of the correct size and do not delay in replacing them.

Above all, maintain your sense of humor. One November, our trails had only a few inches of snow over rough, tussocky ground. When we returned home, the greeting question changed from, "Did you break the sled?" to "What broke?" Another year, we took parts from several broken sleds and built a new one, painting the old boards a bright green. By spring, with more than 1,000 miles of exceptionally rough trails behind the sled, less than half of it was still green. All of the other parts had been broken and replaced — saplings replaced the railings, and an old piece of plywood lined the shattered basket.

We have learned to laugh instead of cry over a broken sled, and sometimes that is the only way to keep going when the odds seem against you.

CHAPTER 11

TEAM TRAINING

One of our leaders would drag a team of scared huskies into danger-ously swift water at our command. We once asked our team, which had never seen a bridge, to cross a long bridge of open steel grating; they were horrified but marched forward without hesitation. Two of our dogs barked furiously at a marauding grizzly but would not leave my side until I ordered them to drive it away — and they did.

These dogs were not extraordinary — they simply understood us. They exercised restraint as we requested, or threw fear to the wind at our command. The serious musher needs dogs that can be counted on in every circumstance, and that is where training pays off.

I Said "STOP!"

Stopping a spirited team with a vocal command often is impossible. If the dogs are trained to stop, get their attention with the brake, then stop them with a vocal command. Do not expect your leaders to stop the team; they must hold that towline tightly to maintain control.

If your dogs are not trained to stop, they will only stop if you can physically halt them. If you want them to stop on command, you must *train* them to stop. Run just three or four dogs so that you can stop them physically, or run a larger team with a heavy wheeled vehicle that has good brakes. Teach them that if they do not stop, they will *get* stopped. Punish them if you must, but do not forget the praise when they respond correctly. Some dogs will not listen to you if they realize that you cannot control them. If you give up and let them go on, you are reinforcing bad behavior, telling them that it is okay to ignore your commands. If you want to run sixteen, twenty, or twenty-four dogs in a team and have them go where *you* want to

Running dogs through deep snow teaches them to appreciate stopping, and they learn to respond to "Whoa!" because they *want* to stop, not because you try to force them to obey.

go, you must train the dogs individually in a small team first, drilling them until they *reliably* do what *you* want them to do.

Team dogs should be trained with a few other commands in addition to "Whoa." (They usually do not need to be taught "Hike!") Teaching them "Stay" could save you a lot of trouble later, because the command teaches them restraint and reinforces your dominance over them.

Speed control is essential in racing teams. You should have a command for more speed — the "kiss," "Get up," or "Let's go" — but keep it consistent. Also have a command to slow down, such as "Easy down," "Slow," or "Steady."

Train the dogs to accelerate by calling the command when you know that they are going to speed up anyway — when they crest a hill, scent game, see another team, or approach the dog yard. Pedaling hard and using an excited tone of voice also helps. (If you use the right tone of voice, an eager team will speed up even if you shout "Tequila!") A few mushers who train with four-wheelers use motor assistance to speed up the team. Once the dogs understand the speed-up command, start demanding obedience. (Here is where the consistency of one command is important.) Teach the dogs to give you an all-out effort when *you* want it, not when they feel like giving it. If a dog does not have what it takes for this all-out effort, he should not be disciplined. He should be culled.

Your team must also slow down on command. You will need to slow your dogs at times for their own safety, such as when traveling on a rough trail or near motorized traffic. On a long race, a spirited team might go too fast and get winded if you do not slow them down occasionally. Do not just stand on the brake to slow them down. Teach them to slow down by braking in spurts while giving the command, or when you are traveling on uphill stretches.

Training the Adult Team Dog

The best teacher for an untrained sled dog is a trained sled dog. To start with a number of untrained, inexperienced dogs and mold them into a united, obedient team is an awesome task, but placing a "green" dog with a few well-trained mates usually reduces your job from teacher to overseer. The dog sees his companions working eagerly and soon catches on with very little prompting from the boss on the runners. Even a single good leader can work wonders with a scatterbrained bunch of trainees.

The untrained adult should be introduced carefully to the team,

Run a new dog beside a calm, friendly team dog who will accept erratic behavior.

because he might be confused or panicked by the speed, power, and tight, unrelenting towline. Use a very small team until he catches on. Be patient, and be reasonable. Some dogs, especially pets, do not have the drive to be sled dogs. Just because he is Aunt Annie's favorite does not mean that he can cut it in a team — any team.

A new addition, whether he is trained or not, should be broken in gently. Even if the dog is a leader, put him in the middle of the team to let him settle in before trying him up front. Start slowly, and do not go very far at first, just in case he does not have as many miles as his previous owner claimed. A dog needs time to adjust to his new home, to his new comrades, to the pace of your team, and to you, your commands, and your voice. Some dogs fit right in, but older dogs might take a year or more to adjust.

Puppy training is more involved; this is covered in Chapter 8.

A Word for Beginners

If you are just starting to run dogs and your dogs are pets or untrained animals, trying to train them will be like the ignorant leading the uninitiated. The best advice that we can give to an aspiring musher is to buy a dependable leader. This dog will teach you, as well as your crew. Good older dogs, perhaps grown too slow for racing, sometimes can be found at reasonable prices.

If your first purchase is a trained dog, your second should be a basic sledding book, such as *MUSH* or *The Joy of Running Sled Dogs* (see the references listed at the back of the book). Or, find an experienced musher who can help you. When we first started mushing dogs at age fourteen, we got four Siberians with two other children. All were so eager that the dogs pulled instinctively, and the kids did not mind running behind — one kid in the basket of a dilapidated sled, one on the runners, and two more dangling off of a tow rope behind the sled. It sure was fun, but without any source of advice, it took us years to figure out how to actually train the dogs.

It takes determination for the uninitiated to try sledding without outside help. Just do not get so desperate that you go overboard like a couple of boys I read about recently. It seems that their two sheep dogs refused to pull their stone boat "sled," so they replaced their dogs with sixteen Corriedale sheep, using horse halters as harnesses. It did not go over very well with the sheep. Things really got out of hand when the sheep dogs dashed out and herded the sheep "team" away.

Dogs That Do Not Pull

If a dog does not pull, has never pulled, and never will pull, he is just a freeloader. If you want him, keep him. If you don't, get rid of him. There are ways to make a dog pull, but some animals simply cannot or will not work in harness.

You must determine why a dog is not working. He might be overworked. He might be lazy. He might be fearful, anxious, or confused. And he might have a physical problem. An overworked dog needs rest; a lazy one needs discipline. A dog that is afraid might do better in a small team or with one-on-one training. Medical problems are covered in Chapter 6. A dog that does not pull because he simply cannot keep up will do better on a slower team or on one that runs fewer miles.

If your dog is not pulling simply because of laziness or a training deficiency, you have a few options. If he knows what you want but is not giving you any effort, stop the team, whack him, and push or pull him forward to tighten his tug. Repeat this until you get results or until it becomes obvious that you will *not* get results. Try moving the dog around — forward or backward in the team. If he is anxious about another dog, remove the other dog. If he is intimidated in a big team, work him in a small team.

A lazy dog *must* work if he is in a three-dog team. He might pull if you run him behind another team. Or, tie a sack of rocks or a short log to his harness and let him run behind your team. Or, leave him home several days so that he will appreciate a workout, then take him only as far as he is willing to pull. Gimmicks include tying a string to the dog's tail and yanking it to make him pull. However, try something more constructive first.

Obviously, if a dog used to pull well and then stops, suspect a problem. Do not discipline this dog. Give him a week off, and start again with a few short runs. If he still will not pull, a visit to the veterinarian might prove enlightening.

Training Leaders

A lead dog can make or break a shaky team. Many dogs can be trained to lead, but the best ones are born for it. Ideally, a potential leader is responsive to praise. He has a sense of responsibility and pays attention. He commands respect from other dogs and is intelligent enough to solve problems but is not a smart aleck. He is enthusiastic but able to handle pressure. He sets a fast pace, but one that the team can handle.

Training Methods

You can train a leader in two ways — one-on-one, or with another leader. One-on-one training develops a stronger rapport, especially if the training begins during puppyhood, but it is very time-consuming. You can start with a harness-broken dog or with a "green" one. First teach him to hold his tug tightly as he stands ahead of you. Then teach him "Gee" and "Haw" by running behind him and pulling him the correct way as you give the command. Frequent short sessions are more effective than long, tedious ones.

Once a dog knows "Gee" and "Haw," teach him to "Come gee" and "Come haw," and to go "Straight ahead" past a fork and "On

Leaders can be
taught commands
by a person
on skis. You are
much closer to the
dogs and can guide
them on the turns.

by" another team or obstacle. When the dog performs consistently,
run him with a couple of steady team dogs to hone his confidence,
and add more dogs as he learns to handle them.

Most leaders are trained by another leader instead of by a person.
If you see a dog with potential, put him in swing (point) right behind
the leaders for several weeks to a year. The dog picks up commands
by taking cues from the leaders. Later, run him in double lead beside
a good leader until he has the ability and confidence to do it alone.
(You may run the trainee on a shorter tug so that the leader is slightly
ahead and can easily shoulder aside his protégé.)

You can also train a leader with a three-dog team. Choose a dog
with the drive to stay out in front, and simply stop at each fork and

Bring only the number of dogs that you *know* you can control when training leaders, so that you can correct the dogs when they make a mistake. This is the only way to train a reliable leader. This is Tim Nelson and his eight Siberians in the sand dunes of Oregon. *Photo by David Waguespack; courtesy Oregon Dune Mushers.*

either wait for the dog to guess the correct reponse to your command, or pull him in the correct direction while giving the command. Skijoring is a great way to train a leader. The dog is not pressured by fire-breathing teammates, and you are close enough to him so that he will pay attention to you. A simple tug on the tow rope gets his attention and turns him the right way. For more information on skijoring, see Chapter 15.

When training a leader, you *must* have absolute control over the team so that you can correct mistakes immediately. To train a dog to *always* obey your command; he must *never* get away with disobedience. Our young leader, Toulouse, was spoiled because we were running a trapline and were not formally training dogs; as a result, he got away with some things. Now he is too smart for his own good. He goes where *he* thinks we should go. With stricter discipline, he would have turned out better. A dog like this needs retraining in a small, controlled team.

If you have to stop the team because a leader missed a turn, do not just stand on the runners shouting. Anchor the team and drag the leader sternly around. If he knew the command but did not listen to you, spank him before pulling him around.

Aside from teaching commands, you must also encourage new leaders to bravely pass obstacles like water, ice, crowds, stray dogs, and other teams. If your leaders will not go forward, your team dogs will also refuse (see "Obstacle Training").

Dogs Are Not Perfect

Some leaders have limited abilities. If you cannot perfect a dog, work around his limitations. Do not punish a dog for his being unable to exceed his potential. This might mean using one dog for finding a wind-blown trail and another for gee-hawing through town.

Single Lead, Double Lead

Double leaders share the pressure and have more power over a bigger team. Often one is fast and the other sharp; therefore, the strengths of one make up for the weaknesses of the other. In a sprint team, a young dog that leaves the chute quickly can be paired with an older one that might start more slowly but come home quickly.

Single leaders do have some advantages. Some dogs perform better alone, plus there is only one dog to make mistakes. A single dog can break trail more easily, and you can trade him with his partner back in the team as he tires. Long ago, mushers sometimes ran a loose leader so that he could find a blown or snowed-in trail without worrying about the dogs behind him. This is rarely done today.

The Gee-Haw Problem

Some mushers expect a leader to turn instantly on command, and others give the command some yards ahead of the turn so that the dog can absorb the situation. This may explain why some people have trouble missing turns. A dog trained to turn instantly will jump straight into deep snow even if he sees a fork ahead. Serious training is required to make a dog leave the trail. He must respond automatically, without thinking. A dog less strictly trained often will miss the fork if you wait until you are right on it.

Once your leaders are well trained, add more dogs gradually so that the leaders learn to handle the others. These trained leaders hold a long string in position during one of Joe Runyan's summer training runs.

Watch your dog as he approaches a fork. He will lift his head when he realizes that a decision must be made. The ears will go forward (which way?) or will turn backward (what does the boss think?). He might even glance backward. The leader is most receptive to your command at this instant. He will not have sized up the situation any earlier than this exact point. A second later, and he will have already decided which way to turn. He might not have time to collect himself and the team to change that direction.

When you buy a leader, you should realize that the dog might have been trained differently. You might need to retrain the dog or adapt to his way of responding.

Stress Control

Leaders are under considerable stress when they are in front of a big team, when they are challenged by an unusual situation, when they are traveling at high speed, or when they are asked to do something that they do not understand or cannot quite hear. Putting two dogs in front relieves some stress. In demanding situations, trade leaders frequently to prevent burnout. A burned-out leader might turn deaf, may jump off of the trail, or may just act depressed. Discipline is more likely to hurt than help. Just move him out of the lead, or leave him home for a few days.

Dogs change as they age. Some get burned out as the years pass, while others gain a better sense of responsibility. One of our leaders was demoted at the age of six because he was not happy in the lead anymore. His replacement was also six, a team dog that needed no training because he apparently already knew it all.

Do Not Confuse the Issue Further

Nothing is worse than saying "Gee!" when you mean "Haw!" — especially when you are training leaders. If you confuse the commands, print the words on their respective mittens, or on the sled handlebow or headboard.

Advanced Team Training

To obtain efficiency, speed, and teamwork, you must run a lot of miles — *quality* miles. This means that you must control your team. If you cannot control your dogs, you will not be training them. You will condition them physically, but they will not learn anything. Teach your dogs the basic commands; train them not to dip snow (if they are sprinters); train them not to play or to chew or to stop for a leak. Train them to pass teams, to ignore distractions, and to keep going under rough conditions. Maintain your discipline, but do not drive the spirit out of your dogs.

For quality miles, avoid training in extreme heat or cold, on extreme terrain, or when the dogs are too tired, sick, or hurt to concentrate on the lessons. Be consistent with your methods. Do not try to solve a problem by making radical changes in training schedules or diet. This just disrupts the team further.

The dogs must take their work seriously, although there is no reason why they should not enjoy it. When your schedule is tough, make it more appealing by running on different trails or with other dog teams. Vary the terrain and the lengths of the runs. Hills are invaluable for teaching endurance, but too much climbing can slow the dogs and make them overmuscled. When the dogs are working or racing hard, spend extra time with them in the yard so that they will still like you.

Team Harmony

You might need to cull a dog for the sake of your team. Even an outstanding dog might not fit in. A dog that works hard might still have a different gait. He might be a fighter. He might disrupt the team by playing or jumping off of the trail. Although these dogs are contributing to your team, they also are detracting from it and should be the first to go when you are culling. Some dogs might fit into the team but may clash with your own personality. For example, if you dislike hyperactive dogs, you might find yourself unfairly punishing a naturally vivacious dog to the detriment of the whole team.

A young dog also can disrupt harmony. He might run great in the puppy team but may not be ready for the main string. He may fight to keep up or may not have learned to change leads on a tight corner. Running him in the main string will be unfair both to him and to the team.

Positioning

Positioning affects team harmony. Pair off matched dogs where they work best. If one dog pulls strangely on the left, do not put him there. It is nice when a dog can run in any position, but if you want a team without jiggles, rattles, and bumps, you will run each dog where he performs best. Remember — a dog might perform better in the back when on a rough trail and in the front when on a fast one.

It is nice to run a dog next to a friend. Running males beside females, and alternating sexes down the towline, helps prevent squabbles.

Dogs that are of the same size and build find it much easier to keep pace with each other. This is important in leaders and makes it easier for them to work together.

This often is not possible, but if fighting is your number-one problem, preventing fights is your number-one priority.

Larger dogs usually run in the wheel so that their power is close to the sled. In fast teams, however, smaller, more agile wheel dogs are less likely to stumble on the towline while cornering. A dog that needs frequent discipline (such as a "leaker," a "dipper," or a "chewer") can be put near the wheel where he will hear you clearly and where you can reach him easily. While two dogs have more power, on a slanted or twisty trail, a single wheel dog can leap from side to side for better leverage and to avoid the towline.

Inexperienced dogs are best run in front of the wheel dogs. This is a visible, laid-back position and is also good for dogs recovering from injury or illness, for burned-out leaders, or for newly purchased dogs.

Obstacle Training

At a mushers' symposium, Susan Butcher was once asked how she

Dogs should be familiar with a number of challenges. Glassy ice takes experience to run on without slipping, but most dogs accept it after a momentary fuss.

Toulouse had never been across a bridge or on a surface like this, but he dragged the rest of the team right out on it.

made her dogs cross glare ice. After a funny pause she said, "They just do."

That is a frustrating answer for the novice, but it is true. An experienced team that has encountered many different conditions does not have to be forced past an unfamiliar obstacle.

Obstacle training starts at puppyhood (see Chapter 8) and continues throughout a dog's life. The more different situations he encounters as a young dog, the more easily he will get through unusual situations in the team. Racers especially need dogs that will not balk when confronted with an unexpected obstacle.

You can expose your dogs to countless situations — crowds, flashbulbs, race chutes, loose dogs, other teams, wild animals, farm stock, horseback riders, deep snow, glare ice, overflow, running water, puddles, banks, bridges, culverts, grates, streets, stairs, ramps, vehicles, strange places — the list is endless. Get your dogs used to your truck. Bring them to town. Take them camping. Let strangers handle them.

Start in a small way — one or two people instead of a crowd; a short bridge, a narrow stream. Stop in the middle of a bridge, a culvert, or a crowd to praise the dogs or even give them a snack. You can also place the subject (a dog, a noisy vehicle, a photographer with a camera flash) some distance off of the trail and move it closer as the dogs grow accustomed to it. Having a strong front end really gives your trainees forward impulsion even when they are startled.

You also can run a young dog loose, where possible, so that he can follow you instead of getting dragged through a scary place. This works especially well on ice.

Conditioning for Events

The dogs must be conditioned for your main goal — the "big race," a cross-country trip, or a major weight pull. While you may be entering other events, your conditioning and training will concentrate on the event in which you most want to succeed. Specific training regimes are detailed in other chapters, but some basic guidelines apply to most goal-oriented training.

To maximize your team's potential, keep the dogs in the best possible condition with good food, current vaccinations, a clean yard, and warm houses. If you do not do this, why bother putting time and effort into training?

Muscles harden in a matter of weeks, but bones and tendons require months — even years — to strengthen fully. Do not start training for a February event as late as December. The dogs might appear fit, but they will be prone to injury because the strength of their bones and tendons will not have caught up with the power in their muscles. Plan your training schedule before the start of the season. The regime you follow will depend upon your dogs, upon your own time, upon trail and weather conditions, and upon the event itself. Some mushers follow a rigid schedule, while others are flexible. Whichever way works for you, do not be so flexible that you compromise improvement, or so rigid that you cannot lay off during severe weather or for other good reasons.

Conditioning should be comparable to what you expect your dogs to do. If you will be traveling with 500-pound loads across sea ice and pressure ridges, expose your dogs to similar circumstances. If you are entering a serious sprint race, do not use those dogs for freighting or for giving the kids a ride. Your training runs should vary in length, but they ought to average out to something less than the distance that you will run in the event. Sprint racers might run distances averaging 80 percent of the race distances; long-distance mushers run thirty to eighty miles per training run, or perhaps thirty to fifty miles for a mid-distance race. Some mushers will test their dogs occasionally by pushing them harder and farther than the "big race" in a series of tough training runs. Others argue that any testing should be done only during preliminary races.

New mushers often make the mistake of overtraining their dogs. If you log 3,000 miles before a long-distance race, your dogs will enter the event worn out. Two weeks of rest before the race will not bring them back. Your dogs will be reluctant to maintain a fast pace or to make an all-out effort. Similarly, sprint dogs can get muscle-bound and lose their sharp edge. Do not aim for the maximum number of miles — aim for the *optimum*. The dogs must be in top form but well rested; they must be controllable but eager to go.

Like human athletes, dogs — especially distance dogs — often train close to the limit of their endurance. Their muscles are stressed repeatedly, energy and nutrients are drained constantly, and their psychological stamina is tested frequently. This means that rest periods are critical. The dogs need enough days off to build and repair muscles, replace drained reserves, heal abused feet, clear out waste products, and regain the cheery outlook that we love to see. Burnout is discussed in Chapter 2. Watch closely for it in heavy training, and be prepared to interrupt your schedule if your dogs need a break.

Training Methods

Training methods are as varied as mushers; all we can do is review some common techniques and let you choose what works for your team. Most mushers run their dogs three to five times a week during training. The schedule varies; it might be every other day, two days on and one day off, or three days on and one or two days off. Dogs will make a stronger showing if you run them hard the first day (or two), then give them an easier run the last day. However, if you are planning to enter a two- or three-day event where the last day is the toughest — such as the North American Open in Fairbanks — have the dogs prepared for a hard run *after* an easy run so that they do not give up on you. Some mushers follow a fairly fixed routine. Others take their team out every day until the dogs lose their enthusiasm, then give the team a few days off. This might involve running the dogs harder on each successive day until they get a break.

Vary the length and frequency of the runs so that the dogs do not pace themselves for a set number of miles. This will keep them interested, plus they will be ready for any length of race that you might plan to enter. Within each run, you might ask for a top speed at the beginning and at the end of a run, or for several peaks during the run, or for an all-out blast the whole way if the sprint is only six miles or less. In his book *The Speed Mushing Manual*, Jim Welch describes interval training, which involves driving the dogs at top speed for one-half mile or so several times during a run to increase their maximum effort and to perfect your control over them.

Peaking the Team

It takes hard training to get a team in top physical condition before the race season. By the time the dogs are hardened, they have lost their eagerness and might even be in a slump. Depending on how tired the dogs are, you should stop the serious training two to four weeks before the race season. Let them rest a few days, then take them on some very short runs. Leave them on the chain *longer* than they want to rest, and do not run them as far as they want to go. This will restore their attitude, and they will be eager to run again. If you can manipulate the dogs so that they are crazy to go while still in top form and still controllable, your team will reach its peak performance. With skill and sound judgment, you can "peak out" the team just in time for the biggest event of the season.

Musher Conditioning

Do not overlook your own condition. My sister and I tend to ignore this factor because our outdoor life keeps us in shape year-round. "Talk about five-gallon deep-knee bends," Miki suggested when I wrote this.

"What's that?" I asked.

"Filling the water barrel from the lake," she chuckled.

However, if your physical activities are limited to four sprint runs with the dogs each week in the snow season, consider a conditioning routine to stay fit. Jogging, swimming, cross-country skiing, and other high-intensity workouts will increase your stamina behind the team. This could mean the difference between winning and losing a race. Although you probably could use a rest after the winter season, you should get in shape *before* you begin training dogs again. Arms, shoulders, back, and legs are tested strenuously when you work with dogs. Three half-hour workouts a week will strengthen your muscles and improve your cardiovascular system.

Champion distance racer Joe Runyan jogs as a hobby, and after his 1985 Yukon Quest victory, a story went around that he wore jogging shoes instead of winter boots between some of the last checkpoints.

Training Without Snow

Summer training is invaluable to a competitive musher with a big team and is indispensable to mushing addits who do not care if there is snow on the ground or not. Summer training is light — usually one or two runs a week, or perhaps three runs if you are training pups. More serious training takes place in the fall, especially in areas where the first snow holds off until December. Some mushers do not train in the summer at all and simply wait for snow.

Gig Training

Fall training with a wheeled rig strengthens dogs and gets some of the discipline out of the way before the snow falls. In areas where snowfall is late and limited, gig training is almost indispensable if you want to build a strong team.

Wheeled rigs are reviewed in Chapter 3. Bring only the number of dogs that you can control safely. This will allow you to train them effectively. Keep the runs to four miles or less, because the dogs are susceptible to injury on hard roads, especially if they are in poor

It can be hard to train dogs during the summer because they overheat easily. A dog that is hot is struggling to combat heat exhaustion and is not concentrating on his job, on his partners, or on his driver. If dogs can be kept cool, summer training can be very productive. *Photo by Pat Brawand; courtesy Oregon Dune Mushers.*

Dog carts should be used only with small teams if the dogs are in training. Larger teams can be run if they are well trained. Rick Armstrong and a four-dog team. *Courtesy* Fairbanks Daily News-Miner.

Joe and Sherri Runyan use a four-wheeler for training young dogs during the summer and fall.

condition. Also, the cart tends to bang them around more than a sled does.

Run the dogs only in cooler temperatures to avoid overheating. This is covered in Chapter 6.

Dog Walkers

Like a horse walker, the dog walker has horizontal spokes that revolve around a wheel; the dogs are hooked to the spokes for exercise and training. Walkers have only recently attracted interest; some mushers swear by them, and others feel that they are useless, harmful, or too much trouble. In addition to conditioning dogs, walkers can be used to teach speed commands, because the rate can be adjusted.

They can gently condition dogs that are weakened by previous injuries and can be used as an intermediate step in puppy training. You can hook a pup to the walker before putting him in the team so that he will not have as many new situations to cope with at one time.

A walker is *not* a time-saver. The dogs must be watched every minute. The musher performs no strenuous work but does not have much fun, either.

Loose Dogs

Running your dogs loose keeps them in good condition, but it must be done responsibly. The dogs should be trained to come to you. Only take dogs that you can control, and do not take too many at one time. Run them in remote areas, preferably in open country where you can watch them easily. Bell collars allow you to keep closer track of them in brush.

Loose dogs can become uncontrollable if they find game or livestock; huskies are especially notorious for losing their heads. Running wild game is illegal, and running stock is not only illegal, but also could result in a fatal case of "lead poisoning." Encounters with skunks, porcupines, snakes, hunters, equestrians, irate property owners, and

Although lumbering and heavy, the stripped-down car chassis allows excellent control for training a large team.

Summer training can include camping trips. The dogs can run free or carry a pack. This not only keeps them limber and healthy, it teaches them to respond to your voice and encourages a close bond between man and dog.

motor vehicles can all have disastrous endings — so be very careful.

Walk or jog with your dogs, or run them with a bike or behind a motorized vehicle. Running them on shore behind a motorboat is great fun; the dogs can cool off in the water, and you can easily evaluate gaits and performance.

Taking one dog on a walk is a great morale booster and provides gentle exercise for pregnant or debilitated dogs.

Sponsors

Racers seldom break even financially; even the top contenders seek sponsorships. Some mushers spend $20,000 to $50,000 per year on their dogs. Nonracers, too, sometimes seek sponsorships for a major cross-country trip or for a trek to the Pole.

Approaching potential sponsors is a difficult and often discouraging chore. Persistence is the key to success. You can call dozens of businesses from the Yellow Pages of a phone book, but you might have better luck beating the sidewalks and looking potential sponsors in the eye. Call on businesses that you patronize, and talk to faces that you recognize before tackling strangers. Check out the sponsors of other mushers and other race sponsors, and the sponsors of other sporting events.

Some businesses will offer merchandise instead of money — dog food, tack, winter clothing, sleds — whatever they might have. Indi-

Advertising your sponsors, on your dog box and in newspapers and trail journals, is one way to repay them. You could also throw a big party for them, offer photographs of your team, or even show them the latest video of the races you have won.

viduals might donate their time to help handle dogs, to build sleds, to sew booties, or to keep the dog yard clean.

When looking for sponsors, bring a resume of your team's accomplishments. Photographs and an invitation to visit your dog yard are other enticements.

Once you find a sponsor, keep him or her happy. If you take $500 and disappear, the sponsor will not be there for you next year. It helps when you win races, but you can keep a sponsor happy by mentioning his or her name at every opportunity — to the press, at banquets, on your dog truck, over your kennel, and to other mushers, neighbors, and businessmen. An advertisement in a local newspaper or magazine is excellent; so is a token of your appreciation — a plaque or a photograph of your team. If a sponsor shows a lot of interest in your team, the greatest reward that you can offer might be a dogsled ride.

CHAPTER 12

THE DOG TEAM TRAVELER

Miki and I stood gazing down a steep, ice-coated road behind the village of Koyuk in western Alaska. The humped road center sloped down to steep shoulders above the willows ten feet below.

"I don't think we should go down there," I said.

"Oh, nonsense," my sister laughed. "With the rough locks, this heavy load, and both of us, we'll just creep down."

The chains wrapped around the runners slowed our forward progress but not the sideways slide. Our heavy sled skidded over the bank and rolled, catapulting us far and wide. One false runner broke, two stanchions snapped, and the handlebow was dislocated from the runner.

I gloomily surveyed the wreckage, but Miki just laughed and set to work. We stuck that sled back together with an impressive array of string, nails, duct tape, and a board hacked from a green willow tree. The sled traveled another 600 miles, completing a 1,900-mile trek across Alaska's wilderness — the rough equivalent of a drive from the eastern Canadian–U.S. border to Miami, Florida.

Recreational or adventuring dog mushers are on their own when traveling across country. No gas station offers repairs at every corner. For days or weeks you live out of your sled, relying solely on yourself and on your dogs to get out of trouble. The bond of mutual respect and affection between yourself and your team grows strong, and the freedom is limited only by your own abilities. The land takes on a new dimension, with every mountain and creek gaining significance and reality.

Your First Trip

Do not trick yourself into thinking that a long-distance race, with its well-planned support crew, is the ideal trip. You will be too tired and under too much stress to enjoy the country, and most back-yard bowsers will be blown away by the highly specialized race teams. Inexperienced people also strain the race organization.

Do not aim high for your first outing. A few overnight trips will accustom you and your dogs to sleeping out in cold, unfamiliar places. Travel with an experienced musher if possible so that you do not have to learn by trial and error. You also will be safer with a competent companion. You should have acquired at least basic mushing skills and also should know first aid, survival skills, and cold-weather camping techniques.

By starting small, you can learn what to bring to get by comfortably. While lists of gear carried by others help, everyone has his or her own ideas on where to draw the line between necessity and extravagance. Do not take shortcuts or put yourself in a survival situation, but leave the TV and the VCR at home. Remember — your dogs have to pull it!

When you discover that you really can camp out comfortably at -10 degrees F., try a longer outing. By going on an out-and-back trip, you can pack a comfortable load, travel until it is half gone, then turn back. With a lighter load and a now-familiar trail, the return trip usually is faster, providing some leeway for problems.

On a five-day trip, you will learn a lot about the capabilities and requirements of your dogs and yourself. Remember that travel conditions can vary widely and change rapidly. You may sail down a hard-packed trail on the way out only to be buried by a two-foot snowfall going home. Severe cold can strike overnight, increasing dog food requirements by 20 to 30 percent. Always pack a little extra grub!

Trip Planning

Where to go? In the north, many trails connect remote villages, and, with some research, routes can be found that offer what you are looking for, be it a ten-mile trackless mountain pass or a frozen river "highway" covering hundreds of miles. In more populated areas, long-distance travel is not as easy to plan. You can follow trails marked for long-distance races *after* the mushers have passed. Mushing magazines and books can provide location ideas. For a few specific locations, see Table 9-1.

Make sure that the trail is open to public use and that dogs are allowed, and obtain any necessary permits. Trails crossing private land may be posted. Some trappers do not like people using their trails, and they may have traps hidden in the trail, aimed at wolves and other furbearers but dangerous to passing dog teams. In Alaska and Canada, trails between villages or on major rivers generally are open to the public. Except in state and national parks and a few other areas, permits for camping are usually not required. Land owned by native corporations may have restrictions.

Once you choose your destination, learn all that you can about trails, terrain, shelters, weather conditions, and availability of supplies before committing yourself. National Park Service personnel, residents, snow machiners, trappers, mushing associations, recreational

If you don't plan your trip carefully, you might end up running into poor trail conditions as winter turns into spring — and spring into summer! A gee pole is a big help on a humped, icy trail like this one.

trail users, and trail preservation organizations can help you. How well used is the trail? If it gets snowed in, will it be hours, days, or weeks before someone opens it up again? Are there any particular hazards? Some rivers have the same open holes year after year. Mountains often have steep, rough terrain and treacherous, unpredictable weather. A few areas in the north are famous for irate moose.

Decide how many days you can take. Then, based on previous experience and available information, estimate your daily mileage. Take into consideration short daylight hours (especially in the north), days of rest, and enforced stays due to storms, sick dogs, or breakdowns.

Daily mileage will vary tremendously depending upon trail conditions, your load, and the size and ability of your team. Once when we were breaking trail through deep, untouched snow, Miki and I took nine days to go sixty miles. The next year, with a good trail, we did the same trip in eight and one-half hours.

At every point en route, update your information, and be sure that you find the right trail out of town! If a phone is handy, call home to reassure your anxious family. This also cuts down on the time required to locate you if you do not show up again.

Hope for the best, but plan for the worst! Make sure that a reliable person knows your route and schedule. Family and friends usually can be counted on to sound the alarm if you disappear. Decide on alternate stopping points should you be unable to proceed as hoped. How will you get out if you cannot reach your pick-up point? We once had to be flown out of a remote area by our father in a two-seater Super Cub airplane. It took three round trips for two girls and eight dogs; the sled remains out there to this very day. If you need rescuing by an organized group, you may be charged. We do everything possible to avoid making demands on strangers or rescue organizations.

Extended trips usually require food and resupply shipments to points along the way. Some mushers scrounge as they go, but this is risky and will cause digestive upsets for the dogs if they jump from dried salmon to Friskies® to beaver meat. Mailing through the post office offers a cheap, fairly reliable method of transporting nonperishables. Sacks of dry feed, bagged in burlap, can be mailed to yourself, general delivery, to post offices along the way. Mark the address tag "Hold for pick-up by —" and put the latest date that you expect to arrive. A letter to the postmaster at each place explaining the situation is good insurance. Be sure to mail everything well in advance. Remember, too, that few post offices are open on weekends. In very small northern villages, the post office may not be open every weekday. (Our own is open only one or two days a week.)

Perishables and frozen meats for dogs usually must be shipped by air freight (an expensive proposition) or, if your route is accessible by road, by a trucking transport company. A private pilot friend with an airplane might be thrilled to fly freight and even dogs into exotic places if you pay part of the expenses. While this is convenient, remember that winter weather can ground planes for days at a time; even feed flown on commercial flights can be delayed. (We once missed a food shipment when a blowing volcano stopped all flights!)

Gear

What to bring, and what to leave! These weighty decisions determine not only your comfort, but possibly the outcome of your trip.

Dog Gear
Well-fitting, well-padded harnesses are important when dogs are hauling a load for long distances. If you anticipate rough ice or abrasive snow conditions, send out plenty of dog booties. A lightweight cable picket line with drops for each dog offers a quick, simple method of picketing dogs in camp. Individual picket cables also come in handy.

If you feed frozen meat or dried fish, you can get by with just a couple of shared water pans. Otherwise, bring a metal three- to five-gallon bucket for cooking and lightweight, stackable feed pans.

Your sled must be adequate for carrying your load over the given terrain. Big or little, toboggan or basket sled, it must be sturdy, roomy enough for your gear, and comfortable to drive. A sled tarp or sled bag lines the basket to protect the load and keep gear from falling out. Lash it down securely with rope or bungee cords.

Camp Gear
Winter camping gear used by mushers is similar to that used by any outdoor winter camper. Some advice pertinent to mushers is mentioned here, but we strongly recommend that you seek out additional information from other winter-camping and survival books or from experienced winter campers if you are unfamiliar with techniques and available gear. New hi-tech gear is continually coming onto the market, and you may find some of the old materials and methods becoming outdated.

Some dog drivers prefer sleeping under the stars to sleeping in a tent. Tents are time-consuming to erect and break down, frost up if unheated, and add to that mountainous pile that you must fit into your sled. They do provide extra warmth, and, more importantly, protection from wind, which can be deadly in open country. Compact mountain tents that can be set up and broken down easily are a good choice.

A canvas wall tent heated with a small stove (usually wood-burning) is very comfortable by our primitive standards. (All dog-team travelers need primitive standards.) It also allows you to dry your gear more easily. But the added weight and bulk, and the necessity of erecting a frame, might make a wall tent more trouble than it is worth unless you intend a lengthy stay in one camp or expect harsh conditions.

Wall tents with a small wood stove offer a temperature-controlled environment much appreciated on cold or wet days; however, they require a large frame and a considerable amount of camp work to set up.

Wall tents do not perform well in moderate to high winds without modification to stabilize them.

A top-quality sleeping bag does more to keep you warm at night than anything this side of common sense. Although good down makes a lighter, more compact, and more durable sleeping bag than fiberfill, down takes longer to dry, causing problems when, with daily use, the bags become damp from frost, snow, and sweat. Good fiberfill bags provide warmth even when wet, and they dry quickly. However, the fibers break down with heavy use, and eventually the bags lose their loft.

Sleeping-bag liners and covers increase the warmth of any bag, and a bivvy-sack or good sled bag breaks the wind. Mattress pads (we prefer closed-cell foam pads) provide considerable warmth as well as increased comfort. Caribou hides make a warm, comfortable bed, but their bulk and tendency to shed make them less desirable; nor can they be found at the local five-and-dime store. When traveling light, your parka makes an acceptable pad.

In remote areas of Alaska and Canada, people often cut spruce boughs for mattresses. This requires extra camp work, and, of course, there must be spruce trees near camp. However, they provide a warm, springy bed that does not have to be packed from camp to camp. Dogs, too, learn to appreciate a warm, dry, spruce-bough bed. Although this is accepted practice in very remote areas, in more populated places this destructive practice is unlawful and will make you unpopular.

Many people carry a camp stove. The two-burner white-gas models have graced many a sled, but charcoal, wood, alcohol, and propane all have been used (see Chapter 3). In wooded areas, stoves might be considered a luxury, because campfires can do the same job.

No sled should be without a good trail ax. A saw is a handy addition; if you carry a wood-burning stove, the saw is a requisite. Snowshoes, too, must be carried unless your route is traveled heavily, and even then you may want them for working around camp. However, you might as well try skiing with your skis on backward as slap on a pair of snowshoes for the first time and expect to get anywhere. Practice *before* you need to depend on them! Even with experience, the rate of travel through very deep snow may be less than two miles per hour.

A headlamp can do everything that a flashlight can and more, and it makes night travel and evening camp work much easier and safer. Good maps, a compass, and the ability to use them have prevented many embarrassing moments and a few catastrophes, especially in unfamiliar or untracked country.

Trail Axes
Left to right: Standard single-bit ax. Lightweight metal ax with rubber grip —
less breakable than the ax with the wooden handle, but the blade is too slim
to split firewood easily. The hand ax is too small to be of any use at all —
avoid it. The hand saw is very useful if you will be counting on wood fires.

A good repair kit saved the day for us after that crash in Koyuk
(see Table 12-1). Extra snaps, lines, and a sewing kit for harness and
clothing repair come in handy on longer trips. A medical kit (for dogs
as well as for humans), along with a basic knowledge of first aid, is
essential. Do not waste money on those little packs made up for RV
campers who have a hospital around the next corner. Make your own,
and know what it contains and how to use everything in it (see Table
12-1). Most physicians and veterinarians willingly recommend and
prescribe medications when you explain the situation. (Leave out the
snakebite kit!)

This lightweight, home-made first aid kit has traveled more than 10,000 miles by dog team. It is small enough to fit into a handlebow bag and light enough to be unnoticed. Yet, it can handle emergencies from severe infections, to open bleeding gashes, to wet, cold feet.

Choose personal gear according to what you need, judging by past experience and by your ability to go three weeks without a change of clothes. Extra foot gear is essential, even if it is just a pair of well-insulated camp slippers to wear while your soaked boots are drying. A full change of clothes could save your life if you fall into deep water. Packing extra clothes in strong plastic bags keeps them dry even if your sled takes an unexpected dip in the hot springs. (If you do get wet, build a fire and dry off *before* you are too cold and stiff to collect firewood or strike a match.) Table 12-1 contains a list of suggested gear to carry on a sled trip.

Table 12-1
Gear for the Dog-Team Traveler

Required (by most people, anyway!)
Sled tarp or bag; rope or bungee lashings
Dog food
Dog food bucket/cook pot
6-dog cable picket
1-dog pickets, enough for additional dogs
Dog booties
People food (see Table 12-2)
Cooking set (minimum: one pot, a spoon, and a pocketknife with a
    can opener)
Matches
Sleeping bag rated to a minimum of -30 degrees F.
Ax
Headlamp and batteries
Snowshoes
Map and compass
Spare towline section; extra tugline, harness, and double neckline
Extra clothes, including spare socks and gloves
Extra foot gear
Overmitts
Personal gear, including sun lotion, hand cream, Chapstick®, and
    premoistened towelettes (as desired)
Sunglasses or goggles
Cash (lots)

First Aid and Emergency Kit
1 roll Kerlix® gauze
Waterproof first-aid tape
1 triangular bandage
1 roll 4-inch Vetrap ® stretch wrapping
1 Ace bandage
1 wire arm splint
1 tube antibiotic ointment
1 small bottle Betadine® scrub
Bandaids®
Assorted surgical pads
Butterfly closures
Thick cotton pad for heavy bleeding
Rectal thermometer and case
Suturing material and needle
Cotton balls
Heavy-duty nail clipper (for dogs)
Dental cap
Skin Bond®

Table 12-1 (Continued)
Gear for the Dog-Team Traveler

People Medication
  Buffered aspirin (also for dogs; see Chapter 6)
  Prescription wide-spectrum antibiotics and painkiller
  Throat lozenges and eye drops
  Kaopectate® anti-diarrheal tablets

Canine Medication
  Tranquilizing tablets
  Oral antibiotics prescribed by a veterinarian
  Nitrofurazone powder
  Opthalmic ointment
  Foot ointment
  Diapect® antidiarrheal tablets

Emergency Gear
  Penlight
  Space blanket
  Waterproof container of matches and tinder
  Hurricane matches and a candle
  Spare army can opener
  First-aid book

Repair Kit
  Pliers
  Nuts and bolts
  Screws and screwdriver
  String, cord, and duct tape
  Spare snaps
  Wire
  Sewing kit (dental floss for thread; needle; harness material; leather patch)

Additional, As Desired or Required By Circumstances
  Camp stove and fuel
  Sleeping pad and additional bedding
  Small saw
  Tent, with or without heating stove
  Caribou hides
  Lamp or flashlight with fuel/batteries
  Pistol or rifle
  Dog coats
  Whip
  More booties
  Ice creepers
  Thermos® bottle
  Books, cards, or other entertainment
  Soap, wash rag, shaving gear, toothbrushes and paste, other personal gear
  Vitamin-mineral supplement for dogs and for humans

Food in a Nutshell

Food can be the best or the worst part of your trip. You do not have to survive on beans and bannock, or on packets of freeze-dried food. Bear in mind that you will eat about twice as much during cold weather and when working hard (pedaling, running, or snowshoeing). Good nutrition plays a major role in your physical ability and sense of well-being. Most nutritionists lean toward a high-carbohydrate diet for athletes, but fats and proteins are also important for the musher working day after day in the cold.

Shipping is a problem with perishable or frozen foods. You may need to forego them, ship them specially, or, when possible, buy them en route. Some foods, like doughnuts and sweet rolls, become very hard when frozen and are best warmed before eating. Other foods, including nuts and dried fruits, can be eaten frozen. Peanut-butter sandwiches can be frozen; sandwiches containing mayonnaise cannot. Stopping for a long lunch break gives both dogs and musher a renewed lease on life but also eats into short daylight hours. Carry snacks for people and dogs to stave off hunger and to increase energy levels later in the day.

Water is a problem in subfreezing weather. Melting snow is the standard method of obtaining water. Natural sources, such as open creeks or overflow, can be used if you know that the water is safe. It may be polluted and may need to be boiled to prevent parasitic infections. Giardia (an intestinal parasite causing flu-like symptoms) can be present even in "pure" mountain streams or remote rivers. It can also affect dogs.

Drinking enough water is a real problem when you must melt snow over a campfire, but dehydration has the same weakening effects in humans as in dogs (see Chapter 6). Hold your nose and drink down that smoky water! Powdered drink or soup mixes help to cover the flavor, and some provide electrolytes that you may have lost during that sweat-popping stint on snowshoes. Carrying a thermos of water, juice, or cocoa allows you to drink during the day without stopping to build a fire. Beware of diuretic drinks like coffee or alcoholic beverages that actually are dehydrating.

Many camping and packing books contain extensive suggestions for camp food and cooking. Most do not take freezing into consideration, so use the information with caution. The *Alaskan Dog Mushers' Trail Food & Old Fashion Recipe Book* contains recipes for trail food, many provided by Iditarod contenders or their hard-working wives.

Mary Shields' book *Sled Dog Trails* also offers some good ideas on food and winter travel. Table 12-2 is a list of food suitable for trail use.

Dog Food

Nutrition is discussed more fully in Chapter 4, but remember that when you ask your dogs to travel day after day instead of just on weekends and occasional evenings, you must adjust their diet accordingly. A top-quality brand of dog food (such as Iams Eukanuba®), containing about 30 percent protein and 20 percent fat, should be adequate for most recreational trips. When feeding dry foods, you must provide water either separately or soaked in the food — or, preferably — both. High-fat foods absorb hot water much faster than cold water, plus this gives the dogs a warm meal before bedding down. On hard runs, feed in the morning and evening. A midday

Packaging the food shipment is a big job for a long trip. Take special care to have the right foodstuffs going to the correct places so that you don't end up with twice as much people food as you can use — and no dog food at all.

Table 12-2
Suggested Trail Foods

Bear in mind you wil eat approximately twice what you normally eat, and be sure to consider weight allowances and shipping requirements.

Breakfast:
Granola or other cold cereal
Instant hot cereal
Pancake mix
Bacon
Whole or skim powdered milk
Sausage
Freeze-dried breakfasts
Hash browns
Cocoa, coffee, or tea
Scrambled eggs, made from freeze-dried or powdered eggs and dried milk

Lunches:
Bread (homemade is best)
Sweet rolls
Sandwiches (with freezable ingredients)
Salmon strips
Jerky
Logan bread or other sweet breads
High-energy snack bars
Instant soup (also used as flavoring)
Bannock (trail bread)
Sandwich meats (freeze slices separately)
Unsalted crackers
Sardines (thaw before eating)
Peanut butter
Jelly or jam, in plastic containers

Snacks:
Cookies
Brownies
Dried and frozen fruits and berries
Gorp
Doughnuts
Candy
Nuts
Granola bars
Squaw candy (dried salmon)

Table 12-2 (Continued)
Suggested Trail Foods

Dinner: Proteins
  Small cans of meat or fish
  Small, flat patties of hamburger or bite-size pieces of frozen meat
  Cheese, milk
  Pemmican
  Jerky
  Dried or smoked fish
  Prepared frozen meats
  Freeze-dried food
  Dried vegetable protein
  Precooked one-pot meals, frozen in a thin layer, then broken into pieces
    and sealed in plastic for easy thawing
  Freezeable takeout restaurant food (chicken, pizza, etc.)

Dinner: Starches
  Instant potatoes
  Instant rice
  Noodles
  Macaroni
  Ramen noodles
  Bannock
  Bread
  Variety baking mix (bake shortcake or bannock slowly in a frying pan on the
    stove or on coals, or make pancakes)

Dinner: Additional
  Dried, freeze-dried, or frozen vegetables
  Instant or frozen cheesecakes and other desserts
  Instant pudding
  Extra snacks

Miscellaneous:
  Sugar, white and brown
  Drink mixes
  Powdered eggs
  Butter
  Crackers
  Flavorings (salt, pepper, soysauce, instant soups, dried onions, parsley,
    cinnamon, etc.)
  Marshmallows
  Popcorn
  Tomato crystals (for soup or flavoring)
  Raisins (for snacks, or add to oatmeal and other food)

Frozen meat chopped into half-pound chunks, makes a good snack when the dogs are taking a short break after a hot run.

snack of frozen meat gives the dogs a break, a shot of energy, and something cold to chew on when they are hot.

Melted tallow, oil, or suet added to dog food increases the fat and caloric content. Adding a little meat increases both palatability and protein content. Unfortunately, meat weighs a lot and creates shipping problems, and on warm days it can thaw and bleed in the sled. Keep it in plastic to avoid some of the mess.

On the long haul, when weight and bulk are at a premium, the diet needs rethinking. The old-time standby of pemmican cannot be found at the local feed store. What should you do? Highly concentrated dry feed may be the best solution. On his polar expeditions, Will Steger used a special formula developed by Hill's Pet Products® that kept his large huskies fit, even under extreme conditions, when fed only two pounds apiece per day. Some manufacturers (including Iams®, Purina®, and Kobuk®) produce food especially for the stress of long-distance sled-dog racing, with ratios of 35 percent protein and

30 percent or more fat. Be sure to get your dogs used to eating concentrated food before your trip, remembering that they will need less of it than regular dog food for maintenance.

Rice, tallow, dried fish, dried meat, and powdered eggs make an acceptable diet with a minimum of weight. (Rice does require extensive cooking.) Rice and tallow are both compact; they may be heavy, but a little goes a long way — two cups of rice make three-quarters to one gallon of thick soup. You can also make pemmican by pounding or grinding jerky and mixing it with tallow.

Your dogs probably will eat roughly twice as much on the long trail

These hard-working dogs really appreciate a rest break and a snack of raw meat. In fifteen minutes they will be happy to see what's around the next bend of the Porcupine River on this cross-country trip.

as they do at home. Sometimes, during hard going or cold weather, they will eat even more. Not only are they working harder, but they have lost the security and warmth of a dog house at night and are stressed by strange places, new faces, and unusual challenges. Feeding a lot is a fact of trail life, and there is no getting around it. Once, while traveling at -30 degrees F., we fed nine seventy-five-pound dogs daily on thirty pounds of meat, twelve pounds of dog food, and three pounds of tallow — forty-five pounds in all. Remember — if you bring too much you can always make friends by giving it away.

Camping in the Cold

This subject is covered in other books, but a few points are worth noting.

Many people cannot bear the thought of winter camping, but the absence of bugs, bears, rain, snakes, summer tourists, and other nuisances makes it well worth the effort, and — honest! — you do not have to be cold. If you dress correctly and stay dry and well-fed, you should never get dangerously cold. (If you do, you are doing something wrong.) Also, a dog team allows you to travel much farther through the backwoods than you could on a hiking trip or even on horseback.

A good campsite must be sheltered from the wind if possible, and it should have a source of dry firewood. Make sure that there is room to picket your team; your dogs, sled, and camp must be well clear of the trail. Some people prefer to camp alone; therefore, do not assume that your company will be welcome by someone else's fire.

Camp early enough to get well set up. You will need to picket the dogs, check their feet, dry their harnesses, and perhaps give them beds of spruce boughs. If there are no trees for anchoring the picket, anchor one end to the side of your sled and the other with your snow hook, remembering that this is *not* a very secure arrangement. Firewood must be gathered and dog food cooked, as well as your own food. If you have a tent, you need to set it up. You also need to make sleeping arrangements, feed the dogs, eat, and dry off.

If you are too tired to make a nice camp and dry off, you will get cold, you will not sleep, and you will feel even more tired the next day. Getting dry is vital to your warmth and well-being. Drying clothes by a campfire presents quite a challenge, but if you fail to do this, you will be cold the next day. You can dry socks and other apparel on a string tied over one side of the fire, out of reach of wayward

If you are in country like this area in Denali National Park, start watching for camp sites early, and don't pass up a good one even if you hadn't planned on stopping yet. By midnight this spot could be in a raging wind storm.

flames. (If you burn your clothes, you will really be cold.) Socks and gloves have a real affinity for fire, and just because you might be wearing them at the time does not ensure them against "spontaneous" combustion.

Before retiring, gather enough dry firewood and tinder for a hot fire in the morning. Climbing out of a warm sleeping bag into a cold winter morning is thrill enough without adding the shock of staggering through the snow scrounging for dry wood. Frost-laden wood will burn well if it is split first.

People with some fat (especially women) have an advantage: once heated by the fire, that fat retains warmth. You can be your own bed warmer! Conversely, if you pop into bed still chilled, that fat will keep you cold.

Chemical or charcoal heat packs add a wonderful warmth inside a sleeping bag and can drive away considerable moisture and chill if they work properly. They are especially valuable when exhaustion prevents your body from efficiently producing heat. A dog snuggled up beside you adds heat, too, but he also drives moisture into your sleeping bag and leaves a mighty cold spot when he decides that he no longer cares for your company. Sleeping next to another person or sharing a double sleeping bag adds greatly to your warmth. Miki and I often share our dogsled; although narrow, it is long enough for us to squeeze in facing opposite directions.

Be prepared to camp out in any weather extreme that you might meet. Learn the all-time record highs and lows for the area. Cold-weather survival (or, ideally, cold weather *comfort*) is not difficult, but you must know what you are doing. *Warm* weather causes problems from damp clothing due to melting snow or rain. You might run into overflow, flooding creeks, punchy trails, or bare ground. Use your resources. Your sled tarp, for instance, can double as a lean-to roof for reflecting warmth and repelling rain, snow, or wind.

Shelter

Shelter cabins are available for public use in some areas. Treat these buildings with respect, whether they are financed by the government or privately maintained. For the next occupant, we always leave enough wood to start a good hot fire, and preferably we leave a pile to last the night. You might find dry standing trees or driftwood nearby, but sometimes no suitable wood can be found and you will be left to your own resources. Ask beforehand where shelter cabins are located and if wood is available. Do not use privately owned cabins, including trapping cabins and empty summer homes, unless you make advance arrangements with the owner.

Many northern villagers open their doors to winter travelers, but on no account should a musher expect or demand a place to stay. Bush hospitality will not last long if it is abused. Keep your dogs staked where they will bother no one, and, if possible, clean up after them. Do not close doors behind you by displaying rude or thoughtless behavior.

Even in remote areas of Alaska and Canada, villages often have a lodge or hotel, and sometimes a laundromat and a health clinic. Bank-

The Iditarod trail is heavily used during March, not just by the competing dog teams but by recreational travelers and snow machinists. Keeping it litter-free is a problem, even in remote areas like this spot near Rohn Roadhouse.

ing usually is done through major towns, so bring plenty of cash to cover incidental purchases. Do not count on credit cards, because many places are not set up to honor them. (We once had to pay about $600 in cash to fly our stranded team from Old Crow, Yukon Territories, to the Dempster Highway when a 200-mile stretch of "trail" proved impassable.)

Camping Ethics

Treat the land with respect, no matter how remote it is. Handle litter economically; if it burns, burn it; if not, pack it out. Some fire precautions apply even in the winter, especially in areas of deep moss where coals from your fire can ignite the underlying peat, causing it to smolder indefinitely. Do not cut live trees or boughs in places frequented by other people, and leave each campsite as you found it.

Respect the rights of others. You may meet snow machiners, skiers, hikers, horseback riders, or other mushers, all of whom have as much right to the trail and shelter cabins as you do. Keep your dogs under control. Respect private property, private trails, historical sites, traplines, and shelter cabins.

This lecture should not be necessary, but unfortunately, we have all too often seen the consequences of travelers who brush off good ethics and ignore basic trail rules.

Some long-distance racers abuse trails because of haste and fatigue. After the Iditarod race, the trail is one long dotted line of thrown and discarded booties. Miki and I have picked up sacks full of booties after the racers had passed through, and our bounty has also included an expensive travel alarm clock, dog harnesses, thirty pounds of discarded meat, a spoon, a leash, bungee cords, a leather punch, a socket wrench, a yellow funnel, a pair of long johns that did not fit, and a fancy cigarette lighter that we used for starting fires. One night I accidentally cremated a glove in the fire — a lefty — and early the next day I replaced it with a brand-new lefty that was thrown down beside the trail.

But booties are the biggest item; we averaged one good bootie per mile, without stopping for those that we missed after one running grab. If we had picked up every bootie we saw and sold them for twenty-five cents each, we would have just about paid for our trip!

CHAPTER 13

THE EXHILARATION: SPRINT RACING

Most sprint races are from three to twenty miles long, but the shorter middle-distance races of thirty to sixty miles are run much like sprint races. Sprint races are held across the nation and also in Canada and Europe. European races are very popular, and often the entire race course is lined with spectators. In Alaska, sprint races tend to be longer with bigger purses, and the teams are larger than in most other areas.

On a good trail, competitive teams average close to twenty miles per hour, with top speeds approaching thirty miles per hour. Unlike greyhound races, where the dogs run very short distances, sprint races can last more than an hour, with the dogs running wide open the full distance. This requires considerable stamina and mental toughness. Although sprint dogs are highly specialized dogs, they also can be trained to run in distance races. They have competed in the Iditarod and in longer middle-distance races. In 1990, a sprint team won the 600-mile Alpirod, which is a series of half-day and day-long races.

The competitiveness in sprint racing has reached the point where a couple of seconds lost on the trail can cost several places at the finish. The speed is fast, the competition fierce, and strategies vital, making the top races a thrill for spectators and racers alike. Because the speed of top teams has become more consistent, the winner often is the musher with the best judgment and strategy.

The Dogs

Before considering conformation in a sprint dog, you must consider

Roxy Wright-Champaine spends a lot of time with her top-notch dogs. A sprint racer rarely cares what his or her dogs look like as long as they have speed and are gaited to match their team.

speed, endurance, and attitude. Sprint dogs *must* be fast and tough-minded enough to run the razor edge between peak speed and exhaustion. In Alaska, Canada, and the Lower 48, sprint dogs are primarily Alaskan huskies or mixed huskies. In the Lower 48, hounds, hound crosses, and purebreds also are popular. In Europe, many races require the entrants to be purebreds, but Alaskan huskies are growing in popularity there also.

Sprint dogs are athletic and have a light build, good feet, a deep, fairly narrow chest, legs that are long but not disproportionately so, a slightly arched loin with a steeper croup than trotting dogs, and a springy back for good extension. Dogs with a short coupling (short back) have less speed and often bob inefficiently. Few sprinters weigh more than fifty or less than thirty pounds, and most average forty to forty-five pounds. The dogs must have a smooth, easy lope with no bobbing or jerking. Ideally, all of the dogs in a team will have the same or very similar gaits.

Some sprint racers prefer all-male or all-female teams, while others do not care. It is easier to keep the sizes more consistent when running dogs of just one sex. Females have finer bones, mature quickly, and might be faster, but they also have reproductive cycles. A bitch in season can cause real problems in a poorly trained team. Females also are drained by heat cycles and pregnancy.

Few racers will sell their best dogs, but if you want to run limited-class races, you might buy a few top-speed dogs that do not have the endurance for longer races. You also might find some heavier dogs with less speed but enough power to carry you through races limited to three or five dogs. These dogs can be valuable in middle-distance races or in offbeat races like triathalon events, which have one heat each of sprint, middle-distance, and freight races. To build a top-notch sprint team, you often must breed your own, pay top dollar for outstanding dogs, or buy young, untrained dogs from top mushers.

Do not race dogs less than one year of age. One- and two-year-olds often are fast, but they lack the endurance and mental toughness of older dogs, and their lack of experience can hurt them and disrupt the team. Young adults do benefit from attending small races where they learn the rules without being stressed. Sprint dogs perform best between three and seven years of age. Many are then retired for breeding, training pups, or running slower races, such as middle-distance and limited-class races.

Training and Conditioning

Once you have a team of the best dogs in the territory, you must train them to win. A team is only as good as its driver. The fastest team in the world cannot win if an undisciplined leader takes a wrong turn.

Fall Training

Some sprint racers train their dogs throughout the summer, but for most, serious training begins in September or October. A number of northern mushers do not start training until after snowfall.

Start the dogs slowly, and concentrate on building endurance and discipline, not speed (see Table 13-1). Do not ask for an all-out effort for at least two months. The dogs are soft, and on the rough autumn ground, injuries are all too likely to occur; and avoiding injuries is a top priority. Running the dogs too hard or too fast depletes oxygen

Table 13-1
Suggested Training Regime (Sprint)

Month	Mileage	Runs Per Week	Goals/Notes
August	2 to 4 (Cart)	2 to 3	Tone muscles
September	2 to 4 (Cart)	3 to 4	Tone muscles; discipline Speed unimportant; avoid injuries
October	2 to 4 (Cart) Or, 4 to 6 (Sled)	3 to 4	Build endurance; discipline
November	4 to 10 (Sled) Fewer on cart More if goal is a longer race	3 to 5	Build endurance; discipline
December	10 to 12 Occasionally 15 or 50 to 80 percent of race distance	2 to 5	Build speed; vary lengths of runs Avoid injuries; ask for top speeds
January - March	4 to 6	Once midweek if racing on weekends	Build attitude; race weekends Avoid injuries

Aim for 250 to 450 miles in training, depending upon conditions, your schedule, your dogs, race dates, and the length and number of races that you plan to enter. Frequency and mileages of runs should be cut in severe weather and on rough trails. If you plan to enter two- or three-day events, train your dogs two and three days in a row before giving a day or two off. If you enter shorter races, train one day out of three, and run them wide open (at top speed) the full distance.

in their muscles and causes waste products to build up, resulting in sore, stiff muscles (sometimes called "stove up").

If you have an ATV or a car chassis, you can run eight or more dogs, but if you have a cart, do not run more than six — or no more than you can control reliably. A very general rule of thumb is to have 100 miles of cart training before snowfall and 200 miles more with a sled before the first race.

Winter Training

When you start with a sled, bring only six or eight dogs until they are better trained and the trails have more snow. You want them to work hard, and you want control. Use a slightly heavier sled or toboggan, carry a load, or drag a snow machine track to toughen the dogs.

Experienced dogs know to run, but younger ones must be conditioned to run — to actually feel uncomfortable trotting. Do this by starting on short runs so that the dogs do not become too winded to stop loping. If they do slow down, stop and rest them. No healthy sprint dog that is kept confined will go out at a trot. Encourage and prolong this attitude, and you can condition your dogs to run all the time. If you must drive them to get any speed, you could be running them too often, too fast, or too far. *Less* hard driving will produce better results in the long run.

You can let your dogs trot occasionally early in the season. They can regain their wind without having to stop, and it helps to get them in shape. As the dogs get into condition toward late November, they should be able to lope six or eight miles or more, depending upon your training regime. In late November and early December, push the dogs harder. Start demanding speed and obedience. Work out disciplinary problems, and weed out poor dogs. Champion musher Charlie Champaine of Salcha, Alaska, takes his dogs into hill country in early December for two or three weeks of intensive training. He takes a big team and brings a handler to help work on his problem dogs. With two people he has more control, and he can easily stop the team on uphill grades. He teaches the dogs not to mess around, to respond to voice commands, and to lope up hills. Dogs that do not respond to the training are culled.

In December, ask for increasingly more speed. Your dogs must learn to hit a top speed, or driving speed, on command. Ask for this speed only when the dogs are ready for it, and only as trail conditions allow, to encourage them to give their full effort. Bring more dogs for better speed and to teach them to work in a bigger team. Specifics on speed control are presented in Chapter 11. If possible, run your dogs on trails that you have measured for distance, and time the runs so that you can accurately judge your team's improvement. (This also is useful for comparing with race times so that you can see where your team fits in with competitors.) Try to develop a sense of speed — it will allow you to judge how fast you are going and will help you in a race.

In his book *The Speed Mushing Manual,* Jim Welch describes a technique for encouraging a fast finish. Stop the dogs near the end of each training run — perhaps one-quarter mile from home — and give them a good rest. Drive them hard going in, and as soon as you reach the dog yard or your truck, give them a good reward, such as a snack. As they learn the routine, give them shorter rests, farther from the end, until you do not have to stop at all.

Toward the end of December, your dogs will be conditioned and trained, but you have been asking a lot of them and they will be tired and perhaps burned out. They will have no enthusiasm, especially if they are overtrained. (These dogs also might be muscle-bound, with a heavy chest and hindquarters. This results in a shortened, tight stride that makes them too heavy to run fast.) In the last week of December (earlier if you are racing early in the season), and especially in January, pay close attention to your team's attitude. The desire to go, and to go fast, plays a critical part in racing. Once your team is in top physical condition, concentrate on attitude instead. Rest the dogs, then take them out on short "fun runs." Do not discipline them anymore. Peaking the team like this is discussed in Chapter 11. If you time this correctly, your team's attitude will come back before physical ability is lost, and both mental and physical ability will peak during the "big race."

Rhythm

As the season progresses, a rhythm, or synchrony, should evolve in your team. Although rhythm can be seen in a matched trotting team, it is particularly important to the sprint racer. Especially in a loping team, rhythm will add efficiency and smoothness and, therefore, speed.

When the dogs run in synchrony, they all move together, and no individual stands out by doing something differently. The heads all come up, and then the rumps, and each dog lands in the tracks of the dog before him. The pace is smooth, and the towline is straight and tight. If the dogs are not running in rhythm, they might be

Dogs must take a sharp turn on the correct leading leg or they may stumble. Young dogs must learn this, and if they stumble in a fast team they may be dragged mercilessly. George Attla in the 1986 North American. *Courtesy* Fairbanks Daily News-Miner.

throwing up their tails for balance, with their hind feet flying around more. They might bump into each other, lean outward, lose their balance, break stride, slow down, or even gear down to a trot for a moment. The towline will have big swags in it.

Practice spotting rhythm in your dogs and in other teams. You can see it more easily from the side of the team than from the runners in back. Have photographs or even videos taken of your team, and study them to identify problem dogs that might be breaking the rhythm. You can broaden your expertise by taping televised dog races on videocassettes and studying other teams in action. (This also is a good way to analyze your opponents.)

Linda Leonard's leaders are running in good rhythm and are leading with the opposite legs. *Courtesy* Fairbanks Daily News-Miner.

You cannot teach your dogs to run in rhythm, but you *can* encourage them to pick it up. Dogs learn rhythm from experienced teammates, but you can encourage rhythm by keeping your dogs uniform in size, build, and gaits, and by pairing dogs in the best possible arrangement. Run them on smooth trails, avoid long runs that fatigue them, and avoid souring them.

You will *discourage* rhythm if you cannot control your sled or if the sled does not track nicely. If the towline snaps the wheel dogs off stride, they might jerk the others off. The seconds that it will take to recover are seconds lost forever. Losing your balance on a corner, pedaling jerkily, or running unevenly also will throw the dogs off. If you add a dog that is not gaited properly, or one that sometimes drops to a trot, he will distract the other dogs. If your towline is short and cramped, a pair of dogs cannot stretch out and land where the forward dogs took off.

A conditioned team can speed up or slow down without losing rhythm. These dogs also learn to rhythmically switch leads on a corner. However, if you have not conditioned them enough, they might not catch the switch on cue; the resulting stumble can unbalance the whole team.

Dogs on the same stride (especially as compared to each one's partner), a towline that is tight, tails down, every foot landing in its proper place — are signs of a team in good rhythm. Here, John Heater's leaders are running in rhythm with the same leading leg. *Courtesy* Fairbanks Daily News-Miner.

Training for Races

You cannot simply train for racing; you must train for specific races. Even if you race every weekend, gear your team to excel in the one race that you most want to win. That is, if your main goal is a long two-day event, run your dogs two or three days in a row over more miles, even though shorter miles will give better performance on weekend meets. Because most races start early in the afternoon, some drivers suggest training dogs at this time.

Dogs that are conditioned on short runs do better on short races that demand an all-out effort. Often, these teams are trained only every third day to keep them spirited. Longer races require more stamina and conservation of energy; therefore, these dogs are trained on longer trails. Dogs that run three-day events are run three days in a row during training. They must have the endurance to bounce back overnight, and you must handle them carefully or they will be appalled to see those harnesses come out on the third day of a tough race. You must be able to draw on their psychological stamina. At some point in training, give this team a test to be sure that all of the dogs are capable of a hard three-day event. Run them twenty-five miles for three or four days in a row. If a dog comes in at a trot, or goes lame or goofs up, consider leaving him home.

Larger kennels keep two teams going — the core team of hardened veterans and a "second string" of younger dogs that run fewer, shorter races. No matter which race you enter, prepare your dogs for the pure drama of it. Review the section titled "Obstacle Training" in Chapter 11. Do not let the dogs get too accustomed to groomed trails or they will have trouble handling the tremendous variety of conditions encountered on the race circuit. Accustom them to the truck and to sleeping in the vehicle at strange places. Have strangers handle the dogs so that race officials and handlers will not alarm the team. These lessons are especially important for inexperienced dogs.

Even if you plan to compete seriously in only one or two major events, the dogs will perform better if you enter them in some smaller races as well. They will understand what's going on and will be less likely to balk, bolt, or rebel.

Before the Race

When you truck the dogs a long distance to a race, consider arriving a day or two early to let the dogs rest. If you are entering a major

A dog team must not only be trained to go fast, but trained to win. This means training them to take commands, ignore distractions such as these people, and drive hard to the finish. Marvin Kokrine in the 1980 Open North American. *Courtesy* Fairbanks Daily News-Miner.

event in a different climate, you might want to spend three weeks in that area to allow the dogs to acclimate to the weather. However, the new environment is very stressful, especially for unseasoned dogs, and some mushers prefer to arrive immediately before the race to avoid wearing out the dogs beforehand. Dogs that live in their truck boxes are less stressed than those that are staked in a strange place.

The Sled

Your race sled must be small, light, flexible, and easy to steer. The way in which it handles is as critical as its weight. A sled that is hard to control can throw the dogs off stride, can cause trouble on the curves, or, worse yet, can "crash and burn" along the course. In a limited-class race like the six-dog class, weight becomes more critical, and you need the lightest sled possible.

The sled should be shod with a plastic appropriate to the trail conditions; this usually means using P-Tex or XH plastic. Many racers use the Quick-Change Runner System so that they can put on fresh plastic before important races. Hot-waxing the plastic before a race also reduces friction. All of this is covered in Chapter 3. If your choice and handling of runner plastic gains you just one-quarter second per mile, you might improve your placing.

The gear that you carry in your sled during a race depends upon the race and your own needs. However, it usually includes required items like a dog bag and any promotional material that you are given. Also, it may include an extra neckline or two, a tugline, a sharp knife, perhaps an extra snow hook, booties, a stopwatch, an AM/FM radio to monitor the race, and some candy or fruit for a longer race.

The Dogs

You can give your dogs a small, high-powered snack a few hours before the race. Also give them a cup of water per dog three hours before the race, or one-half cup two hours before the race. (Avoid electrolytes before a race.) Extra water helps to prevent mild dehydration, which can seriously affect performance. It also helps to stop "dippers" from grabbing snow during the run. A squirt of water in each dog's mouth right at hookup might stop dippers, too. Some mushers think that lemon juice squirted on the dog's tongue prevents dipping; others disagree.

Some racers give their dogs suppositories to clean out the bowels; others let their dogs run loose for a few minutes in the morning before a race. Dogs that simply refuse to "poop on the fly" benefit most from the use of suppositories.

Dogs heading into a tough event should be a little fatter than those running short, one-day races.

Conditions

Check local weather forecasts and consider snow, temperature, and trail conditions when deciding which dogs to run and what gear to take. If possible, run over the racetrack with a dog team or snow machine, or check out areas visible from the road, especially if you are not familiar with the track. Race conditions affect your strategy, and the more research you do, the better you can plan your race. If you plan to monitor the race on a radio as you run, find out which station is broadcasting the event.

Strategy

The more thought you put into your strategy, the more effective the strategy will be. Consider every possible variable — dogs, weather, other mushers, equipment, and track layout — and jockey what you can control to complement your team. Having a game plan will give you more confidence and will make the race go smoothly; it also will give you a straw to grab when things go wrong. The broader your thoughts, the more good ideas you will have. During one major race, George Attla was contending strongly with several other closely matched competitors who were following his every move on the radio so that he wouldn't get a lead on them. George made his move in a long stretch of trail that had no radio reporters alongside it; by the time the radio silence was broken, he had first place sealed up. *That* is strategy! Do *you* know where the reporters are situated along the trail? Find out!

You must decide which dogs to leave home; how many to bring; which ones to run in lead, swing, and wheel; and the kind and amount of food and water to give them. Decide which mushers you want to trail, which ones you want to pass, and which ones you need to stay ahead of. Do you want to drive hard throughout the race, or do you want to let the dogs just cruise midway before pushing for a fast finish? Or would you prefer to let them run their own race? Many of the decisions will depend upon current conditions, your competitors, your dogs, and your starting position.

Old-time Canadian musher Emile Martel is credited with first saying that races are run by the dogs left behind. Your team is only as fast as the slowest dog. Leave that dog behind, and the team is as fast as the next slowest. If you take a dog that habitually messes up or burns up or freaks out or dips snow or that refuses to pass or to cross ice or to poop on the fly, then you are taking a liability that could cost you the race.

On any given day, you might leave a fine dog at home because he did not feel good last time, or maybe he looks stiff today. Although females in season are allowed on most racetracks, if you have trouble with them, you should leave them home. Other dogs cannot tolerate a fast run in hot weather and should not race on warm days. On a very cold or hot day, you might switch to a more suitable sled plastic, bring different dogs, or run the dogs in different positions. If the snow is especially sharp and icy, watch your dogs' feet. Sprint racers are reluctant to use booties in a fast race, and top mushers have been

With years of racing behind her, Roxy Wright-Champaine has the skill she needs to handle eighteen dogs in a race. If you have never run more than twelve dogs, don't show up on race day expecting to run eighteen. You'll be sorry, and so will your competitors. *Courtesy* Fairbanks Daily News-Miner.

known to scratch from a major race rather than risk damaging their dogs' feet on bad trails.

The number of dogs that you run in an open (unlimited) competition depends upon how many you can handle and upon the expected trail conditions. Many novices make the mistake of bringing too many dogs, causing problems not only for themselves, but for their competitors as well. Every additional dog is one more piece of potential trouble. Anyway, it is preferable not to bring extra dogs that are slower than your core team unless the race is very long. If the course is complicated or poorly marked, fewer dogs are easier to stop and turn. Your team is shorter, allowing you to look ahead of it for trail markers and hazards. If the course is extremely rough or icy, fewer dogs give you more control, and you will risk fewer injuries.

On the other hand, a soft course with fresh snow or slush requires extra dog power. During a long, tough race, your slower dogs can take over the load as the speedy ones get winded. On a three-day event, you want to start with a few extra dogs in case you must drop some by the third day. (These races do not allow dogs to be added after the first day; they may only be dropped.)

Training leaders is covered in Chapter 11. If you are lucky, you will have three or four leaders in your team. On a three-day race, use hotshot leaders the first couple of days, and strong, reliable leaders the last day if possible. Rotating leaders after each heat helps to avoid burnout. Spare leaders can save the day if the front end fails. One bush musher borrowed a trapline dog to lead his team in a race that followed the dog's home trails. The dog stopped the team at every trap along the way, expecting the driver to step over and check the trap. An extra leader in the team might have saved this musher the last-place red lantern.

Some mushers might try to psych you out before a race. By challenging or irritating you, or by confiding a "secret strategy" that they do not intend to follow, they hope to shake your confidence and cripple your judgment. These mushers study their competitors and know how to play on them. Be wary of racers who try this; just laugh them off.

A rookie starting near the front of the pack may be passed by several mushers, while a top contender can expect to overtake a few teams. If you anticipate a pass and plan for it with the other musher before the race, the maneuver will go more smoothly on the course and will save time for both of you, no matter which team is faster. Some mushers find it uncomfortable to approach their compatriots, either

The race start is your last chance to go over your race strategy and study the contenders. For the novice, attending races is a good way to pick up tips and to study the different gear and techniques used by the top competitors. *Courtesy* Fairbanks Daily News-Miner.

from pride or modesty, but if it is done courteously, there should be no call for animosity.

While hooking up your dogs, place a handler behind the leaders to absorb the shocks of the lurching team. This helps especially on the last heat of a three-day race when the tired leaders tune in to any reluctant dogs behind them. Also, try to have a handler hold any females in heat. Maybe tension will shorten your temper, but restrain yourself if the handlers have trouble following your instructions in the noise and excitement. Do not let the dogs sense any fear from you. They will go out more smoothly if you are calm and in control,

Anything can happen at a race start, and a mass start like this one in Nome, Alaska, can get explosive real fast. The 1986 Salmon Lake Derby.

so do not get upset or overly excited. Dogs pick up even subtle hints, like a trembling hand or a shaky voice — so play it cool and relax.

When you leave the chute, drag your feet enough to keep the dogs strung out. In the noise, your leaders might not hear your commands; therefore, keep that pressure on the towline until you are safely away. (On the racetrack, avoid using the sled brake if possible to prevent tearing up the carefully groomed trails.) Do not discipline your dogs in a race. All that should be behind you. A bit of slacking can be tolerated. If you are too harsh, you will just bum out the dogs, and they won't run on excitement anymore.

Linda Leonard keeps driving her dogs despite the tangle in her team. When races are won by fractions of a second, it is usually better to let minor problems slide rather than stop the team and fix them. *Courtesy* Fairbanks Daily News-Miner.

Once on the trail, you may need to vary your strategy slightly. However, the closer you stick to it, the more effective your game plan will be. Watch other competitors and their teams. If a team overtakes and passes you but is showing signs of exhaustion, perhaps you can stay with it and pass it again later. If a team flies by forcefully, do not burn up your dogs trying to stay with it. Remember, though, that the musher might be one of those who drives too hard at the start, burning up the dogs before the finish. If you know that, be prepared to pass that team later. (Some mushers save their dogs for a hard drive at the finish, while others let their dogs run at their own speed the entire way. Get to know these mushers, and plan to take advantage of their running styles.)

If your team is strong, pass the slower teams early. If a faster team catches you and your dogs are not too tired, you might be able to "ride" that team to the finish by letting it set your own team's pace. Do not try to pass the team; the musher will drive your team into the ground. Stay behind, and let your dogs chase it — that way *you* will be doing the driving. (Always follow race rules, and use courtesy in passing. This is discussed in Chapter 10.)

If you carry a light radio with headphones, you can keep track of other racers. Do not let the news scare you into driving too hard or losing sight of your plan. A stopwatch, too, can help you pace the team, especially if you practice with it during training.

If your dogs are flagging toward the end, be cautious in asking for extra speed. Do not force them to pass another team if they are saving energy by following it. Do not push the sled forward so hard that the dogs bunch up; keep them strung out as they cross the finish. Dogs that come in tail-wagging and ready for more could have been pushed harder in the race. Most come in ready for a break; however, if they are not on their feet again in an hour or so, you have pushed them too hard. File away your experiences and observations and apply them to future races.

Take the dogs on a light run a day or two after the race to check for any lingering lameness incurred in the race. If the dogs are racing every weekend, it is the only run that they need during the week.

The Media

The more you win, the more you must deal with the press. For some mushers this is an ego trip, but for the more retiring or shy ones, it can be excruciating. However, good media coverage sparks interest among spectators and race sponsors and ultimately affects the success of the races. Sprint races in particular are subjected to constant coverage, and it behooves racers to cooperate with reporters even during the frenzied starts. Keep your comments succint, understandable, and positive to best benefit the sport — and your own reputation.

Shorter Middle-Distance Races

Middle-distance races fall into two fairly distinct categories — those less than about sixty miles in length, where the dogs lope virtually the entire distance, and those of eighty or more miles that require a more conservative pace, rest breaks, snacks, and extra trail gear. We will discuss the shorter, sprinting races here and the longer ones in the next chapter.

Shorter middle-distance races, which are usually thirty to sixty miles long, are run very similarly to sprint races; therefore, we do not need to add many details. The dogs lope most of the way and rarely stop. Snacking the dogs on the trail takes too much time because of the fast pace. Avoid snacking unless more than seven or eight hours will be required to run the trail.

These race dogs require more mileage and conditioning (see Table 13-2). Avoid excessively long runs, except for an occasional fifty-miler to toughen the dogs and to weed out weak ones. Quieter dogs perform better on these races because they do not wear themselves out at the start. Dogs too old for sprint racing often make good middle-distance dogs. They have years of conditioning, and while they have lost that keen edge of speed, they have the endurance to lope for miles. Jane Cosgrove of North Pole, Alaska, is a successful sprint racer, and her husband Bruce puts her older dogs into his team for mid-distance races.

Pacing and speed control are vital so that the dogs do not exhaust themselves. If you let a spirited team run wide open, the dogs will not reach the finish line. Plan your race carefully, taking into consideration the terrain (dogs can cruise and rest on downhills). If a team starts too fast, it might burn out; you can keep the dogs going better if you stop and let them catch their breath when they get winded.

These races usually are run with race sleds or with slightly larger basket sleds, and only rarely with toboggans. Required gear usually includes booties. Anticipate dehydration, especially if the weather is extra hot or cold or windy, and take steps to prevent it. Watch also

Table 13-2
Suggested Training Regime (Shorter Mid-Distance Races)

Month	Mileage	Runs Per Week	Goals/Notes
August	2 to 4 (Cart)	2 to 4	Tone muscles
September	2 to 5 (Cart)	3 to 4	Tone muscles, discipline; avoid injuries
October	2 to 6 (Cart) Up to 15 on sled	3 to 4	Endurance, discipline Trot or easy lope
November	15 to 30 (Sled) Fewer on cart	2 to 5	Encourage loping Build endurance, discipline
December	30 to 40 (or 50 to 80 percent of race distance)	2 to 4	Build speed, endurance, discipline Add 1 or 2 50-mile runs to cull weak dogs, or 3 40-milers back-to-back. Vary length of runs; avoid injuries
January - March	Short runs between races	2 to 3	Cut mileages 3 or 4 weeks before heavy racing. Watch for burnout if on a heavy schedule. Avoid injuries.

Total mileage depends on the length of the races that you will enter but probably will not exceed 1,000 miles. This basic regime must be adapted to your situation, taking into account training conditions, your dogs and your schedule, race starting dates, and race lengths.

The middle-distance teams should be quierter and should conserve energy more than the sprint-race team, but the dogs should still be able to lope for most of fifty miles. Charlie Boulding on the Tour de Minto near Fairbanks, Alaska. *Courtesy* Fairbanks Daily News-Miner.

for overheating if the trail is long and hot. In cold weather, have a little extra weight on your dogs if the race is long.

After the race, check each dog carefully for dehydration, weight loss, sore feet, and harness sores. Give them a little water, but not too much until they have cooled off. If the weather is hot, let them cool off awhile before loading them into the truck. Except for these differences, the shorter mid-distance races are run much like sprint races, with similar strategies and equipment.

A number of good books have been written on sprint racing that describe different training methods and strategies. We have listed a few in the references at the back of the book.

CHAPTER 14

THE CHALLENGE: LONG-DISTANCE RACING

Long-distance racing is the most demanding mushing sport; a full year often is invested in just one race. Although the future holds promise for additional events, currently only two major long-distance races are held each year: the 1,100-mile Iditarod from Anchorage to Nome, Alaska, and the 1,000-mile Yukon Quest from Whitehorse, Yukon Territory, to Fairbanks, Alaska.

Several shorter races also can fit into the distance category, including the John Beargrease 500-mile race in Minnesota and the Montana 500. Much of this information also will apply to 100- and 200-mile middle-distance races.

Being a relatively new sport, long-distance racing is still evolving. We have much to learn, including details about optimal nutrition and foot care.

You should have at least two or three years of serious mushing behind you before entering one of these races. You will need every bit of experience and knowledge that you have gained, and the information in the chapters on psychology, nutrition, health care, foot care, breeding, team training, and camping is needed.

Which race you enter depends primarily upon your dogs and upon the type of training that you can do. The Yukon Quest demands tough, strong, durable dogs capable not only of going the distance but of pulling a sizable load. The Iditarod, with larger teams and shorter distances between checkpoints, requires dogs capable of somewhat more speed and able to cover more miles per day without breaking down. If your dogs do well on steep, hilly terrain, a race in the Rockies or the John Beargrease will be more suitable than a flat, fast race like the Kusko 300. The Alpirod, held in the Alps, actually consists of a series of one-day mid-distance races, demanding fast dogs that bounce back quickly. Some major middle- and long-distance races are listed in the appendix. Obtain a copy of the race rules the summer before so that you will be familiar with all of the requirements and with the trail distances and checkpoints. Major distance events usually require early entry — even months before the start. Most are held in mid- or late winter.

Do not consider a long-distance race unless you are financially prepared for a very expensive vacation. Ten thousand dollars is probably a minimum amount required to run the Iditarod, *not* including the initial purchase of top-quality dogs (see Table 14-1). Most mushers rely in part on sponsorships (see Chapter 11).

The Dogs

If you plan to start with sixteen dogs, you must maintain at least twenty so that you can drop a few in case of injury, illness, or other problems before the race. Most distance mushers maintain thirty or more. Some keep enough to run a second string.

The number of dogs that you run will depend upon the number of good dogs that you have available, upon the number of dogs that you can handle, and upon the race that you intend to enter. The Yukon Quest limits teams to twelve dogs. Most mushers in the Iditarod run sixteen to eighteen dogs, while some unlimited races have twenty- or twenty-two-dog teams.

Get your team together as early as possible, preferably by the time fall training begins, so that you can mold each dog and the team as a whole into what you need. You will know much more about the requirements of dogs that you have had for years than about a dog that you lease three weeks before the start of the race. Health issues, including parasite control and feeding a top-quality diet even when the dogs are at rest in the summer, should be of primary concern year-round. These dogs are world-class athletes. Teams have been getting faster and stronger due to excellent diet, improved health, and sound breeding programs. Instead of having two or three outstanding dogs, a top team might have ten or fourteen. Mushers often win the Iditarod in eleven days, yet keep their dogs in better condition than when it was won in fourteen days.

Look for dogs from stock that has been proven on long-distance races. (If you are a novice, try to run veteran dogs.) Sprint dogs often lack the fast trot and durable feet of dogs bred from generations of

Table 14-1
Yukon Quest Race Expenses

This list does not include additional expenses such as summer feeding, other training sleds and rigs, or the initial expense of buying or raising top-quality dogs. Figures provided by Jeff King, 1989 Yukon Quest winner. The Iditarod is somewhat more expensive.

Entry fee	$ 750
Food shipment	$ 250
Dog food, October through February	$4,000
Musher food for race	$ 350
Headlamp batteries for the season	$ 250
Vaccinations (20 x $10)	$ 200
Equipment: clothing, sled, towline, hardware, harnesses, maintenance, dog trailers	$1,000
Expense for truck and trailer, travel between checkpoints	$1,200
Veterinary expenses	$ 900
TOTAL	$8,925

Joe Runyan and Furlin, one of his main leaders who has been in many major long-distance races. Furlin is an Alaskan husky.

top distance dogs, but some of the better sprint dogs can do long distances if they are retrained to pace themselves at a trot. Avoid dogs that require extra care on the trail. Administering daily thyroid pills, booting up twice daily, or spending fifteen minutes coaxing a dog to eat can be more time-consuming and demanding than traveling with a slower dog that requires no special care. Weigh each dog's capabilities against his weaknesses and against your determination and ability to deal with them.

Three- to eight-year-old dogs in the forty- to sixty-pound range have proven best. The dogs should be matched in size and ability, and ideally, all should trot and lope at the same speed. They will work more efficiently if their gaits fall into rhythm. Distance dogs generally tend to have a flatter back and croup than sprint huskies, but the back should slope gently from withers to rump. Look for elbows that are close together and set well underneath the chest. Longer legs give a longer stride. A loping dog is more likely to burn out or to suffer injuries than a fast, smooth-trotting dog built for the job. As usual, though, dogs are judged by their capabilities rather than by appearance. They should be able to trot at least ten to twelve miles per hour for a sustained period of time.

Training

Training for these events is more time-consuming and physically demanding than training for shorter races, partly due to the sheer number of miles that you run. Details of training from nine months ago, or even from two years ago, come back to help or to haunt you.

Training starts at puppyhood, when you can ingrain good habits in your dogs. Make them good eaters by allowing them to eat their fill and then immediately removing the food. When pups compete over a small amount of food, they quickly learn to eat immediately and to leave nothing behind. This does *not* mean shorting them on food! (Unfortunately, this can encourage fighting in more aggressive pups.) Having eager eaters is a big advantage on longer races. Expose pups and young dogs to different surfaces (ice, water, rocks, grating), and have other people handle them.

A year-round training program for your athletes is vital. It takes months and years to develop a durable body. (This is why a veteran dog needs much less conditioning than a green dog that has never been physically stressed, regardless of age.) Light, occasional summer runs keep the dogs' condition from deteriorating. In September, start

Plan on doing a lot of long, lonely mushing before you even get into a long-distance race. Note that the dog in the wheel has a weak pastern that hyperextends when she brings her weight down, making it more susceptible to spraining.

running with a wheeled rig (see Chapter 11). Get the dogs conditioned and trained so that they will be ready for heavier workouts in November.

When the snow falls, hopefully by early November, switch to faster sled work. Increase mileage gradually from fifteen miles per run up to twenty-five miles (see Table 14-2).

Train the dogs to trot. Dragging a snow-machine track behind the sled, carrying a load, or going long distances keeps them from loping much, and they need to learn about pulling heavier loads anyway. Once you have a trotting team trained, new additions will learn quickly to travel at this pace. Train them to slow-trot, to fast-trot, and to lope on command so that you can speed up or slow down as needed during the race.

Table 14-2
Suggested Training Regime (Long-Distance)

Month	Mileage	Runs Per Week	Goals/Notes
August	3 to 4 (Cart)	2 to 3	Tone muscles
September	3 to 10 (Cart)	2 to 4	Tone muscles; discipline
October	5 to 10 (Cart) 10 to 15 (Sled)	3 to 5	Conditioning; discipline
November	15, working up to 20	3 to 5	Enforce response to commands. Train to trot by running with a load, then decrease weight to increase speed. Vary mileage.
December	20, working up to 50	4 to 5	Toughen but look for some speed. Vary mileage. Run with weight (50 to 100 pounds) in sled most of the time. Include some fast runs.
January	Run about 150 miles per week; vary mileage, up to 80 miles per day	3 to 5	Toughen; speed; attitude; no injuries
February	25 to 30, a few 50	3 to 4	Attitude; speed; no injuries or sore feet
Last 2 weeks before race	15 to 30	2 to 3	Attitude; no injuries or sore feet

Aim for 1,000 to 1,600 miles before the start of the race, depending upon your trail conditions and upon how early you start training. Vary all of these mileages to suit your training conditions, the size of your team, and the date of the race start. Run proportionally fewer miles for long mid-distance races (increase the mileage more slowly to lessen the chances of injury at higher speed); some loping is encouraged. Expose the dogs to training in severe weather, but cut mileage and the frequency of runs.

In December, increase distances again, aiming to develop physical and psychological endurance. Run them 80 to 150 miles per week, varying the distance to accommodate trail conditions and the response of the team. Aim for optimal, not maximum, mileage. If your dogs hide at hookup time, mess up repeatedly, or never lope, you are probably training too hard. Conversely, if they lope most of the time and are not controllable at the start, yet seem exhausted at the end of a long run, you have not put enough miles on them. The optimal distance varies from dog to dog, and veteran dogs can get by with much less mileage. When I ran the Yukon Quest, I leased a dog named Stevie in late January that had not been run all winter. In the month before the race, we ran him less than 300 miles, but he finished the race with flying colors. This dog had raced in the Iditarod, and he needed very little training to bring back his physical and mental abilities.

In December, you should run four or five days a week, including both back-to-back long runs and shorter runs to keep up the dogs' speed. Some dogs fall by the wayside — better now than during the race. Give them plenty of breaks during the longer runs so that they learn to rest at every opportunity. This also encourages speed.

Train under as many different conditions as possible, and expose the dogs to as many obstacles as you can (see Chapter 11). You are apt to run into a wide variety of conditions over a 1,000-mile race. In the Iditarod, for example, you may have heat (well, 45 degrees F. and rain) in Anchorage, cold in Sulatna (try -60 degrees F.), and sixty-mile-per-hour winds on the coast. Add a sled-eating canyon, killer climbs, a "glacier" of steep, glazed ice, a buffalo herd, and a passel of reporters at every stop. The more your dogs have seen, the less these obstacles will stress them. The same is true of yourself!

Distance dogs must be accustomed to eating and drinking in strange places and to being parked in harness for extended periods of time. They must learn to rest comfortably in the team, because they are rarely unharnessed during the race.

Drop injured dogs from training until they are fully recovered. Then give them a few extra days off (or even weeks if recovery was slow). An injury often seems completely healed, but when the dog is stressed, the injury reappears, sometimes even months after the original insult occurred. If your dog was in decent shape before his sick leave, it will be easier to tone him back up than to deal with a recurring injury. Some mushers believe that having strong, sound dogs is more important than having dogs with speed.

Running on trails used by other mushers exposes your dogs to

Your dogs must learn to relax in strange places and to rest comfortably anywhere, anytime, in harness, without chewing ropes or getting distracted.
This Iditarod team sprawls out at the checkpoint at Kaltag.

various diseases, including intestinal flu and kennel cough. This allows them to build immunities now, before they are stressed in the
race. If they do get sick, you can rest them.

Entering a middle-distance race toughens the dogs and prepares
them mentally for longer competitions. These races are especially
beneficial for young dogs who learn that they *can* keep going and that
they *will* reach the end of the trail. Mid-distance races also help you
to practice efficient feeding techniques and to speed trail chores. Cutting down on chore time is critical. You can test your dogs, your gear,

and your own abilities. Participating in one mid-distance race by early January generally helps, but more than that might take too much out of your team.

Cut back on training the month before the race. Emphasize attitude and health. Keep the dogs tough, but give them time off to heal over-used muscles, minor injuries, and sore feet. A couple of fifty-mile runs keep the dogs on their toes, but more long miles are apt to hurt their attitude and lead to a risk of injury too close to the start of the race. Late additions, or dogs dropped earlier for recovery, do need some long runs, but watch them closely for souring or other problems. Fatten up the dogs a bit so that they will go into the race with some reserves. Check out any signs of ill health well before the race.

The Food Shipment

The food shipment is critical to the outcome of your race. Send out much more than you think you will use (race dogs require three to four times their normal diet on a long race). Do everything possible to cut down on trail chores, from preparing meals to chopping up meat (see Table 14-3).

Pay particular attention to dog food. Diet is discussed in Chapter 4. Concentrated dry dog food offers a lightweight, relatively cheap, well-balanced diet. More precise formulas are now being produced, with promise of further improvement. Meat is much more palatable; debone and reduce it to small pieces before shipment. (You can chop frozen meat up with an ax, saw it with a band or Skill® saw, or have it slabbed commercially.) Include a high level of fat (up to 50 percent).

Do not drastically change the diet of your dogs. Feed them more, and be prepared with a variety of food for picky eaters. However, if you have not fed beaver during training, do not feed large amounts of it on the race. If your dogs are accustomed to several different kinds of food, you will be able to switch from one to another as needed with little affect on the dogs' digestive systems.

Beef, beaver, and lamb are favored meats. Beef by-products, turkey, chicken, horse meat, and frozen eggs are used to tantalize dogs with poor appetites. A little liver daily provides vitamins and minerals and stimulates the appetite. Frozen fish provides water in a trail snack or can be boiled into a soup. Soak all dry food to help prevent dehydration; you also can bait water with it to encourage drinking. Some mushers mix wheat germ oil, honey, ground liver, powdered egg, and dry dog food, making preformed, bite-size pieces for a quick,

Top mushers like Rick Swenson know the value of having everything in order for the food shipment — and being able to prepare inside! *Courtesy* Fairbanks Daily News-Miner.

tasty pick-me-up. It can contain a vitamin-mineral supplement, or this may be given in other food. Some mushers use electrolytes daily during the race (see Chapter 6), but this is probably not good policy.

Send out extra food to each checkpoint in case of delays or losses. This will also help you if the food shipment cannot get through. In the 1985 Iditarod, the race was officially stopped twice because planes could not make the deliveries due to weather. Consider the distances between checkpoints, the possibility of bad trails, and whether you might spend extra time at a checkpoint. In the Yukon Quest, you need food for that race's mandatory thirty-six-hour layover in Dawson

Table 14-3
Gear and Food Shipments

Carry in Sled:
Sled bag
Stove, fuel
Cook pot and pans for dogs
Cable picket (or have cable in your towline)
1-dog pickets (for dropped dogs)
Dog food
Food
Sleeping bag
Mattress pad (or use parka)
Snowshoes
Ax
Headlamp, batteries, extra bulbs
Penlight
Booties (at least 8 per dog)
Maps, compass
Promotional material (provided by race committee)
Overmitts
Raincoat or poncho
Spare clothes (minimal — one set of quilted long underwear [top and
    bottoms], extra socks, gloves, and footgear)
Thermos® bottle
Sunglasses or goggles
Extra collar, harness, double neckline, towline section
Fire starter (commercial)
Minimal cooking set for yourself
Cash (lots)
List of everything sent to each checkpoint; mileages between checkpoints
Personal gear, First-aid kit, Repair kit (See Table 12-1)
Optional: saw, plastic sled, dog coats, pistol or rifle if needed for protection
    (handguns not allowed in Canada)

Send to Every Checkpoint:
Dog food (lots — see following list)
Your food (about one day per 50 miles, to allow for delays — see Table 12-2)
1 to 3 pairs each socks and gloves
Straw (if you choose — trail committee will not transport for you)
Batteries (1 set per 50 miles)
Fuel for stove, if not provided
Booties (at least 4 per dog; more on long hauls or rough trails)
Surgical gloves (for applying foot ointment)
Matches

Table 14-3
Gear and Food Shipments

Send to Selected Checkpoints:
  Runner plastic
  Extra harnesses, lines, double necklines, collars
  Headlamp bulbs
  Personal gear (see Table 12-1)
  Additional first-aid gear and repair gear
  Fire starter (commercial)
  Extra headlamp
  Additional dog food (in case of delays; dry dog food is the cheapest and
    is an acceptable food if the dogs are staying in one place)
  Sled (you may want to change sleds en route, if allowed; you might break
    your first sled, or you may wish to switch to a smaller sled for the last
    200 to 300 miles of the race)
  * The farther apart the checkpoints are, the more supplies you must send
to each one.

Dog Food Shipment:
  Send out roughly 2,000 pounds of dog food for 16 to 18 dogs on a 1,000-mile
race. Send out proportionally less for a smaller team or for a shorter race;
send out more for a larger team. For exmple:
  300 pounds beaver (deboned; high-fat, highly palatable)
  300 pounds lamb (high-fat, palatable)
  300 pounds beef (lower in fat, use in warmer weather)
  200 pounds beef by-products (lower-quality protein, but highly palatable;
    it seems to soak up water better)
  100 pounds fish (whitefish preferred; high in water content, low in fat;
    good for warm weather)
  300 pounds highest-quality dry dog food, made for racing sled dogs
  60 pounds each chicken, horse, turkey, egg (less palatable food, but some-
    times good if the dogs need a change)
  150 pounds fat source (preferably balanced premix for sled dogs)
  100 pounds liver (use as daily treats)
  Appropriate vitamin and mineral supplements; bone meal
  Electrolytes if you plan to use them (carry at least a few)

  Know your dogs and what they like — humor them! You may choose a
diet based on dry dog food instead of meat; if so, be sure to send out an
additional fat source, and include some meat for picky eaters and for snacking.

City. Rohn Roadhouse on the Iditarod trail is really in the middle of nowhere, and no outside food or gear is available. At this point, your team will have just crossed the Alaska Range, and if the dogs are not holding together well, you might take this race's required twenty-four-hour layover here instead of farther down the trail. The better you know the race trail, the easier these decisions are to make.

Ship out a lot of your own food, too. Do not count on hospitality at checkpoints. Precooked meals save time, and you are more likely to eat food that does not require an hour to prepare. High-calorie snacks like cheesecake; frozen fruits (which can be thawed in your camp stove or in the hot water of your dog food if the package is sealed); and carry-out restaurant food (including pizza and chicken) are popular. Give yourself a variety of tempting foods, because stress and exhaustion can quell your appetite. (See also Table 12-2.) *Alaskan Dog Mushers Trail Food & Old Fashion Recipe Book* has many ideas provided by racers.

Unfortunately, frozen foods, including your frozen dog meat, may thaw. It is wise to pack everything in plastic. Clear bags allow easy viewing of the contents. The bags are then packed in burlap sacks (sometimes provided by the trail committee). Keep them to less than fifty pounds, and label each sack so that you know its contents. Carry a list during the race of everything shipped to each location.

Straw can be mailed to checkpoints, addressed to yourself in care of the Trail Committee. The committee usually will not ship it. The post office should accept it if you package half-bales in heavy garbage bags.

Race Gear

For the most part, you will use the same gear mentioned in Chapter 12. Your sled must be lightweight but adequate for the trail and terrain. Toboggans and modified toboggans are popular, but a few people prefer stanchion sleds, especially in areas of high wind. Five- to seven-foot models are typical for longer races. Send out extra runner plastic (QCR is popular), and change often to minimize drag. Some sleds sport a folding seat, allowing the driver to sit down on smooth sections of trail.

You can use a cooler to keep dog food warm. This allows you to feed your dogs as soon as you stop, when they are most likely to eat. Put frozen meat inside the cooler and cover it with hot water. It will thaw for the next feeding. If food stays hot for more than a couple

Sonny Linder's gear must be tried and true to see him through the Yukon Quest. It includes snowshoes, a cooler for meat, and a cooker. *Photo by Ron Lambert.*

of hours, dump in some snow to cool it and thus prevent fermentation. Rinsing the cooler and dog pans periodically in hot water will cut down on the likelihood of diarrhea occurring in your dogs from food poisoning.

Carry a high-quality, very warm fiberfill sleeping bag that will keep you warm even when you are too tired to dry off. A good sled bag that can be closed securely over you serves as a wind-break, because you will not carry a tent. Dog coats help to protect your dogs, especially those with shorter hair, from cold weather. Bring lightweight snowshoes, because you probably will not be using them much; however, they must be functional. An efficient stove for melting snow and cooking dog food is a must. Also, a dependable, strong headlamp is needed for night travel. Send two or three sets of batteries to each checkpoint, and be sure to carry a couple of replacement bulbs. Good lighting is so critical that some mushers carry two headlamps.

Carrying a heavyweight, extra-warm sleeping bag lets a weary musher crash down on the nearest available surface without worrying about the cold, even if that surface happens to be the roof of your truck's dog box. Kathy Wardlow on the 1987 Yukon Quest. *Courtesy* Fairbanks Daily News-Miner.

Additional gear is covered in Chapters 3 and 12, but keep your load to a minimum. The gear required by race rules varies from race to race and from year to year but typically includes a cold-weather sleeping bag, an ax, snowshoes, booties (usually eight per dog), maps, a compass, and promotional material. All required gear must be durable, of high quality, and well secured in the sled.

Before the Start

If the climate or terrain in your training area is dramatically different from that of the race, your dogs will benefit from a training period of a few weeks or even months in the race area. If you have been training on the Yukon at -30 degrees F., and in Minnesota it is 45 degrees F., your dogs will suffer. (Dogs raised and trained on Alaska's barren coasts have never seen trees and respond unpredictably when

Some distance race mushers use warm dog coats to conserve body heat at severe temperatures. Joe May on the Yukon Quest. *Photo by Ron Lambert.*

first confronted with these tall, unearthly beings.) This time period also allows them to rest if the trip from home has been very long and tiring. You may be able to find housing with another musher living there.

Otherwise, reaching the start just before the vet check (see below) allows less time for possible confusion, catastrophies, and stress from the strange place. Most mushers truck their dogs, and if the dogs are well accustomed to the routine, they live comfortably in their boxes while the mushers stay in hotels or at the homes of other mushers. The Trail Committee makes an effort to locate volunteer housing for entrants and their dogs before and after the race. No matter where you stay, clean up after your dogs!

The Vet Check

All dogs are required to be examined by a race veterinarian for health and soundness, and their vaccination records are checked. You need a rabies vaccination certificate and a health certificate for crossing many state and federal boundaries. Some European countries have a quarantine period of weeks or months.

The vet check occurs a few days prior to the race start. This gives you an opportunity to ask questions or clear up any uncertainties. Your dogs probably will have blood drawn for drug testing at some point in the race. The amount of blood taken is not enough to affect their performance. It will ensure that you are not competing against dogs that are running on drugs instead of on ability, training, and competence.

The Trail Committee

The Trail Committee is responsible for opening and marking the trail and for transporting your food drops from a central holding area to the appropriate checkpoints. It often provides white gas for mushers' stoves, and it provides tags for dogs in case they are lost or dropped during the race. The Trail Committee also provides and transports veterinarians and ham radio operators along the trail and and keeps track of each musher's progress.

The Race

Your pit crew at the start should consist of experienced handlers. (If a well-meaning but uninitiated friend insists on "helping," put a camera in his or her hands and say, "Take pictures!")

This is usually the last time that you are allowed prearranged help. Family or supporters meeting you at checkpoints usually cannot assist you with any trail chores or dog handling.

Leave the start with a handler on your sled, or on an extra sled towed behind yours for maximum control, until the mob of teams has sorted itself out. Many professional racers push hard to get ahead of the others to avoid tangles and the possibility of disease spreading among the concentration of dogs. However, one of the most common mistakes made by rookies is to drive too hard early in the race. If this is your first long race, take the first 300 miles with caution and keep an eye on learning what you and your dogs can do. If you have a realistic shot at Rookie of the Year, stay within a day of the front-runners, but remember that many of your colleagues also expect to win the title. Often, twenty or even thirty entrants fully expect to finish in the top ten. The most intense racing occurs in the last 300 miles, but if you are two days behind, you do not have much hope of catching up.

An additional note to rookies: Enter a long race with three goals. Winning is *not* one of them. Try to finish the race. Learn as much as you can. And enjoy yourself, your dogs, and the magnificent country through which you travel.

Watch closely for trail markers, especially when leaving and entering villages. Flagging tape, reflective markers, or surveyor's stakes with blazing orange tips are all used. Unfortunately, some villages use similar markers for local races. While race volunteers make every effort to avoid these problems, it is ultimately your responsibility to stay on the correct trail.

When to Run, When to Rest

Dogs run best at dawn and dusk. On a 1,000-mile race, roughly half of the time is spent actually traveling. By adjusting your schedule, you can run your dogs when they go best and let them rest during the afternoons. This allows them to sleep in the warmth, when they can sprawl out and relax. (When you stop to rest after running underneath a hot sun, let them sleep in the shade so that their muscles will cool off. This reduces both stiffness and dehydration. Stiff animals should be rubbed and walked before you head out.) Starting again before the air cools lets the dogs loosen up slowly; their speed then picks up impressively as night approaches.

Some mushers run on a strict timetable, such as four hours of running followed by four hours off. (Joe Runyan lengthened this time schedule, running longer periods and resting longer periods, when he won the 1989 Iditarod.) Dogs do benefit from a dependable schedule. If allowed to travel at their own pace, they can continue on through the hot afternoons (watch for overheating and dehydration).

When you stop, get the dogs well off of the trail and snub them securely, preferably just behind the leaders as well as at the sled. Do not feed them in the trail, because this blocks other teams and distracts other dogs with leftover food, even after you have moved on.

Know your dogs so that you can tell when they will or will not benefit from a rest. Maybe they will bounce back and go faster after a break, or maybe they will go just as slowly or even more slowly.

Sometimes dogs will actually travel too fast, resulting in burnout or injury. Slow them down by command if possible, or by gentle, occasional braking, by running behind a slower team, or by feeding them to make them a little sluggish.

Dogs often run better at night or very early and late in the day. This often means getting ready to go in the dead of the night. Bill Cotter and Jon Gleason during the 1987 Yukon Quest. *Courtesy* Fairbanks Daily News-Miner.

Rotate leaders frequently to decrease stress. Put them far enough back in the team so that they are not still watching where they are going. Fast leaders can burn up a team quickly; save them for when speed is needed. You may have to catch up to someone, or whiz through a mountain pass ahead of a storm, or shoot ahead at the end of the race. Save hotshot command leaders for snarled village trails, and save trail-finding dogs for storms and blown-in or snowed-in places.

Your team cannot be pressured into racing 1,000 miles. They must do it by virtue of their training and natural ability, aided by your handling and guidance. Keep discipline to a minimum. When you punish one dog, the whole team feels the pressure. Young dogs especially should never be pushed too hard. If one starts acting up or getting tired or sore-footed, drop him or he may be ruined. Keep your dogs wanting to go by making them feel that you are holding them back (see Chapter 2).

You are likely to be with a group of matched competitors striving to beat each other, whether in the top or bottom of the race pack. However, as always, care of your dogs comes first. Take care of them even if you fall behind in doing so. It will pay off farther down the trail; if not in this race, then in the next one.

Watch your dogs constantly for signs of burnout. These signs include diarrhea, dehydration, rebellion, lack of appetite, lethargy, and refusal to go, any or all of which are signs of physical stress or illness.

Switch leaders frequently, especially if you are breaking trail. Running behind another team also reduces some of the pressure on your leaders if they do not try too hard to overtake the team ahead. Bruce Lee and Martin Wiener passing Eagle Bluff outside Eagle, Alaska, during the 1986 Yukon Quest. *Photo by Ron Lambert.*

(They also can be due to poor training, psychological weakness, sore feet, or other problems.) Physical stress usually can be relieved by rest and plenty of food and water. Mental problems sometimes can be overcome by resting, then running just a short distance and surprising the dogs with another rest, or by stopping frequently and giving plenty of one-on-one attention. Discipline may or may not help and should never be used on a dog that might be physically incapable of continuing.

Snacking during rest breaks keeps up the dogs' strength. Frozen meat or fish provides some water and cools the dogs, and saves time cooking. If the dogs are going to be sleeping for awhile, or if they are already cold, thaw the food so that they do not burn calories just to warm it. Give them a lot of fat when they are cold and more fish when they are hot.

Checkpoints

Distances between checkpoints may be 15 miles or 250 miles. You are required to sign in and may be required to sign out as well. Veterinary care and communications usually are available, and most

In Alaskan races, the checkpoints are usually at widely scattered villages along the route. This Iditarod team is following spruce-pole trail markers off the Bering Sea ice coming into Koyuk on the Iditarod trail.

When you arrive at a checkpoint, like this one at Circle City, you will have to locate your bags out of the stacks — not an easy task in the dead of the night after an exhausting run. The easiest way to do it is to be the last one into the checkpoint! *Photo by Ron Lambert.*

checkpoints are designated dog drops. Although you may find numerous people ready to help you, be aware that race rules usually allow only incidental help, such as guiding a team to the checkers.

Water usually is available — use it! Feed and water your team now to save time melting snow on the trail. Park well away from the center of activity, and bed down your dogs in straw if you have it. You might want to travel a short distance before bedding down, because dogs rest better away from the distractions of the checkpoints.

Remember that your hosts at each checkpoint must bear with up to eighty teams, not to mention race officials, veterinarians, spectators, and the press. They might be as short on sleep as you are; therefore, try not to strain their hospitality or it may be withdrawn from future races (this has happened in some places).

Some checkpoints provide hay for dogs; others do not. Take advantage of whatever they have to offer, including stove fuel, water, and food. Some checkpoints, like this one at Chena Hot Springs on the Yukon Quest Race, even have hot springs that you can soak in — if you have time. Julie Collins on the Yukon Quest, 1985.

The press must often be dealt with, especially at checkpoints. Here, CNN is filming Kathy Swenson, a long-distance racer and the wife of top racer Rick Swenson. *Courtesy* Fairbanks Daily News-Miner.

Strategy

Some people run their own race, driving their teams as fast as the dogs are capable of going over that distance. Others watch the competition, traveling just fast enough to keep within striking distance of the leaders and not pushing their dogs unnecessarily. As you travel, judge the strength of your competition. Are their dogs thin, unhealthy, tired, or balky? Have they dropped a lot of dogs? Do the dogs have diarrhea? Teams like this may keep up the pace for awhile but may then fall back. Mushers will sometimes psych out or trick their competitors and may even lie outright. Pacts for stopping over for a period of time cannot be trusted.

Get forecasts from checkers or on radio stations. If you push ahead when a big storm is imminent, others may be cut off behind you — or you might get hopelessly lost in a whiteout and even freeze to death. Knowing the peculiarities of each area helps. For instance, Eagle Summit on the Yukon Quest trail is notorious for high winds and white-out conditions.

Shave minutes and seconds from your camp time with a smooth routine polished before race time. Fast cookers, prepared foods, spare dry socks and gloves, and warm sleeping bags all cut down on labor. Efficiency is critical. Getting the dogs fed quickly speeds their recovery, and then you can all rest. Do not stand around doing nothing — *rest*!

Common Medical Problems

Medical problems are discussed in Chapter 6. Check your dogs once or twice a day for sore feet, dehydration, harness sores, and other problems. Keep a written record of medication that you administer, because you do not want to forget when you gave what dog which pill. (One musher mixed up his little yellow anti-inflammatory pills for himself with the little yellow anti-estrus pills for his dogs!)

Feet are so important that we have dedicated a whole chapter to them (Chapter 7). Diarrhea caused by changing diets, stress, viruses, and possibly food poisoning is common. It also occurs when a dog eats more than he can physically digest. A trail veterinarian can provide treatment. Dehydration demands constant preventative treatment.

Sprains and strains are common. A mild one can heal while the dog works. If the dog is not limping too badly, you may want to leave him in the team to help prevent stiffening. In some cases, the dog must be carried in the sled. He may recover if you carry him long enough, but usually a dog injured this badly should be dropped. Wrist problems tend to heal unless the dog is limping severely or is limping from a recurring injury. Injuries higher in the leg and shoulder are generally slower to heal. Remember — if a dog is not pulling, he actually is hindering you by taking up your precious time, energy, and care.

Making tired, stressed, or sick dogs eat challenges nearly every musher at some point. Some dogs have a habit of refusing food for hours and then suddenly consuming a heavy meal — humor them! Remember, however — a dog that eats or drinks a lot when he is hot (from running) is likely to vomit, especially if he runs immediately afterward. Overeating also makes a dog sluggish. Dogs that refuse food may be tired, sick, or stressed (physically or psychologically) or

Villagers must put up with a horde of volunteers, sight-seers, race officials, and the press, including ham radio operators and their gear. Radio operators can often get messages in and out for you when no telephone or other communication is available.

may have sore feet. Sometimes just getting a little food into them, even if it is force-fed, is enough to start them eating. Thawed meat is more palatable than frozen meat, commercial food, or soup. Teasing the dog with it makes him want it more. A burnt layer on the bottom of your cooking container taints food and must be cleaned off completely or the dogs will refuse all food cooked in it. If you must force-feed a dog, give him chunks of food about one inch in diameter, and gently push them down his throat as you would a pill. To force-water a dog, use a bulb syringe or squirt bottle to inject small amounts of water back into his cheek pouch, making sure that he swallows the water. Stomach tubing should be left to trained people.

Veterinarians at the checkpoints can hand out foot ointments, vitamin B and iron injections, antibiotics, anti-diarrheal drugs, and other

When a dog is sick or injured, he must be carried in the sled to the next checkpoint. Having the dog trained to accept this before the race makes it easier. Ideally, the dog is low in the sled, where he will be protected by the sides and will be less likely to get tossed around. *Photo by Ron Lambert.*

allowed pharmaceuticals. Some do not look over a team unless requested; others go over every dog. They also will treat dropped dogs when requested to do so. Experienced trail veterinarians can offer sound advice on anything from poor appetites to bizarre foot conditions. You have been working with ten or eighteen animals; they have been supervising fifty times that many. However, in order to provide enough trail veterinarians, the race committee often must bring in green ones who lack experience in trail-related problems.

If you drop an injured dog, you must leave him with a picket and some food. The Trail Committee may transport him back to a holding facility until he can be picked up (a boarding fee may be charged). Dogs are dropped because they are tired, injured, or sick, or because they are messing up or are not pulling. They may also have some other problem that prevents them from being an asset to the team.

Living with Yourself

Long-distance racing is very stressful. On longer races, mushers travel hard for ten or twenty days. They get by on two to six hours of sleep a day, despite numerous physical and psychological pressures. By the end of the trek, these people can be hard to get along

If you leave Dawson City on a trail that is unbearably soft and slow, and the sun is burning down hotly, don't despair because all of your competitors are going through the same thing.

with. Be especially careful that a quick temper or a lethargic mind do not affect the treatment of your dogs. Decisions become more difficult. Long stretches of trail become extremely tedious. Many mushers carry a lightweight cassette tape player to entertain themselves and to keep them awake. A radio allows you to listen to forecasts and race updates within the range of stations. (Unfortunately, radio reports are often outdated.)

Exhaustion and emotional swings affect your moods and your body's ability to handle stress, cold, fear, depression, and other internal and external forces. (This is also true for your dogs.) Depression can be a problem, especially among less experienced mushers and among those whose dogs are not up to their aspirations. Being aware of this can help. You *can* modify your moods by telling yourself in a very determined voice, *"This too shall pass!"*

Remember, too, that everyone has to deal with the weather, with the trail, with dog problems, and with other race challenges. When your dogs are slowed by a heavy snowfall, other teams will be, too, so don't let it bother you. Do not let your dogs become aware of despair or anger. They need the security of knowing that you are in control, whether you are or not. Fear, ignorance, and depression are your worst enemies — not the trail, not the other mushers, and certainly not your troublesome team. (Remember, this whole thing was *your* idea.)

Scratching

The most difficult choice (especially for a rookie) is whether or not to scratch. Do *not* scratch because of depression, because you are not having fun, or because you are behind schedule. You will regret it later. Do scratch if your dogs cannot go on without risking serious injuries or illnesses, or if a veterinarian advises it. Do scratch if you are so injured, sick, or tired that you can no longer take care of your dogs or yourself, or make rational decisions in a crisis. Problems that seem insurmountable during the race may appear much less significant once you are home. If you wait twelve hours before officially scratching, your outlook may change.

The Finish

When you march into downtown Nome, Fairbanks, or Whitehorse, you have the intense satisfaction of knowing that you have completed one of the most grueling competitions ever devised by man. Let your dogs know it. Let them know that you couldn't have done it without them. Give them the best of care, whether you came in first or whether

Winning a major long-distance race is an international accomplishment. It is extra special when it runs in the family. Five years after Dick Mackey won the Iditarod in 1978, his son Rick repeated the performance. *Courtesy* Fairbanks Daily News-Miner.

your tardiness surpassed your wildest reckoning.

Just finishing is a great achievement for a rookie. Finishing in the money is an achievement for anyone, and winning is an international accomplishment. Always remember that your dogs are the ones responsible for the feat. Their paws still hurt, their muscles are still sore, and they still need you. Even if someone else takes over the chores, the dogs will appreciate seeing you frequently. After all, the bunch of you have been living in intimacy for the past couple of weeks, and that habit can be hard to break.

Longer Middle-Distance Races

Some mushers run middle-distance events as practice for long-distance races. Others concentrate on winning these events, or are

The last miles are special beyond words. Joe May and his team winning the 1980 Iditarod. *Courtesy* Fairbanks Daily News-Miner.

just out to have fun and see some country. Shorter mid-distance races (less than 50 or 100 miles) are run like sprint races (see Chapter 13). In longer races, you will use many of the same practices as on the true long-distance race. The dogs must trot at least part of the time, and if running time exceeds about eight to twelve hours, you will need to stop to feed and water them or they will give out. In races less than 200 miles (and even some 300-mile events), you are unlikely to get any sleep at all.

Do not run as many training miles for these races as you would for a 1,000-mile race. Speed is more critical — keep it up during training by putting on fewer really long runs (keep the distance below fifty miles, with plenty of fifteen- to forty-mile runs) and by running less often. You still need the psychological toughness; the dogs do not have to last as long, but you will be pushing them more throughout the race. With the higher speeds, injuries are also more likely to occur.

Train the dogs to trot fast, and do not discourage loping. Encourage loping in races less than 200 miles long.

Know the race conditions, and train for the race that you really want to win. The Kusko 300, for example, is run on fast, flat, icy trails and you may experience extremely severe windchill factors (down to -100 degrees F.). You must expose your dogs to running on ice in the wind during training. Several mid-distance races are held in the Rockies and have numerous slopes and wildly variable weather and trail conditions. Your dogs must be able to run in heat, cold, wind, snow, and rain and must maintain a decent pace whether going uphill or downhill. The race trail on the Montana 500 (Governor's Cup) reaches elevations of more than 7,000 feet and crosses the continental divide four times. The Alpirod, held in the Alps of Italy, France, Switzerland, and Germany, actually consists of eleven one-day heats that vary in length from 18 to 124 miles (totaling 621 miles). Sometimes one or more heats are canceled due to bad conditions. Again, if this is *the* race that you want to win, prepare your dogs by running in variable weather conditions (including warm weather), in mountainous terrain, and through crowds of spectators. The dogs should be fairly fast and should be capable of bouncing back overnight.

In Alaska, just reaching some races is a challenge. Many host villages are inaccessible by road, and teams must be flown in. Airlines often offer discount rates for racing teams but require kennels for the dogs. Chartering a plane is sometimes cheaper.

Longer races have checkpoints and food drops. Speed and efficiency in cooking and in doing camp chores are critical. If water is available, use it. If you know in advance that you will be able to get water at every checkpoint, you might not have to carry a stove.

Dogs can be pressured a little more than in true long-distance races, but be careful — teams have quit close to the finish when they were driven too hard. Dogs familiar with the end of the trail, whether the race is a fifty-mile event or the Iditarod, recognize the area and often speed up when they realize that the end is near.

In 1985, Miki and I trained our team in the Fairbanks area for the Yukon Quest. Our longest one-day training run was over the final seventy miles of the race trail, from Angel Creek to Fairbanks. That weeded out a couple of dogs, but the others finished easily with a feeling of accomplishment.

When I reached Angel Creek during the race, my dogs were slow to recognize the route that they had been over once before. Night was falling. I had traveled all the way from Dawson City, Canada, with just six dogs; young Raven, only eighteen months old, was nearly exhausted. Then, magically, they started to pick up. As the day's heat seeped away, one by one they realized something.

They were almost home!

They started to lope on the easy stretches. Raven was running on excitement alone. Legs, in the lead, pushed the team so fast that I had to stop and give the dogs frequent breathers for fear they would burn up.

Down the Chena River toward the finish they sped. Right at the end, they broke into a lope. They knew that the race was over and that the truck with its hay-filled boxes was waiting. And they knew as well as I did just how much they had accomplished.

CHAPTER 15

MUSHING MISCELLANY

Some years ago, before the villagers of Alaska abandoned their trusty dog teams for faster transportation, a bush pilot landed his plane at a small community with a load of freight. As he was taxiing, the ski plane suddenly sank into deep overflow hidden beneath the snow. The slush instantly froze onto the skis, immobilizing the plane. The engine could not budge it. (And you thought that a dogsled in overflow was bad!)

Out came the villagers with their dogs. Two teams of forty dogs each were hooked up, one team on each ski, and the helpless airplane was ignominiously towed to safety.

Sled dogs are not limited to running races on well-groomed trails. Our dogs are trained for skijoring as well as for sledding. They have shouldered packs and skidded poles from the forest. Single dogs have pulled our heavily loaded red plastic sleds or hauled a child's wagon loaded with mail and packages. We have used them to chase off bears and to pull canoes over spring ice. They provide us with transportation in the winter and companionship year-round.

Some entrepreneurial mushers earn money carrying tourists or hauling freight. Even if you can keep only a couple of dogs, you still can work them seriously and even compete in skijoring or weight-pulling events.

Skijoring

In many northern European countries, skijoring, with or without a pulk (small sled) in tow, has been the preferred method of dog-powered travel. Even in America, skijoring competitions have been held for years. For the skier who wants an extra thrill, for the mushing

Skijoring dogs can be run in fan style, as shown here, or with one leader in the front of two swing dogs. Note the set of this girl's skis, which acts to hold back her dogs. *Photo by Polly Walters.*

enthusiast who cannot afford a full team, or for any dog person who has a good sense of balance and some derring-do, skijoring has much to offer.

A three-dog team pulling a skier can easily run twenty miles per hour and is roughly comparable to a six-dog team pulling a sled and driver. Even one dog can pull a skier four miles in less than twenty minutes. The dogs get a charge out of it, and because of the close proximity, the feeling of unity cannot be matched. Each dog's gaits and abilities can be analyzed without viewing him through half a dozen other wagging tails. Leaders are trained more easily. It is also a lot easier to transport two dogs and a pair of skis than seven dogs and a sled that will not fit in your Volkswagon.

Equipment

Harnesses and lines need no special adaptations except for the end of the tow rope. Instead of hooking to a sled harness, the towline

Even Jermstad demonstrates skijoring at the Tanana Valley Fairgrounds. *Courtesy* Fairbanks Daily News-Miner.

One can skijor with
a belt and ski poles
for extra balance and
drive. *Photo by
Polly Walters.*

connects to a rope that you tow from as if you were water-skiing.
The rope can be attached to a spreader bar, to a loop, or to a wide
belt around your waist by means of a steel hook or a quick-release
snap. A belt frees your hands for ski poles and can actually improve
your balance by lowering the center of gravity; however, it also prevents the automatic separation of skier and dogs in an emergency.
Belts should be at least four inches wide across the back to spread
out the pull and should be made of heavy fabric or, preferably, leather.
They fasten around the waist just loosely enough to allow some give
as the dogs move. A quick-release system is imperative for safety.
    Miki does a lot of skijoring and frequently tows behind my dogsled.

. . . Or you can just
grab a rope and
hang on.

She prefers gripping a spare dog harness, hooked backward to the
towline so that she can hold the lined part. The padding provides a
warm, sure grip, and she can loop an arm through the harness to
rest her hands on long eight-hour runs.

With one dog, a single line runs back to the belt or tow bar. More
dogs usually are paired as in a dog team, with or without necklines.
You also can run them fan-style (three abreast). The tow rope must
be long enough to allow room between you and the dogs if you slide
forward, but not so long that the power of the dogs is lost or the rope
tangles too easily. Some people insert a shock line or bungee in the
lines to absorb the jerks as the dogs and skier go over bumps. This

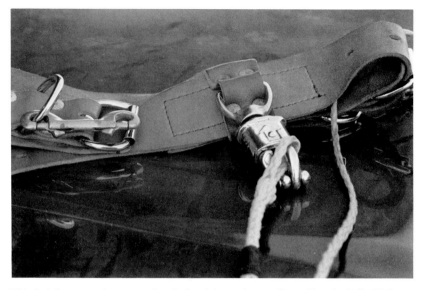

This belt has a panic snap to hook the skier to the towline. *Photo by Polly Walters.*

is not necessary when you are holding the rope instead of using a belt, because your arms act as the shock absorber.

Cross-country skis are most popular, but mountaineering or downhill skis also are used. Short, wide skis offer more stability, decreasing foot fatigue. They are less tiring over long distances and are more maneuverable and easier to "untangle" if you fall. Toe bindings allow you to move your feet more for better maneuverability and balance, but they do require special boots.

Ski poles make balancing easier and allow the musher to ski cross-country style more effectively. They are best used in combination with a belt. Using one or two ski poles while gripping a spreader bar can get complicated when you are racing along at eighteen miles per hour; it's easier without them.

Ski equipment is readily available from ski and sporting goods shops, although you may need to request a special mounting of ski bindings if you want cross-country bindings on downhill skis. Dog equipment for skijoring is available from many mushing outlets.

Training the Musher

Training is very important for the skijorer. If you cannot ski, you will get where you want to go faster if you turn the dogs loose and walk. A cross-country skier knows how to skate along, helping the dogs out and lessening the strain on the back and arms. Downhill skiers are attuned to the awesome velocity and split-second maneuvering, and water skiers know how to keep the elbows as well as the knees bent to absorb the give and take of the tow rope. All have developed a vital sense of balance.

Skijoring is faster than cross-country skiing and lasts longer than the fleeting thrill of downhill skiing. Because skis have little friction, the physical effort of holding the rope is insignificant compared to staying upright and pointed forward, not to mention feigning a semblance of balance. With experience, this, too, is effortless.

If you doubt your ability to control yourself *and* your dogs, hone your skijoring abilities by towing behind a dogsled or snow machine, or even behind a horse and rider (which is thrilling enough in itself!). This way you do not have to worry about what's happening up front. Start out on level terrain and work up to bumps, banks, hills, and turns. Keep your knees and (when not using a belt) your elbows supple, bending them so that they act as springs and shock absorbers. Do not lean back against the pull of the rope — if it goes slack, you might fall backward. Instead, crouch against the pull so that you can absorb both increases and decreases in speed. This also lowers your center of gravity, which makes balancing easier.

Once you have mastered the basics, try skiing with the dogs. You should be able to ski automatically without needing to concentrate on your balance — because now you must pay close attention to your crew. It is actually easier to skijor behind two well-trained dogs than behind just one, because two have enough power to pull you readily.

To slow down when skijoring, snowplow with the skis by pointing the toes inward and the back ends outward. Put your weight on the inside edges, keeping your legs rigid to hold that position. If your dogs do not respond when you tell them to stop, you can sit down and drag. This will stop them eventually. Keep your ski tips pointing straight forward, or snowplow just slightly. Try to control your skis when dragging, or one might dig in and break, get torn off, or race away in the wrong direction, taking your foot along with it.

Training the Dogs

Ideally, all of your dogs are perfectly obedient and are trained to

334 Dog Driver: A Guide for the Serious Musher

stop on command. They must have the drive to stay out in front. Sometimes an inexperienced dog gets confused or scared when he realizes that you are *right there* instead of a sled-length away. This usually passes quickly. Some dogs are afraid of the skis, and others quickly learn to fear the skis if you run up on the dogs' heels. Running these dogs ahead of an experienced dog usually cures this difficulty. Traveling behind another team helps the dogs to learn this new skill quickly.

A misbehaving dog runs better behind a leader that can pull him around. You can then tap the offender on the side of the rump with a ski pole or with the tip of your ski for correction without stopping — *if* you know that he won't spook.

Most dogs are eager to run, whether they are pulling a sled or a skier. It's when they stop — or take a wrong turn — or do *not* stop — that the situation gets complicated. First, you have no brake. Second, once you drag your seat long enough to stop the dogs, you have no way of anchoring them short of tying off to a tree. Untangling these eager dogs is trouble enough without doing it when they are un-anchored and your feet are six feet long and slippery as all get-out. (A single-prong snow hook might be the answer, if it can be secured safely to your waist when not in use.)

Consequently, having dogs that are mild-mannered, tangle-free, and trained to "Stay!" are important in keeping your blood pressure within safe limits. Strict training may be needed, and while this takes some of the fun out of the sport for awhile, in the long run you will enjoy yourself much more. Most dogs can quickly be trained to stop and stay if you run one dog alone, or if you run three dogs with a small sled and a good brake. The key is to drill effectively and consistently.

Experienced skijoring dogs learn to stop when you fall down, or to slow down when you lose your balance. I have even had dogs learn to slow down after scrambling over fallen trees, giving me a chance to hippity-hop over. Dogs pick up "Gee" and "Haw" faster than when they are in a team because they are essentially running in the lead, and you are right there to correct them and lever them quickly in the right direction. Young lead prospects can be trained without the often overwhelming pressure of staying ahead of a bunch of dogs. Even dogs with no experience in leading can do very well in skijoring.

We prefer using three dogs, which provides great power without the wasted effort of additional dogs. This usually means having a trained leader in front and a pair behind. When we are running down

Skijoring races are growing more popular and are held with or without other racing events. *Photo by Polly Walters.*

a narrow ski track, the dogs are run in single file. (Do *not* run dogs on someone else's ski trail without permission; they usually punch the neat track full of holes.)

Skijoring with Many Dogs

An acquaintance once mentioned that he did not skijor because the one time he had tried it, he had hooked up seven dogs. "I couldn't control them," he said.

To run a large number of dogs for skijoring, you use the same principle as for running a twenty-dog team. You must train the dogs in small teams until they are completely controllable, then gradually increase the number of dogs.

Miki once had to get a sled out to a trapping cabin, where it would be left for the next winter. She hooked up seven dogs, threw a pair of skis in the sled, and took off. At the cabin, she cached the sled, slapped on the skis, turned one dog loose, and sped home with the other six without a hitch.

When running many dogs, you must match them for speed. The faster dogs are not slowed by pulling more than their share as they are when hauling bigger loads. The one dog that Miki turned loose would have dragged; her team actually went *faster* with six dogs than with seven. A dragging dog not only is inefficient, but he slows down the other dogs, causing all of them to feel demoralized.

When you are running seven dogs on skis, only three or four are really pulling, and you are only going as fast as your slowest dog. Running a big team is *not* the way to train dogs or people for the sport. However, with well-trained dogs and a confident skier, it is immensely thrilling, and provides more power when breaking trail.

Pulks

Pulk races have been held for years in northern Europe and are starting up in America. The pulk is a small sled that is towed between the dogs and the musher, or sometimes behind the musher, allowing a load to be carried. Unlike most skijoring races, which are only one-quarter to fifteen miles long, pulk races can be two hundred miles long, with food and camp gear stowed in the pulk.

A good pulk is flexible and durable. Some have a hand-operated brake. Some pulks are equipped with shafts to prevent them from running up on the dogs. (Special harnesses for pulk attachment are required.) If they have no shafts, run a line from the end of the sled back to the tow rope as a hold-back line. If just a light load such as a snack is brought, one dog can carry a pack instead, but he will not be able to pull as hard and should be turned loose on high-speed or challenging trails. He should be pack trained before doing both jobs.

For those unwilling to invest in a good, dependable pulk, a little red sled makes an admirable substitute. I am referring to those marvelous creations known as Red Bombers® and Thunderbolts®, found in stores at Christmastime and used by little kids to slide down hills, crash into trees, and get nosebleeds. These devices withstand a remarkable amount of abuse, carry up to 100 pounds, and glide easily on most types of snow. The weak point is the sled harness. Instead of tying the tow rope into the provided holes, run the line through the front holes and then down the sides of the sled. It is tied off at the holes for the back handle so that the plastic will not rip out.

These sleds can be tied one behind another for hauling larger loads. Miki has used three loaded sleds and five dogs while she skied behind.

Joring without Skis

Sled dogs can also pull an ice skater. Familiarize the dogs with glassy ice first, and remember that sprains, strains, and muscle soreness are not uncommon when the dogs are run on slippery surfaces. Wise dogs will not run flat out, but they can move right along even on very slippery ice. Try roller skates on pavement or other hard surfaces, but be careful not to stub your toe! A forceful tumble on pavement will ding you up a lot more quickly than a fall into a snowbank, or even on hard ice. A biker's helmet and thick elbow and knee pads are wise investments.

Bold bicyclists have hooked up one to five dogs for a speedy, effortless ride. This, too, demands the use of a helmet and a certain disregard for personal safety. Do not hit the brakes, or the dogs will spill the bike. Dogs used for these sports should be well trained and responsive.

These two dogs are having fun, but they are evidently experienced as they take this girl for a ride. *Courtesy* Fairbanks Daily News-Miner.

Along with sprint races and skijoring races, a number of "fun races" are scheduled during race weekends, including lead-dog's revenge (man-pulls-beast) and children's races. Here, Jennifer Smith tries to hold back her dogs long enough to grab some money during a fun race in 1972. *Courtesy* Fairbanks Daily News-Miner.

As with any nonwinter work, watch your dogs closely for heat exhaustion.

With the cost of keeping a team always on the rise, more people are turning to skijoring to satisfy their competitive spirit. Instead of keeping thirty dogs and picking the best sixteen, you can maintain five dogs and have the same caliber team — in a three-dog skijoring class. Events are growing in popularity, clubs are materializing, and skijoring seems ready to be accepted here as it has been in Europe.

Weight Pulling

Organized weight pulling competitions are held regularly in the United States, Canada, and other countries. When snow is lacking, pulls are done with wheeled rigs. Due to advances in hi-tech runner material, training, and breeding, records are still being broken regularly. One well-trained dog can pull an incredible load. Many can pull one ton, and some have pulled more than 5,000 pounds (5,280 is the official record at this writing). One dog unofficially pulled a 10,000-pound truck and trailer down a paved road. A fellow who we knew had an untrained MacKenzie River husky chained by the collar to a Volkswagon, and he was pretty surprised when his neighbor phoned to report that the dog was coming down the road unsupervised — car and all!

Most pulls have weight divisions, allowing even smaller dogs to compete, and sometimes the top dog is considered to be the one that pulls the most per pound of body weight. The North American Championship Weight Pull, held in Fairbanks, Alaska, has divisions for dogs less than 60 pounds, for dogs 60 to 90 pounds, for dogs 90 to 120 pounds, and for dogs more than 120 pounds. Runner or wheel type, temperatures, and terrain all affect the outcome.

The weights are often sacked dog food, but anything can be used, from concrete blocks to volunteer people.

The historic three-dog pulls recently have been reintroduced. For these events, the dogs must be well trained, because the driver is not physically in control of the dogs, and the dogs must pull in unison to be effective.

Dogs take turns pulling in rounds, starting with loads of 200 to 500 pounds. Weight is added, usually at the rate of 100 pounds per turn, and dogs are eliminated when they cannot pull the additional weight in the time limit. No leashes, treats, or physical contact are allowed. Because every round is more difficult than the last, and because the dog competes until he cannot pull the weight, competitions take quite a toll psychologically. You must recognize this and offer plenty of encouragement and praise for success. You need to let the dog realize that while he is expected to do his best, if he cannot pull the load, that's okay. Such close work allows a strong bond to form between you and your dog, especially because you are working with only a few dogs. That bond gives the dog added incentive to please you. People who have the ability to instill a strong desire to please can get more from their dogs.

The Dogs

Malamutes are the most popular weight pulling dogs, but many northern and robust non-northern breeds compete successfully, including Alaskan huskies, Saint Bernards, Newfoundlands, and Mac-

SOFA (Son of Famous Amos), a MacKenzie River husky owned by Mark Weller, weighs in at 134 pounds during this competition. *Photo by Sue Renkert.*

Look how well coordinated these dogs owned by Norm Stoppenbrink are as they pull 3,320 pounds to win the three-dog pull in the 1988 North American. *Courtesy Sue Renkert.*

Kenzie River huskies. Even Labradors and Pit Bulls have been used. Because of the weight divisions, almost any of the stouter breeds can compete if the dogs are trained properly. Temperament and conformation, with well-balanced, powerful hindquarters and good angulation, are important. The dogs must have controlled drive and a strong desire to please. Shy dogs are apt to spook, and aggressive, excitable dogs might fight the load, leaping and plunging ineffectively.

Harnesses
Use a padded freight harness with a spreader bar so that the pull comes straight off of the chest and shoulders. The weight must be distributed evenly with no interference to the dog's movements, breathing, or hind legs. Adjustments may be required as the dog muscles out.

Training
Ideally, training begins by exposing older pups to crowds, to handling, and to the feel of a harness. A very light drag can be added at three to four months, but keep all training positive and gentle. As the dog matures, the weight can be very slowly increased. He should

Yukon Pride's Nanook Horizon, WWPD, owned by Gordon Heppner, shows good form here. A steady, head-down, digging-in pull is the best way to reach the finish line. *Photo by Ken Bade; courtesy Sue Renkert.*

Weight pullers need encouragement, especially as the loads reach their upper limits. In most competitions, this dog handler's leash would not be allowed. *Courtesy* Fairbanks Daily News-Miner.

not be asked to pull a heavy load until he is physically mature.

The dog must *always* be able to pull his load. Training with loads that are too heavy discourage a dog from giving his all when it counts — in competition. Adult dogs can be trained to pull tires or other weights. Teach them to feel good about what they are doing by offering praise and encouragement, and by making the training fun.

Breaking out the load is the hardest part. Discourage leaping and banging against the line; a steady, head-down, digging-in pull with three paws always on the ground is most effective. The weight must be far enough back so that it does not interfere with the dog's action or slide up on his heels.

Build up a dog's strength first, teaching him what to do and how to pull. Only after he is well muscled-out and well trained should you start asking for much larger loads, always keeping within a weight that the dog can pull. You may want to train him with a routine similar to a competitive routine, by adding weight several times during each session; however, do not let the dog get discouraged.

Dogs can be either driven from the back or called from the finish line, which is probably more effective. When urging the dog forward, crouch to encourage him to keep his head down. He should be taught to respond to you even from a distance, as he must do during competition.

During events, the dogs usually are exposed to crowds, photographers, and other distractions. If they are accustomed to these situations, they can concentrate better on the task at hand. Always give your dog heartfelt praise for pulling the load, even if he is not able to do so in the required time. Some handlers will help the dog pull his load if he is disqualified so that he does not feel defeated.

Packing Dogs

Almost any dog can be trained to carry a pack, but the larger, heavier breeds can carry bigger loads. Dogs used for heavy harness work take to packing readily. A high-strung race dog usually requires more training, plus his racing abilities may be dulled.

Once trained for the job, most dogs are capable of carrying up to one-third of their own weight. Our seventy- to eighty-pound huskies carry fifteen or twenty pounds each all day long, over rough ground, brush, beaver dams, and creeks.

Dog packs have two pouches that ride on either side of the dog. The weight should be well forward, resting over the withers and rib cage to avoid back strain. Balance is the single most important factor in loading. An unbalanced pack may swivel until the heavier pouch is dragging under the dog's belly, while the light one is over his back. Not only is this very awkward, but the harness may be digging in and causing sores. Even a slight imbalance throws a dog off stride. Bulkiness also should be balanced.

Before a dog can be trained to pack, he must learn to stay close to you or to accept leashing. (Sled dogs *can* be trained *not* to pull against a leash, but don't do this until they have been trained *to* pull against

Pack dogs cannot carry as much as pack horses, but they are much more versatile in the terrain that they can cover, and they have a lesser impact on the environment than horses.

a harness.) Many huskies love to range, and this habit can be difficult to break. Dogs that are frequently turned loose and handled as individuals generally respond to commands more readily.

Let the dog wear an empty pack until he is used to it. If he is brought on an outing each time the pack is put on, he will associate it with good times and will look forward to it. A few minutes a day, or one outing a day for a few days, should suffice unless the dog is afraid of the pack. Gradually fill the pouches with a lightweight material so that the dog leans to dodge trees and other obstacles — because the pack increases his width by up to three times. Once he can handle the bulk, add weight slowly over a period of days to condition him for heavier loads.

A dog in good shape that will accept strange jobs and that will come when called can learn to pack in just a couple of sessions, although he will need a few weeks of conditioning before he can carry a heavy load. Occasionally, a dog will freeze up when the pack is put on for the first time. This can be overcome with encouragement, especially if other dogs are tearing around happily. If he staggers or falls, the load is too heavy or he just has not learned to handle that much yet.

Dog packs come in many styles and sizes, and many mushing outfitters supply them. The harness arrangement must prevent the dog from backing out of the pack or from simply throwing it off somewhere. A breast strap, one or two cinches, and a britchen (the strap circling the hindquarters under the tail) are used frequently. Make sure that packs and buckles are padded if heavy loads are carried. The harness usually does not need padding unless harness sores appear. If you see rub marks or sores, check first for a proper fit and be sure that the load is balanced.

Load heavy gear at the bottom of the pack for greater stability. Breakable, hard, or sharp items must be well padded (perhaps wrapped in clothing) so that they do not dig into the dog's ribs. You can further protect breakables by placing them inside an empty tin can or wooden box. Unless you will be traveling in very dry or frozen country, assume that the pack and its contents will get wet, and plan accordingly. Wrap anything that might be damaged by water in plastic. Because dog packing always involves some risk of loss, breakage, or water damage, avoid letting Fido carry your valuables and absolute necessities.

Pack dogs can overheat quickly, and sometimes this can become a real problem. The load, combined with the thick, insulating pack, contributes to the trouble. If your dog pants heavily, weaves his

Pack dogs learn that if they lie down, their load rests on the ground.

hindquarters, or persistently tries to bury his face in cold ground, stop and remove the pack. Let him rest at least ten minutes or until he seems ready to go; you may not be able to put the pack back on if he continues to overheat.

Most dogs hesitate to swim while wearing a pack because it might sink them, but they can step off of a drop-off without warning. Keep your dogs at your side when crossing deep water, and support them if they have to swim. If *you* have to swim, take the packs off so that the dogs can fend for themselves.

Working for Wages

From the gold-rush days at the turn of the century until airplanes took over the mail routes in the 1930s and 1940s, "dog punchers" in the north could find employment with their teams. During the winter months, dogs moved passengers, freight, and mail all across Alaska and through parts of Canada and the northern United States. These days, finding a steady income with a dog team is considerably more difficult. Instead of freighting life's necessities, the musher must usually rely on clients interested in recreational outings.

Some mushers take tourists for sled rides, while others take out clients on excursions lasting a day or more. Building up a good business requires an investment of several years' work, an effective advertising campaign, and the ability to run an outfit that is both reliable *and* exciting enough to build a good customer base so that people will spread the word.

The going rate of hire for a dog team varies. Forty dollars per hour or eighty dollars for a half-day trip is charged by one outfit. For a full day including lunch, the charge is $160. Another outfitter who takes clients on trips charges $100 to $120 per day. This covers feeding and care of clients and dogs. This may sound like a get-rich-quick-while-having-fun job — $1,200 for a ten-day trip — but consider the year-round cost of your dogs; vet bills; gear; food; wall tents or cabins (clients must be pampered or they won't be back); advertising; insurance; transportation of dogs, clients, and freight; and countless other investments. Each trip requires precise planning and preparation. Trips lasting more than two days need additional support from extra dog teams, snow machines, trucks, or airplanes, because you cannot haul passengers *and* a lot of dog food.

Clients may ride in your sled or may follow a guide with a sled and small team that they drive. Be sure to match the team and the trip to the client's abilities. If you suspect that the client's enthusiasm surpasses reality, play it safe. At least have an alternate plan should your self-proclaimed mountain man not be quite the wilderness scout that he thought he was. Be prepared to handle with grace, and without patronizing, people who are smart, dumb, rude, too brave, too timid, obnoxious, unthinking, or ignorant. If you cannot get along with all kinds of people, you are in the wrong business.

Commercial ventures involving clients should be insured (a skyrocketing cost, unfortunately), and you may have your customers sign a statement of non-liability. While this might not stand up in court if negligence on your part can be proven, it can help in the event of a lawsuit.

Before attempting such a business, you must be experienced in people handling, dog driving, wilderness camping, survival, and first aid, and you must have an intimate knowledge of the land you travel

Dogs can be used for any number of chores, from hauling wood and water to getting the mail, going to the grocery, or taking the kids to school.

through and of the vagaries of local weather. The responsibility cannot be taken too seriously.

Occasionally, dog teams hire out to carry freight or to run support for skiers and other wilderness travelers. Dog drivers are responsible for the freight but not necessarily for the clients. When motorized access is restricted by law or terrain, dog teams can carry freight for people. In Denali National Park, for example, mountain climbers sometimes pay to have their supplies hauled by dog team up to a base camp. You might also find big-game hunters who will pay you to haul out their meat.

Before starting a business, check applicable laws covering dogs, concessions, and the land that you want to cover. Parklands may require insurance and special permits or may have other restrictions. Some allow no dogs at all. Crossing private land requires permission from the landowners, and this must be obtained every year. On public trails, treat skiers, snow machiners, and other users courteously. Your business does not give you title to the trail. Remember, too, that the business end will require advertising, bookkeeping, and many other details — you are not going to be simply sledding.

Trapping by Dog Team

Trappers are among the few dog drivers who still use their teams for serious transportation. Although most trappers switched to snow machines during the 1960s, a few still prefer using dogs. If trained and fed properly, dogs are extremely dependable. They can traverse country that machines cannot, including vertical banks, deep overflow, thin ice, and piles of deadfall. They offer a companionship that has never been built successfully into a machine. They come with a built-in repair system, an orchestra for the late evening, a bear-and-burglar alarm, and a self-energized heater. They burn renewable resources, start at the first shout even at fifty below, float when they fall through ice, and willingly eat the burnt half of the cornbread. Depending upon what a trapper feeds his dogs and upon how many dogs he or she keeps, they may or may not be more expensive than repairing, replacing, and fueling snow machines. They are slower (except in extremely rough country) and have a limited mileage that they can be run.

Training and power play a greater role than speed. The dogs that we run on our eighty-mile trapline weigh seventy to eighty pounds, and some are much bigger. Teams of four to ten dogs get the trapper where he or she needs to go without wasting energy on extra dogs. Because team maintenance is dictated by economics rather than by the need for peak performance, diets need not be sophisticated. The goal is to catch fur, not build a hotshot team. However, because good maintenance enhances the team's ability to cover miles, and hence catch more fur, the wise trapper does the best that he or she can for the dogs. We do not give our dogs vitamin/mineral supplements (except as pups), because we have not seen any increase in performance from doing so. However, we do give them liver and meat snacks during the winter, because that does significantly increase the number of miles that we can put on them.

Most training and conditioning take place on the trapline in the course of the work that must be done. A good trapline team stops on command, needs no anchoring, and will not run off as the trapper works. My team will stop on command even if I am some distance away. The dogs must be trained not to jump fur animals caught near

Trapline dogs tend to be big but fairly leggy, so they can pull a heavy load through deep snow. This old leader was also used for packing, sledding, and skijoring, and he occasionally tracked down escaped animals.

the trail, because you do not want the pelts to be damaged. A good, strong leader will drag the excited team past a fighting animal. Some dogs can even be trained to track game that has escaped.

Poor trails and frequent stops to service traps means a slow rate of travel. Although the teams often travel twelve miles per hour, speeds of three to eight miles per hour are more common. Distances range from five to thirty miles per day. Our team runs 80 to 130 miles per week for three or four months of the season. Traps must be checked whether the dogs need a rest or not, even if their condition and attitude are hurt by the additional work. In return, we probably give our dogs more one-on-one treatment, as well as special care.

One chilly ten-below day, Miki and I set out to explore the upper reaches of a creek that we trapped. Overflow and glaciering soaked the dogs, and open stream crossings drenched them even more. The nine huskies were crusted with ice when we returned to our cabin at dark.

We unhooked the towline and sent all nine dogs inside the tiny cabin. The vapor from their panting filled the cabin with a dense fog until a roaring fire in the wood stove warmed the air. Wading among the grinning beasts, my sister and I started their supper of boiled rice, fish, tallow, and commercial feed. The dogs lay dripping under the table, on the bed, under the bed, by the stove, and across the floor like living wall-to-wall carpeting. We were awash in dogs, surrounded by dogs, living with dogs.

That's just the way we like it.

GLOSSARY

Alaskan husky: A variable and versatile breed of northern dog known for speed, stamina, and drive, originating in the Alaskan bush. Because these dogs are selected for performance rather than for appearance, they are not a standardized breed.

Anabolic steroids: Male hormones (see "Drugs" section of Chapter 6).

Analgesic: A painkiller, such as aspirin or phenylbutazole.

Anemia: A subnormal amount of red blood cells or hemoglobin (responsible for transporting oxygen in the blood). Anemia causes the gums and mucous membranes to become pale.

Anesthetics: An agent that causes a loss of feeling or pain.

Angulation: The angle between the long bones of the leg, and the shoulder or pelvis, when the dog is standing square. A dog with poor angulation has straight legs, vertical shoulders, and a horizontal pelvis with the tail generally set high.

Anti-inflammatory: A drug that decreases inflammation (pain, heat, redness, swelling).

Backline: Same as tugline.

Basket sled: A sled with an elevated basket set up on stanchions, as opposed to a flat-bottomed toboggan. Same as stanchion sled.

Bivvy sack: A sack that fits over a sleeping bag, serving as protection from wind, rain, and snow when camping out without a tent.

Bolt: When a team runs uncontrollably or leaves the trail or runs into a crowd, usually caused by overexcitement or confusion.

Break out: To loosen a sled that has been standing on snow long enough for the runners to freeze to the surface. Or, to start a sled moving forward.

Breast plate: The wide, elongated section of most modern harnesses that rides over the dog's sternum (breastbone) between his front legs (see Fig. 3-2, page 72).

Bridle: The rope rigging of a sled to which the towline attaches. Same as sled harness.

Brush hook: Same as snow hook.

Burnout: The depressed condition of a dog that has been worked too hard. Burnout can be physical, psychological, or both.

Bushbow or brush bow: A curved bow attached to the front of the sled, that deflects the sled off of trees and other obstacles, to prevent breakage or a sudden stop (see Fig. 3-1, page 59).

Cargo bag: Same as sled bag.

Checkpoints: Designated spots along a race course where the teams are checked to be sure that everyone follows the prescribed route. On mid- and long-distance races, they also allow for resupply and dog drops.

Chute: The fenced-in area at the start of a race that guides the dogs onto the correct trail and keeps spectators at bay.

"Come Gee!" "Come Haw!": Command to make the leader bring the team around a full 180 degrees to the right (gee) or left (haw).

Command leader: A lead dog trained to follow vocal commands, such as gee, haw, and on by, as opposed to a trail leader who will take a team down a trail but will not necessarily obey commands.

Conformation: The physical form of a dog or an animal, especially the way in which the bones and muscles are put together. Conformation affects how the animal moves.

Coupling: The dog's back between the fore and hind limbs; the back "couples" the front to the rear.

Coursing dogs: Hounds that hunt by eyesight and speed (rather than by scent), including Greyhounds, Afghan Hounds, and Salukis; they typically have a double-suspension gallop in which they are airborne during two phases of every bound (as opposed to huskies and most other dogs, which have only one period of suspension during each bound). Generally known for their high speed without long-range stamina.

Crabbing: A sidewise movement, usually at the trot, when the dog is traveling straight ahead but his body is at an angle to his line of travel. Dogs may crab to avoid interference, or because of pulling beside the towline. It is a fault.

Croup: Rump, or pelvic area at the end of the back ahead of the tail; especially the slope on the top leading down to the tail.

Cyanosis: The bluish discoloration of mucous membranes and gums when an animal has insufficient oxygen in the blood.

Dehydration: Loss of water from within the body which can be life-threatening.

Dewclaw: A small toe with a claw on the inside of the lower leg. It often is removed to prevent it from being torn or from causing sores when the dog is booted.

Dipping snow: When a dog bites a mouthful of snow while running. Although this combats dehydration, it can disrupt the team; sprint dogs especially are discouraged from dipping. Dogs dip because they are hot or thirsty, because they have a dry mouth, because it is a habit, or because they see other dogs dipping.

Diuretic: A substance or drug that causes an increased urinary output. Caffeine and alcohol are diuretics.

DMSO: Dimethylsulfoxide, a colorless anti-inflammatory compound that passes readily through the skin, carrying certain other chemicals with it.

Dog box: A box, usually made of plywood, which sits on a pickup truck or trailer, with individual compartments for each dog; used to transport teams.

Dog drop: A point along a race trail (mid- or long-distance) where injured, sick, or tired dogs can be dropped from the team.

Dog yard: The area at home where sled dogs are tied or kenneled.

Double lead: Running two leaders side by side (as opposed to a single lead).

Double neckline: A short line with a snap on each end which connects to the collar of each leader; used when running a double lead.

Drive bow: Same as handlebow (see Fig. 3-1, page 59).

Electrolytes: Minerals such as sodium, chloride, and potassium which are essential to body function. They can be lost especially through diarrhea, vomiting, and blood loss (and, in sweating animals, through sweat). Either an excess or a lack of electrolytes causes dehydration.

Extend: To open (straighten) a limb; the opposite of flex.

Femur: The large bone of the upper leg (thigh).

Flex: To bend a limb (closing the angle); the opposite of extend.

Foot pad: A nonskid pad on the back of the runner on which the musher stands. It prevents the musher from slipping off and provides a wider surface on which to stand.

Free zone: No-Man's-Land.

Gait: The manner of movement at a walk, trot, or lope ("the dog has a choppy gait"); can also mean a specific pattern of footfalls, such as a trot or a lope ("The dog's preferred gait was a lope").

Gangline: Same as towline. Or, a stake-out line with individual drops, used for picketing dogs temporarily.

"Gee!": Command to turn right.

Gee-Haw leader: A lead dog that will reliably take the commands to turn. A command leader.

Gee pole: A pole extending forward from the right side of the sled. It is gripped by a driver on skis, on foot, or on a ouija board, to give better leverage for steering the sled.

Gene: A unit within a cell that controls or influences hereditary traits, affecting how the body will look, work, and act; a particle of genetic material.

Genetics: The study of heredity.

Gig: Same as a wheeled rig.

Glaciering: Occurs when water seeps or floods repeatedly, causing layers of ice to build up as it freezes. When this occurs on a slope or in waterfall form, the result is sometimes called a glacier. Glaciering occurs most commonly in areas of permafrost, or on shallow streams.

Handlebow: The upright handle at the back of a sled that the driver holds onto; it may be curved or squared. Also called a driving bow (see Fig 3-1, page 59).

Handler: An assistant, often helping to harness and hold dogs at a race start; may also be an assistant who does chores in the dog yard, hooks up sled dogs, or trains a team for someone else.

Harness-banging: When an excited dog leaps against his harness, trying to start the sled, either prior to a run or when stopped during the run.

"Haw!": Command to turn left.

Heat stroke, heat exhaustion: Conditions brought on by excessive overheating of a dog, leading to collapse and death if the dog is not cooled promptly.

Hematinic: An agent used to increase the oxygen-carrying capacity of the blood (such as iron, copper, and other minerals used by hemoglobin); often given as a dietary supplement; higher levels can be toxic.

"Hike!": Command for go. Also used by some mushers to encourage the team to go faster or pull harder.

Holding area: The area at a race where the dogs are organized and harnessed prior to the race start.

Hot-wax: Treating the plastic on sled runners with wax to improve glide and decrease friction, similar to waxing cross-country skis.

Hound: Among mushers, a hound frequently refers to any non-northern breed. Otherwise, it is a hunting dog, either a coursing (speed) hound or a tracking (scent) hound.

Husky: A catch-all term covering most northern-type sled dogs. In its broadest interpretation, it can include all northern breeds and strains, including purebreds.

Hybrid vigor: The increased size and vitality often seen in the offspring when two unrelated, but previously inbred, strains are mated.

Hypothyroidism: A condition caused by decreased hormonal output of the thyroid gland, common in some lines of huskies, which can lead to a number of symptoms, including reduced speed and stamina.

Ice hook: Similar to a snow hook, this anchor generally has sharper prongs that can be pounded into ice; it lacks the fins and high handle of many snow hooks.

Inbreeding: Breeding closely related animals, such as father-daughter or sister-brother crosses, with the intention of concentrating characteristics. Can also refer to breeding any two related animals even if they are only distantly related.

Indian dog: A general term for a husky originating in a northern native village.

Individual start: A starting order at a race in which each team leaves at intervals, usually one to three minutes apart, to avoid tangles and confusions; in this type of race, the mushers are timed and the one with the fastest time wins (see mass start).

Interference: When the hind feet overreach and hit the front feet, most commonly at a trot. This can be caused by legs that are too long, a back that is too short, or bad angulation in front combined with powerful hindquarters. These dogs may pace or crab to avoid interference.

Jingler: A noisemaker, usually made of bottle caps or little bells, used to get a team's attention; it often replaces a whip as a noisemaker.

Lead coupler: Same as double neckline.

Leader: The dog at the front of the team that guides the team and takes orders from the driver.

Leading leg: The foreleg that extends the farthest forward and hits the ground last at a lope; the entire weight of the dog breaks over this one leg (see Fig. 1-2, page 28).

Limited race: A race that limits the number of dogs in each team, such as five-dog class; usually a shorter race.

Linebreeding: Breeding dogs that are related to each other but not closely, such as grandfather-granddaughter crosses; linebreeding results in a small amount of inbreeding.

"Line Out!": Order to the dogs to line out or to tighten the towline.

Lope: The canter, or run, with a long, easy stride.

Mass start: A race start in which all of the teams line up at the starting line and leave at the same time; the team crossing the finish line first is the winner (see individual start).

Metabolism: The chemical and physical processes within cells that produce energy for life and activity and that change compounds into living tissue; the work done constantly by living cells to maintain life.

Metacarpals: The long, slender bones found within the wrist (pastern) of a dog; the bones in the back of a human hand.

Metatarsals; The long, slender bones between the hock and the hind foot of a dog; the bones in the human foot.

Muscle-bound: A condition affecting dogs that have been worked very hard, perhaps with very heavy loads; characterized by a broad chest and heavy muscles; causes overmuscling and a shorter, less limber stride.

Mush: To run a dog team; also a command to "Go!" (rarely used).

Neckline: Line running from the towline to the dog's collar to keep him from turning around or swinging out of line.

Necklining: When a dog is pulling back against the neckline, or dragging.

No-Man's-Land: A predetermined stretch of race trail, as it comes to the finish line, where a lead musher is not required to give trail to an overtaking team (although interference also is not allowed). Also called free zone.

"On By!": Command to go straight ahead, on past an obstacle or a distraction, such as another team.

Ouija board (pronounced "wee gee"): A short toboggan or board fastened to the towline between the team and the sled; a driver stands on it when using a gee pole.

Overflow: Water flooding the snow, usually on rivers, lakes, or swamps. Overflow can occur even in extreme cold and is potentially dangerous.

Overreaching: When the hind foot reaches too far forward and strikes the front foot as the dog trots, causing interference.

Pace: A specific gait, also called sidewheeling, in which the front and back legs on the same side move forward and backward together. It is similar to a trot, in which the front left leg moves with the back right leg. Pace can also refer to a speed at which a dog travels ("he set a fast pace"), or to the way in which the speed of a team is regulated so that it does not burn out ("he paced his team carefully during the race") (see Fig. 1-3, page 30).

Peak out: To bring a team to its maximum potential both physically and psychologically.

Pedaling: When the driver stands on the sled runner with one foot and shifts his or her weight to the opposite foot on the ground, pushing the sled forward; or more commonly, just taking the weight off of the team. Also called pumping or kicking.

Picket line: A long cable or chain line with shorter drop lines for securing a number of dogs.

Point: The two dogs running directly behind the leaders; Alaskans usually call these dogs swing dogs.

Prepotent: A particularly strong ability to pass characteristics on to offspring; more common among inbreds.

P-Tex: A type of plastic that can be glued onto the bottom of sled runners; P-Tex is very slick but is less durable than some plastics, and it is popular among sprint racers.

Pumping: Same as pedaling.

QCR: The Quick Change Runner System, invented by Tim White. A system of sliding plastic shoes through rails mounted on the sled runners, making changing plastic easy and fast.

Recovery time: The lapse of time that dogs require to recover from a run; the period of time that they must rest before they feel ready to continue. Or, the time required for the pulse and respiration rates to return to normal after exercise. Often used to determine a dog's physical condition; a dog in good condition has a short recovery time.

Rig: A wheeled cart used for training dogs under snowless conditions; made especially for the purpose of running sled dogs; generally, a rig is much lighter than the motorized three- or four-wheelers also used.

Saddlebag: A dog pack.

Second string: A team of younger dogs or lower-quality dogs that is kept in training in addition to the main racing string.

Sesamoid bones: Tiny round or irregularly shaped bones found in some tendons, where they act as fulcrums; the ones in the feet are sometimes broken, causing lameness.

Shoes: Material placed on sled runners to improve glide, decrease friction, and protect the runners; usually made of plastic or metal.

Single lead: A single lead dog, as opposed to a double lead.

Singletree: A spreader bar at the back of a freight harness that keeps the side straps from rubbing or pinching the hind legs.

Skijoring (also spelled "skijouring"): Running sled dogs with skis instead of with a sled. Or, towing on skis behind a dogsled, horse, or vehicle.

Sled bag: A formed sack or lining fitted to the inside of a sled basket; used instead of a sled tarp to protect and hold the load in place.

Sled basket: The area of a sled (including a toboggan sled) that holds the load.

Sled harness: Same as the bridle of a sled.

Snow anchor: A snow hook.

Snub rope: A rope used to tie the sled to a tree or post, to hold the dogs while stopped, especially during hookup. Novice drivers sometimes have a very long snub rope, up to thirty feet in length, trailing behind the sled so that they can grab it if their team gets away. (This is illegal in some races because it can interfere with a team running behind.)

Sour: A dog that is psychologically sick of dogsledding. Dogs are made sour by overwork, improper training or management (including an inadequate diet), or a bad experience.

Spooky: A dog that is easily frightened or that shies away from humans or other things.

Spreader bar: A singletree.

Sprint race: A shorter race, usually thirty miles or less, in which the dogs are expected to lope all the way.

Stabilizing rudder: A skatelike blade attached to the runner; the driver can stand on the rudder to press it against ice, preventing a sidewise skid on glare ice.

Stake-out chain: A chain with drop chains for staking out dogs temporarily while hooking up in a dog yard or at a race, or when in camp. Or, an individual dog's chain that keeps him confined at home.

Stanchion sled: A basket sled, as opposed to a toboggan (Fig. 3-1, page 59).

Steroids: Compounds including anabolic steroids (male hormones) and corticosteroids (anti-inflammatory agents).

Stimulants: Drugs that cause a temporary increase in activity, frequently affecting the nervous and cardiovascular systems.

Stove or stove-up: Lame or injured, or stiff.

"Straight On!": Command for go straight ahead, instead of taking a fork angling away from the trail. Or, go straight ahead past a distraction.

Swing: The dogs immediately behind the lead dogs. Also called point dogs outside of Alaska.

Systemic: Affecting the entire body. For example, a local infection in a small wound can become systemic if the infecting bacteria or their toxins spread throughout the body.

Team dogs: Dogs running behind the leader, especially the dogs behind the swing (point) dogs and in front of the wheel dogs.

Toboggan: A flat-bottomed sled, usually with no stanchions. Modern toboggans, or toboggan sleds, have plastic beds elevated on runners; old-time toboggans have no runners and ride with the full basket against the snow (see Fig. 3-1, page 59).

Topical: Pertaining to a specific area, usually the skin; for example, a topical steroid is applied on the skin, as opposed to a steroid that is injected or given orally.

Towline or tow rope: The rope extending from the sled, onto which individual or paired dogs are attached. Also called a gangline.

Traces: The towline, necklines, and tuglines; all the ropes by which the dogs pull the sled. Also called rigging.

"Trail!": A signal from an overtaking musher to alert the team ahead that he or she wishes to pass; the advance musher must give trail (allow the overtaking musher to pass, even if he or she has to stop his or her team).

Trail leader: A dog that will stay in front of the team and lead the team down a trail, but that will not necessarily take commands from the driver. He may be highly skilled in judging trail hazards and locating obscured trails.

Tugline: The rope attaching a dog's harness to the towline. Same as backline.

Unlimited race: A race in which no limit is placed on the number of dogs that can be run on each team; usually a longer sprint race. Teams of sixteen to twenty-two dogs are not uncommon.

Vetrap®: A brand-name stretchy bandaging material that clings to itself; similar to elastic bandages.

Village dogs: A general term referring to huskies originating from Alaskan villages; many have been interbred with southern breeds in the past. They also might be called Indian dogs or Alaskan huskies, although not all Alaskan huskies are considered to be village dogs.

Wheel: The position directly ahead of the sled.

Wheel dogs or wheelers: The dogs running in the wheel position that take the brunt of the load and tend to be banged around more than other dogs; they also steer the sled by pulling it around corners.

"Whoa!": Command for stop.

Withers: The top of the shoulders; usually the highest point along a dog's back, at the base of the neck.

REFERENCES AND SUGGESTED READING

The accompanying notes merely reflect our own opinion. Many breed books also are available, as well as countless reference books covering every topic from physiology to breeding.

Books

Alpo Pet Center, *Feeding and Training Dogs for Hard Work*. Allentown, Penn.: Alpo Pet Foods, Inc., 1985. An informative booklet on nutrition published by Alpo in collaboration with Harris Dunlap of Zero Kennels.

Attla, George. *Everything I Know About Training and Racing Sled Dogs*. Rone, New York: Arner Publications, 1972 (revised 1975). The sport has evolved since this book came out, but George Attla is still winning, and much of his advice still holds true.

Barve, Betty. *Dog Mushers Trail Food and Old Fashion Recipe Book*. Wasilla, Alaska: L&B Color Printing, 1989. A collection of recipes and trail hints, including dog-food recipes for long-distance races; many originating from mushers and their wives.

Barve, Lavon, editor. *Mushing North*. Wasilla, Alaska: Lavon Barve, n.d. A pictorial book on the Iditarod done by a veteran racer.

Brown, Curtis M. *Dog Locomotion and Gait Analysis*. Wheat Ridge, Colo.: Hoflin Publishers, 1986. An in-depth and technical discussion of conformation and gaits.

Carlson, Delbert G., DVM, and James M. Giffin, M.D. *Dog Owner's Home Veterinary Handbook*. New York: Howell Book House, 1980. This is our favorite layman's reference for medical problems.

Collins, Donald R., DVM. *The Collins Guide to Dog Nutrition.* New York: Howell Book House, 1982 (revised 1987). This is a good nontechnical reference for mushers, although it lacks some of the recent strides made in racing sled dog nutrition.

Collins, Julie and Miki. *Trapline Twins.* Edmunds, Wash.: Alaska Northwest Books (GTE Discovery Publications, Inc.), 1989. Dog mushing, trapping, and Alaskan bush life-style adventures, including cross-country dog-team treks and distance racing.

Cooper, Michael. *Racing Sled Dogs, An Original North American Sport.* New York: Clarion Books, 1988. A children's book on the sport, covering racing, history, and breeds; a nice book, but it does contain some inaccuracies.

Coppinger, Lorna, with the International Sled Dog Racing Association. *The World of Sled Dogs.* New York: Howell Book House, 1977. A comprehensive work covering everything from history and famous mushers to sled-dog clubs around the world.

Dart, Joe. *Mush! Or, How To Make an Alaskan Dog Sled.* Fairbanks, Alaska: Joe Dart, 1979. Diagrams detail the steps in building a small basket sled.

Dorland's Pocket Medical Dictionary. Philadelphia, Penn.: W. B. Saunders Company, 1977. A good reference for medical terms.

Elliot, Rachel Page. *The New Dogsteps.* New York: Howell Book House, 1984. A nicely illustrated, understandable presentation of conformation, angulation, gaits, and gait faults.

Fishback, Lee, and Mel Fishback. *Novice Sled Dog Training,* and *The Sled and Harness Book.* Snohomish, Wash.: Bastion Press, 1972. The Fishback books, although outdated, offer advice from veteran mushers.

Fishback, Lee. *Training Lead Dogs.* Nunica, Mich.: Tun-Dra, 1978. One man's method of meticulously training a quality lead dog.

Flanders, Noël K. *The Joy of Running Sled Dogs.* Loveland, Colo.: Alpine Publications, 1989. An up-to-date book on basic mushing, including breeds, equipment, training, racing, and care of sled dogs.

Frankling, Eleanor. *Practical Dog Breeding and Genetics.* New York: Arco Pub., 1977. Anyone working to breed better dogs should have a few books like this one.

Holst, Phyllis A., MS, DVM. *Canine Reproduction: A Breeder's Guide.* Loveland, Colo.: Alpine Publications, 1985. An in-depth, technical, informative book on the physiology of reproduction in dogs, without getting into genetics.

Hubbard, Bernard R. *Mush, You Malamutes!* New York: The American Press, 1938. The historical adventures of the Glacier Priest.

Jones, Tim. *The Last Great Race.* Seattle, Wash.: Madrona, 1982. Day-by-day account of the 1979 Iditarod, in a readable style.

Kaynor, Carol, and Mari Hoe-Raitto. *Skijoring: An Introduction to the Sport.* Delta, Alaska: Dragon Press, 1988. A booklet on skiing behind sled dogs, including information on training, equipment, commands, and the skier.

Levorsen, Bella, editor. *Mush! A Beginner's Manual of Sled Dog Training.* Westmoreland, N.Y.: Arner Publications, 1976. This is a good book for a new musher just entering the sport.

Lyon, McDowell. *The Dog in Action.* New York: Howell Book House, 1985. A readable and thought-provoking, widely read book on dog locomotion.

Monks of the Brotherhood of St. Francis. *How To Be Your Dog's Best Friend.* Boston: Little, Brown, 1978. The monks of New Skete present training methods for the general dog owner, including many ideas popular among mushers.

Nielsen, Nicki J. *The Iditarod: Women on the Trail.* Anchorage, Alaska: Wolfdog Publications, 1986. Includes history of the trail and sketches of women who have run the race, 1974-1985.

Onstott, Kyle. *The New Art of Breeding Better Dogs.* New York: Howell Book House, 1978. Genetics as it applies to the serious breeding program.

Rennick, Penny, editor. *Dogs of the North.* Anchorage, Alaska: *Alaska Geographic*, vol. 14, no. 1, 1987. A colorful review of dog mushing in Alaska.

Riddles, Libby, and Tim Jones. *Race Across Alaska.* Harrisburg, Penn.: Stackpole Books, 1988. "What I feel is, if I died right now, it'd be okay." The Iditarod adventures of the 1985 winner; well written, informative, and exciting.

Rutherford, Clarice, and David H. Neil, MRCVS. *How to Raise a Puppy You Can Live With.* Loveland, Colo.: Alpine Publications, 1981.

Informative book on raising puppies, including valuable information on imprinting. Be aware that this is aimed at raising a *pet*
puppy; not all of the advice is good for raising a *sled-dog* puppy.

Shields, Mary. *Sled Dog Trails*. Anchorage, Alaska: Alaska Northwest
Books (currently published by Pyrola Pub., Fairbanks, Alaska),
1984. A warm book detailing Mary's adventures on Alaskan trails,
including her account as the first woman to finish the Iditarod.

Siegmund, Otto H., editor. *The Merck Veterinary Manual*, 5th edition.
Rahway, N.J.: Merck & Co., 1979. An extremely detailed reference
book covering everything from pharmaceuticals to farm animals.

Smythe, R. H. *The Breeding and Rearing of Dogs*. New York: Arco Pub.,
1979. Details breeding, whelping, and raising dogs without getting
into too much genetics.

Steger, Will, with Paul Schurke. *North to the Pole*. New York: Random
House, 1987. The story of Steger's 1986 dog-team trek to the North
Pole. Includes equipment and logistics information.

Sternberg, Mike. *Teach Your Dogs to Pull*. Post Falls, Idaho: Self-
published, 1984. A valuable booklet for weight-pulling, including
equipment, training, conditioning, and International Weight Pull
Association rules.

Stuck, Hudson. *Ten Thousand Miles With a Dog Sled*. New York: Charles
Scribner's Sons, 1914. Reprinted by the University of Nebraska
Press, 1988. Like Stuck's other books, this is a marvelous account
of the archdeacon's travels in the early 1900s.

Swenson, Rick. *The Secrets of Long Distance Training and Racing*. Wasilla,
Alaska: L&B Color Printing, 1987. Although it contains excellent
advice from a veteran musher and is required reading for aspiring
distance racers, the quality of this small book could be better.

Thompson, Raymond. Miscellaneous bulletins and booklets. Lyn-
wood, Wash.: Raymond Thompson Company. Although outdated, Thompson offers considerable information on sled dogs,
gear, skijoring, and training.

Turner, A. Allan, Ph.D., editor. *The Iditarod Arctic Sports Medicine/
Human Performance Guide*. Anchorage, Alaska: The Alaska Regional
Chapter of American College of Sports Medicine, 1988. This is a
well-researched text on human physiology in the Arctic but is
not actually based on studies of Iditarod mushers.

Uncle Elmer, Vol. I and II. Center Harbor, N.H.: Team and Trail Pub., 1981 and 1986. These anonymous booklets present some really advanced ideas on sled-dog training and care in a folksy and readable style.

Ungermann, Kenneth A. *The Race to Nome.* New York: Harper & Row, 1963. A historical account of the *real* race to Nome — the life-saving 1925 Nenana-to-Nome diphtheria serum relay run.

United States War Dept., Basic Field Manual. *Dog Team Transportation.* Seattle, Wash.: Shorey Book Store, 1975 (facsimile of the 1941 edition). An outdated but detailed account of dog-team travel, army-style.

Vaudrin, Bill. *Racing Alaskan Sled Dogs.* Anchorage, Alaska: Alaska Northwest Books, 1976. Although growing outdated, this is a highly informative collection of essays done by the masters of the 1960s and 1970s.

Walden, Arthur T. *A Dog Puncher on the Yukon.* Boston: Houghton Mifflin, 1928. An excellent account of dog-team freighting and travel during the gold-rush days.

Welch, Jim. *The Speed Mushing Manual.* Eagle River, Alaska: Sirius Publications, 1989. Contains the most up-to-date and usable information on sprint racing, including dogs, nutrition, conditioning, training, equipment, and strategy.

Whitney, Leon F. *Dog Psychology: The Basis of Dog Training.* New York: Howell Book House, 1971. An older but detailed textbook that includes the author's favorite training methods.

Magazines

Many clubs and associations put out their own newsletters and magazines. A few magazines are of interest to most mushers.

The Gangline, Bruce Meyer, 8191 E. 17th, Terrebonne, Oregon 97760. A small magazine covering Alaskan races and containing information, historical articles, and adventure stories.

INFO (Official Magazine of ISDRA, the International Sled Dog Racing Association), HC 86, Box 3380, Merrifield, Minnesota 56465; 218-765-4297. Informative magazine covering the political scene and including knowledgeable articles on dog mushing; aimed primarily at racing. It also contains addresses of regional directors.

Mushing, P.O. Box 149, Ester, Alaska 99725-0149. A full-size classy magazine covering most aspects of the sport, including new ideas, technology, book reviews, and stories. Around-the-world coverage.

TEAM & TRAIL, P.O. Box 128, Sibley Rd., Center Harbor, New Hampshire 03226-0128. Includes race coverage and other articles.

Videos

Videos are available for some major distance races, each one covering a year's race; they are sold by the race association and sometimes by mushing outlets. We hope to see more general-interest and informative videos released in the future.

KYUK Video Productions. *Tales of the Tundra: Supernatural Lore From Western Alaska.* Includes three dog mushing tales. One hour. KYUK Video Productions, Pouch 468M, Bethel, Alaska 99559.

Lugo, Bob and Pat. *Sled Dog Basics.* Free Spirit Kennel & Outfitters, Rural Route 3, Milaca, Minnesota 56353. Although not as professionally done as Maryís video (below), this one covers many basic questions for beginning mushers, including information on equipment, on training pups, and on commands.

Shields, Mary. *Season of the Sled Dog.* Pyrola Pub., P.O. Box 80961-M, Fairbanks, Alaska 99708. A professionally taped video portraying well-known musher and adventurer Mary Shields, including her bush life-style, the Yukon Quest race, and cross-country travel (not a how-to video).

ORGANIZATIONS

Mushing clubs and associations are organized around the world. A few addresses are included here. Because addresses can change frequently, you may have trouble contacting an association. If this happens, try writing to ISDRA for current information. If that fails, ask local mushers, feed-store owners, or mushing outlets in your area, or write to one of the mushing magazines for information.

ISDRA (International Sled Dog Racing Association), HC 86, Box 3380, Merrifield, Minnesota 56465; 218/765-4297. Addresses of regional directors can be obtained by writing ISDRA and are also listed in *INFO*, the association's magazine. (USDRA has members in forty-two states, Canada, Europe, and New Zealand.)

International Federation of Sleddog Sports (IFSS), Prospect House, Charlton, Kilmersdon, Bath BA3 5TN United Kingdom.

International Siberian Husky Club (for working Siberians), N7002 Peck Station Rd., Elkhorn, Wisconsin 53121.

Alaska Dog Musher's Association, (holds the North American championships), P.O. Box 70662, Fairbanks, Alaska 99707.

Alaska Skijoring & Pulk Association, P.O. Box 82843, Fairbanks, Alaska 99708.

Alaskan Sled Dog & Racing Association, (holds the fur Rendezvous world championships), 3400 Tudor Road, P.O. Box 110569, Anchorage, Alaska 99511.

DSSV (Deutscher Schlittenhunde Sport Verband) Geschaftstelle, Postfach 1420, D-67448 Hassbloch, Germany.

Eskimo Dog Club of Great Britain, Jenny Mai Handford, The Gore, West End, Herstmonceux, East Sussex BN27 4N2 United Kingdom.

Finnish Federation of Sleddog Sportmen, Radiokatu 20, SF-00240, Helsinki, Finland.

Great Lakes Sled Dog Association, 5875 McCrum Rd., Jackson, Michigan 49201.

Inland Empire Sled Dog Association, 207 Thain Rd., Lewiston, Idaho 83501.

Lakes Region Sled Dog Club, P.O. Box 382, Laconia, New Hampshire 03247.

Mid-Union Sled Haulers (MUSH), 4480 Hendershot NW, Grand Rapids, Michigan 49544.

Montana Mountain Mushers, P.O. Box 905, Seeley Lake, Montana 59868.

Narragansett Bay Sled Dog Club, 72 Hamlin Street, Acushnet, Massachusetts 02743.

New England Sled Dog Club, RR 2, Box 262H, Lyme, New Hampshire 03768.

North Alberta Sled Dog Association, 10123 97th Ave., Edmonton, AB T5K 0B3 Canada.

Northwest Sled Dog Association, P.O. Box 551, Roy, Washington 98580.

Rocky Mountain Sled Dog Club, P.O. Box 57, Grand Lake, Colorado 80447.

Sierra Nevada Dog Drivers, 5220 Sierra Road, San Jose, California 95132.

Wisconsin Trailblazers, 11032 Four Duck Lake Rd., Three Lakes, Wisconsin 54562.

RACE ADDRESSES

Many middle- and long-distance races are run under their own organization instead of being affiliated with a regional club. Some of them are listed here, but there are many more.

Iditarod Trail Committee, (1,100 miles across Alaska), P.O. Box 870800, Wasilla, Alaska 99687-0800.

Yukon Quest International, (1,000 miles in Alaska and Canada), P.O. Box 75015, Fairbanks, Alaska 99707.

John Beargrease Sled Dog Marathon, (330 miles near the Canadian border in Minnesota), P.O. Box 500, Duluth, Minnesota 55801.

Kusko 300, P.O. Box 758, Bethel, Alaska 99559.

Race to the Sky, Montana Sled Dog, Inc., P.O. Box 854, Helena, Montana 59624. (Also educates through rendezvous and grade school curriculum.)

OUTFITTERS

Here are some outfitters who cater to dog mushers or who sell mushing-related items. We are not necessarily endorsing them or their products. There are many, many more whose addresses can be found in mushing magazines and newsletters. Ask your fellow mushers who they patronize in your area. Most of the ones listed here will send you a catalog or price list on request.

Adanac Sled and Equipment, 4108 Highway 93 North, Kalispell, Montana 59901.

AKKO Outdoors, Box 977, Hudson, Quebec, J0P 1H0, Canada.

Alyeska Sled Dog Products, 237 Camp 20 Road, P.O. Box 627, Hovland, Minnesota 55606.

ATIM, 4210 25th Avenue, Vernon, British Columbia, V1T 1P4, Canada. Also has veterinary supplies.

Bernd Weschle, Lindenbergweg 15, D-7730 Villingen - Tannheim, Germany.

Black Ice Dog Sledding Equipment, 3620 Yancy Avenue, New Germany, Minnesota 55367.

Dog Pack Supply, Shane Hansen, General Delivery, Nanton, Alberta, Canada, T0L 1R0.

Equipment de Traineau a chiens Nordic, 650 Herve, St. Amable, Quebec, J0L 1N0, Canada.

Evenstar Supply (Snaps, harnesses, and hardware), 6537 Marsh Road, Kingsley, Michigan 49649.

Frank Hall Sleds, 5875 McCrum Road, Jackson, Michigan 49201.

Free Spirit Kennel & Outfitters, Rural Route 3, Milaca, Minnesota 56353.

Kaleb's Kart Company, W5770 Wildwood Road, Neillsville, Wisconsin 54456.

Kayak Mushing Company of Great Britain, Prospect House, Charlton, Kilmersdon, Bath, BA3 5TN, United Kingdom.

Kebo Dogsupply, Oostsingel 76, 3751 Av Spakenburg, Netherlands.

Kema Sleds, P.O. Box 870415, Wasilla, Alaska 99687.

Klondike Shop, Aberenstr. 51, CH 8712 Staffa, Switzerland.

Konari Outfitters, P.O. Box 752, 52 Seymour St., Middlebury, Vermont 05753.

Nordische Freizeit Schlittenhundeausrustungen, Auf Der Reide 15, Box 330134, D-4000 Duesseldorf 30, Germany.

Nordkyn Outfitters, P.O. Box 1023, Graham, Washington 98338-1023.

Northwoods Outfitters, N4088 Pine Mountain Road, Iron Mountain, Michigan 49801.

Nova Equipment, Box 383, Yellowknife, Northwest Territories, X1A 2L8, Canada.

Omaha Vaccine Company (veterinary supplies), 3030 L Street, Omaha, Nebraska 69107.

Piragis Northwoods Company, 105 North Central Avenue, Ely, Minnesota 55731.

QCR System (formerly Tim White Sleds), 881 County Road 14, Grand Marais, Minnesota 55604.

Rae's Harness Shop, a division of Taku Enterprises, Patricia Rae, 401 W. International Airport Rd. #3, Anchorage, Alaska 99518.

The Real Alaska Mushing Company (RAMCO), 471-M Fleshman St., Fairbanks, Alaska 99712.

Resha Sled Dog Equipment, HC 1 Box 101, Lewis Run, Pennsylvania 16738.

Risdon Rigs, P.O. Box 127, Laingsburg, Michigan 48848.

Rustic Outdoor Supply, R.R. #2, Shanty Bay, Ontario, Canada.

RV Enterprises La Kometic, 660 Rang St-Charles, St-Thomas de Joilette, Quebec, J0K 3L0, Canada.

Tanzilla Harness Supply, 407 Alexander St., Whitehorse, Yukon Territory, Y1A 2L8, Canada.

Tun-Dra Outfitters, 16438 96th Avenue, Nunica, Michigan 49448.

Windigo Outfitters, HCR Box 22A, Iron River, Wisconsin 54847.

Yukon Trading A/S, Skjebstadasen 20, 4500 Mandal, Norway.

INDEX

Note: Italicized pages contain detailed information; photographs are in parentheses.

feet, effects of diet on, 152
food shipment, distance race, 302-306
"homebrew," 97-99
malnutrition, 136
people, *260-263*, 282, 306
pups, 172-173
supplements, 92-97, 142
trail foods (dog), 261, 264-266
Discipline
when and how, *35-39*, 43, 49, 50, 115, 212, 230, 233, 237, 273-276, 314
when not to, 46, 230, 233, 235, 288, 312
Diseases, *122-124*, 132, 301
pups, 177-179
Distance dogs, (24), 29, 87, 150, *294-297*
See also Long-distance racing
DMSO, *141-143*, 162, 163
Dog bags, 80, 282
Dog boxes (on trucks), *80-83*, 281
Dog yard, 105-115, 117, 119
Dragging. See Necklining
Drive bow. See Handlebow
Drugs, *140-144*
banned, 96, 137, 141-144
testing for, 141, 310
Dunlap, Harris, 3, 93, 113, 167

Echinococcus tapeworm, 96, 119-121, *145-146*
Elbows, 22-27
Electrolytes, 92, 132, *134*, 282, 303, 305
Emergency gear, 199, 202, 204-205, 222, 256-259
Enzymes
digestive, 92, 100-102
lack of, 102, 136, 172
Epilepsy, 134
Eskimo Dog, 14
Estrus cycle, 21, 107, 124, 138, 273, 283

irregular, 18, 137
Fainting. See Collapse
Fat (in diet), 87-90, 92, 93, 97, 102, 133, 302
Fatigue, 32, 134, 145-148
Feet, 22, 47, 119, (150-151), *147-165*
abrasion, 147, 151, 154, 158, *161*
cracks and swelling, 147, 151-153, 157, *161-163*
diet, effects of, 89, 91
ice and snow balls, 147, 151, 154, *158-160*
infection, 147, 149, 152, 153, (159), 161-163
injuries, 128, 131, 147, *157-163*
lacerations, 147, *161*
licking, 149, (158), (160), (164)
ointments, 143, *163-165*, 199, 319
prevention of problems, 110, 112, *149-157*, 283-285
sore, 38, 47, 125, (126), 137, 147, 149, 152, 153 (158), 314
"tougheners," 152
See also Booties
Fiber, 90-91, 133
Fighting, 23, *49-52*, (108), 145
injuries from, 128-129
in pups, 179, 297
prevention of, 137, 138, 179, 236-237
wolves, 14, 50
See also Aggression
Firearms, 50, 144, *214-215*
Fish (dog food), 93, 95-99, 121, 302
Flu, 132, 260
See also Coronavirus, Giardia, Parvovirus
Food. See Diet
Food poisoning, 99-100, 132, 307
Food shipment, (261), 302-306, (315)
Freighting, 5, *216-221*
conformation of dogs, 27
cross-country, 198-199, 201, 240, 249
dogs, 13

ABOUT THE AUTHORS

Twin sisters Miki and Julie Collins grew up in the Alaskan bush and have been mushing dogs since 1974. Their working dogs run 2,000 to 3,000 miles each year, hauling freight and firewood and pulling gear on an eighty-mile trapline. Although the sisters have raced dogs occasionally, they prefer going on cross-country journeys in remote wilderness areas; most of these trips cover from 300 miles to almost 2,000 miles of trail in Alaska and Canada.

In addition to mushing sled dogs, Miki and Julie are freelance writers. They appear frequently in local and regional newspapers and have published in magazines such as *Mushing, Dog Fancy, Western Horseman,* and *Field & Stream.* Their first book, *Trapline Twins,* describes their life in the bush and their many adventures with their one great love — sled dogs.